COASTING

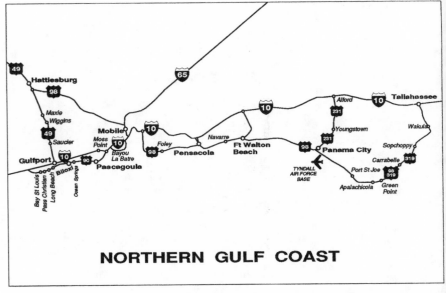

NORTHERN GULF COAST

Permission to reprint map granted by Keith Map Service, Inc.

COASTING
An Expanded Guide to the Northern Gulf Coast
THIRD EDITION

**Judy Barnes
Jolane Edwards
Carolyn Lee Goodloe
Laurel Wilson**

PELICAN PUBLISHING COMPANY
Gretna 1998

First edition, 1992
Second edition, 1994
Third edition, 1998

*The word "Pelican" and the depiction of a pelican are trademarks
of Pelican Publishing Company, Inc.,
and are registered in the U.S. Patent and Trademark Office.*

Library of Congress Cataloging-in-Publication Data

Coasting : an expanded guide to the northern Gulf Coast / Judy Barnes
   [et. al.] — 3rd ed.
     p. cm.
   Includes index.
   ISBN 1-56554-343-2 (pbk. : alk. paper)
    1. Gulf Coast (U.S.)—Guidebooks. 2. Gulf Coast (U.S.)-
Description and travel. I. Barnes, Judy, 1938- .
F296.C64 1998
917.604'43—dc21   98-11529
                                                     CIP

*Information in this guidebook is based on authoritative data available at the
time of printing. Prices and hours of operation of businesses listed are subject
to change without notice. Readers are asked to take this into account when
consulting this guide.*

Printed in Canada
Published by Pelican Publishing Company, Inc.
P.O. Box 3110, Gretna, Louisiana 70054-3110

Contents

Acknowledgments

We are grateful to Page Stalcup, Winston Groom, Jim and Peggy Poteet, Jim Neilson, Tara Steiner, Vincent Bosarge, Tom Hutchings, Green Nurseries, Kit Brinkley, Dr. Bob Shipp, Dooney Tickner, Jay Higgenbotham, Gary Johnson, Linda Monroe, Lane Weavil, Venetia Friend, Norman Nicolson, Wayne Hanthorn, Beverly Loper, Chick and Cathy Huettel, Stevie Gaston, Johnny Carwie, Laura Delegal, Dr. Larry Allums, Nancy Irvin, Richard Wilkins, Willoweise Langham, Alice Jorgensen, Janet Reid, and Vickers, Riis, Murray, and Curran, L.L.C.

For general advice and encouragement, we would like to thank Roy Barnes, Bill Goodloe, and Jack Edwards. Special thanks go to artist Jo Patton for allowing us to use her sketches from her notecard series and to Richard Scott, Jr., for permission to use his father's sketches from *Battles Wharf and Point Clear* and *Montrose* by Florence and Richard Scott. We are grateful to Tom Keith for the use of his Northern Gulf Coast, Mobile, and Midtown/Loop area maps in this book.

Coasting *covers the land that I was thinking about when I wrote* Forrest Gump. *This great little guidebook is a must for all visitors to the Northern Gulf Coast, as it really does take you through the heart of "Gumpland."*

Winston Groom
Author of *Forrest Gump*

Introduction

Once again *Coasting* has a new edition covering the ever-changing Gulf Coast. Each time we revisit the sights from Mississippi to Florida we are aghast at the explosion taking place. We hardly finish an edition before another one is needed and although we may mourn a favorite place closing, we are in awe of all the exciting new developments.

With this edition we feel that *Coasting* has taken on a new mien and we have dug deep to include more colors in the Gulf Coast's kaleidoscope. We have added more "child friendly" places this time, investigated more historical sites, and have found some nice hideaway spots to stay. As always, we have restaurants galore; we were glad to find many of our old favorites are thriving and still believe the small family business offers the best quality.

Alabama is our stomping ground . . . we know it and we love it. Mobile is where Mardi Gras is king and history takes a front seat. Across Mobile Bay, Fairhope makes you believe you are in Provence and Gulf Shores has white beaches unequal to any other place in the world.

The Panhandle of Florida is for dining. From Pensacola to Apalachicola, it is a moveable feast. The Forgotten Coast has had its wakeup call and now is the time to drive U.S. Route 98 while you can still glimpse fields of wetlands and palmetto forests.

If Mardi Gras is king in Mobile, gambling is king on the Mississippi Coast and is putting on quite a show; but the real show is the charming old Mississippi towns of Ocean Springs, Pass Christian, and Bay St. Louis and the beautiful architecture seen along the way.

We do not profess to be experts but years of experience come with *Coasting* and we believe it is your best bet for traveling along the Gulf Coast. Only one thing plagues us . . . hours. Businesses often change hours, so call before you visit. Get in your car and explore this dazzling region. Simon and Garfunkel sang, "We've all come to look for America." Well, America is here on the Gulf Coast.

COASTING

ALABAMA

Alabama

Cliff-dwelling Indians lived in the Alabama region more than 8,000 years ago (in fact, the name *Alabama* comes from the tribe, Alibamu, which once lived there). Some historians believe that the Spanish sailed into Mobile Bay in 1519. What is agreed upon is that Hernando DeSoto led an expedition into Alabama in 1540, but the first large group of white men were the French in 1702.

Known as the "Heart of Dixie," Alabama occupies a central place in the history of the South, serving as the first capital of the Confederacy. Today "Alabama the Beautiful" is just that—from its mountains in the north to the seashore in the south.

The Oaks on Adams Street
Montrose, Alabama

The Oaks on Adams Street, Montrose, Alabama. (Sketch courtesy of Richard Scott, Jr., from *Montrose* by Florence and Richard Scott.)

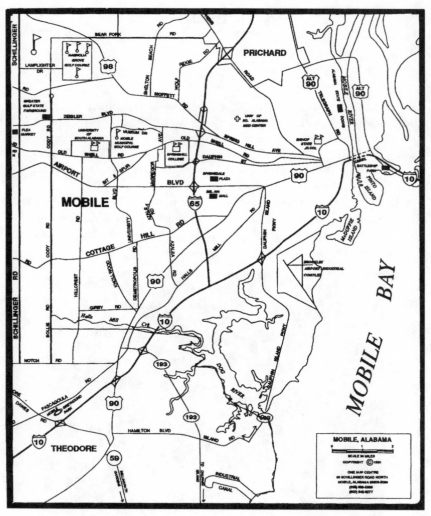

Permission to reproduce map granted by Keith Map Service, Inc.

Mobile

Mobile, Alabama's only port and one of the largest ports in the United States, lies on the Mobile River, 31 miles north of the Gulf of Mexico.

Founded in 1702 as Fort Louis de la Mobile, Mobile is the only city in America established under the direct auspices of the fabulous Louis XIV. Its individuality comes naturally, because as one flag (of an eventual six) was lowered to be replaced by another, each country left some of its distinctive culture and character to be adopted and adapted into the new culture. Mobile has maintained these influences and preserved its varied past in many historical districts.

As you approach the downtown area, you will drive under huge, moss-draped oaks towering over historic Government Street (U.S. Route 90); from the east, you enter Mobile through one of two underwater tunnels that handle the traffic under the Mobile River. There are quite a few museums, four of them in the downtown area: the **Phoenix Fire Museum,** the **Museum of the City of Mobile,** the **Conde-Charlotte House,** and the **Mobile Museum of Art.** While downtown, do not miss **Fort Conde,** the 1711 French fort that was discovered during excavation for the Wallace Tunnel. In Mobile's city museum, you'll find an exciting collection of Mardi Gras gowns and robes as well as one of only three Napoleon death masks in the world.

Toward the west, the **Exploreum** is a hands-on museum for children located on Springhill Avenue; and the **Mobile Museum of Art** is located at the west end of Springhill Avenue in the 720-acre **Mobile Municipal Park,** which offers golf, tennis, paddleboat rides, and the **Botanical Gardens.** After visiting these sites, head toward Dauphin Island and see **Bellingrath Gardens,** which contains more than 75 acres of flowering plants and is located in Theodore.

Downtown

The impressive, sprawling structure called the **Mobile Convention Center** (1 South Water Street), located along the riverfront in downtown Mobile, covers seven acres on the west bank of the Mobile River and is

Mobile Convention Center

making Mobile a premier convention city. Until now, the port city has offered little opportunity for people to enjoy the feeling of being on the water, which makes the location of the Mobile Convention Center one of its most appealing assets. There are terraces and a riverwalk for the public to enjoy watching harbor traffic, and architects achieved an open-air feeling inside the center by using lots of glass and high arches. There are 16 meeting rooms, a grand ballroom, and a 100,000-square-foot exhibition hall. For information, call (334) 415-2100.

Next door to the Mobile Convention Center is **Cooper Riverside Park,** which is lovingly dedicated to Ervin S. Cooper, a native Mobilian and founder of Cooper/T Smith Stevedoring. A bronze statue of Mr. Cooper sits on a park bench overlooking the Port of Mobile and forever watches the comings and goings of international commerce—much as he did when he was a boy.

Although it is much changed from Mr. Cooper's day, the Port of Mobile is still fascinating. Tankers, ships, and barges from all over the world conduct business and then are off to places unknown. Take advantage of this special park where the best show in town appears every single day—and it is free.

Mobile's major convention hotel is the **Adam's Mark Riverview Plaza** at 64 North Water Street, with 32,000 square feet of meeting space. It is conveniently connected to the Mobile Convention Center by a skywalk and is a full-service hotel. Most of the 375 rooms have a superlative view of the Mobile River, the busy harbor, and the city.

In a great-looking building at 80 St. Michael Street is **Justine's.** With large streetfront windows showing crisp white linen on the tables, this distinctive restaurant will make you feel welcome even before you enter. Once inside, you'll notice a definite "New Orleans feeling."

Justine's offers duck, quail, an outstanding turtle soup, and great bloody Marys. Some of the specialties, which you can enjoy in the courtyard, are Sautéed Dover Sole and Veal in Porcini Port Cream Sauce. The freshly made, in-house desserts are wonderful—try the Orange Bread Pudding with White Chocolate Sauce. Prices are moderate to expensive. It is open for lunch, Wednesday through Friday, from 11:30 A.M. until 2:00 P.M.; for dinner, Monday through Saturday, from 5:00 P.M. until 10:00 P.M.; and for brunch on Sunday from 11:00 A.M. until 3:00 P.M. The telephone number is (334) 438-4535.

Eric and Sonya Buckner have been a shot in the arm to downtown Mobile by conscientiously restoring the Van Antwerp Building, located at 101 Dauphin Street, into a fine restaurant and bar—**Drayton Place.** The Van Antwerp family have owned the property since 1884 when they opened a drugstore at the corner of Dauphin and Royal; in 1906, architect George Rogers designed the present structure, which is still family-owned.

The young Buckners have breathed life into the building, carefully using as much of the original brass fixtures and mahogany woodwork as they could. The long mahogany bar stretches the length of the restaurant with an antique humidor adorning the cigar section. A small poolroom has a separate entrance if you want to play pool and sample any one of the 10 draft or 20 bottled beers.

Drayton Place is age blind—the older crowd loves it for its sense of history and the young crowd loves it for its live music and activity. They all love it for its food. If you stick with the specials, you cannot go wrong. The hot crab dip is the best start, followed by the shrimp and grits or the soft-shell crab dishes. Good sandwiches and salads are served for lunch. Never go to Drayton Place for a small, intimate dinner; go to make a night of it with friends—to enjoy good jazz and good food.

Drayton Place has lunch, Monday through Friday, and dinner, Tuesday through Saturday. The hours are sometimes seasonal and may be checked by calling (334) 432-7438.

Chandler's Café has opened a new branch in downtown Mobile for on-the-go businesspeople who do not have time to sit down for lunch, although a few tables and a food bar are available if you do have time to sit awhile. A good menu offers salads, sandwiches, soups, and desserts that most Mobilians have come to expect from this fine café.

The downtown branch of Chandler's is located at 107 Dauphin Street and, if you want to order by phone, the telephone number is (334) 432-2402.

Downtown Mobile has a jewel of a restaurant that offers a European twist on traditional Southern cooking. **Loretta's** is located at 19 South Conception Street.

The dining area has jewel-colored place mats scattered over tabletops with silver palm trees planted around the room and, to really add sparkle to the 1940s feeling, glitter is sprinkled over the floor. The ladies' room is adorned with brightly colored stones and the walls are papered with pages from *W.*

Owners Christopher and Lori (the chef) Hunter serve food that is just as unusual and pleasing as their decor. In order to use the freshest of local seafood and vegetables, there are seasonal menus. Lori says, "It's like having a dinner party every night."

The "down South" eggroll, filled with sweet potatoes, black-eyed peas, and turnip greens, with a hell-fire mustard sauce, will start you off right. A popular entrée is the Pork Tenderloin stuffed with pecans and parsley. There are always pasta dishes on the health-conscious menu.

Loretta's is open for lunch from 11:30 A.M. until 2:00 P.M., Monday through Friday; for dinner from 6:00 P.M. until 10:00 P.M., Wednesday through Saturday; and from 11:00 A.M. to 3:00 P.M. on Sunday. Reservations are necessary and the telephone number is (334) 432-2200.

Quatorze, tucked away at 54 South Conception Street, is like a secret garden; once you find it, you want to go back again. The restaurant is quite small with panels of glass surrounding the room. White linens cover the carefully spaced tables and everything is precisely set. This is the ultimate in intimate dining. There are a few tables in the outside courtyard at the back of the building and pots of fresh herbs and fragrant flowers decorate this small space.

But Quatorze is much more than just an intimate dining place; Chef Yannick Merchand, who grew up in the Loire Valley in France, is there. He prepares everything that is served in the restaurant. Although the menu changes periodically, there is usually duck, lamb, rabbit, or fish. The Duck Comfit in a phyllo purse with guava sauce is a delectable way to start the meal. All salad greens are organically grown and are garnished with the freshest of dressings. The main course dishes are all prepared to the high standards of Chef Yannick and are often enhanced with wonderful sauces and relishes famous to his region in France. There is a nice wine list to accompany each beautifully served course.

It may cost a little more to enjoy this chance to indulge, but that is not what one remembers. Quatorze is open Tuesday through Saturday from 5:30 P.M. until 10:00 P.M. and on Friday from 11:30 A.M. until 2:00 P.M. for lunch. For reservations, call (334) 690-7770.

Beginning as a promotion for the radio station WZEW 92.1 FM in Mobile, **Brown Bag in Bienville Square** has evolved into something unique. In 1986, Catt Sirtin, operations manager of the station, came up with the idea of Brown Bag Bienville. "The day before the first Brown Bag Day," Catt said, "there were two people in Bienville Square." Today, however, on Brown Bag Day (the last Wednesday in the months of April through October, from 11:00 A.M. until 2:00 P.M.), not only will you find lots of people, but tables and chairs are set up and food vendors sell their fares while live music is played from the grand old bandstand by various artists.

Bienville Square is a beautiful old park (the purchase dates back to 1836) and, courtesy of some magnificent live oaks, it is quite shady. Bring your lunch or buy your lunch, but you will have lots of company in this pleasant place.

Operating within the same block for 76 years, **Three George's Candy Shop** is truly a tradition. Begun by George Pappas, it is the ultimate in sweets.

Candies of all varieties are displayed in three original marble-based cases; and original glass candy jars, holding jelly beans and rock candy, line the shelves of two magnificent mirror-backed, mahogany cases that run almost the length of the store. The shop's specialty, however, is chocolate, made on the premises in copper kettles and on marble tables, all hand dipped—a real art.

In 1992, Siobhan and Scott Gonzalez bought and restored the circa-1870 building. After the business changed hands, daughter-in-law Euple Pappas, who had dipped chocolate for more than 40 years, taught the new owners the difficult art of hand dipping.

The busiest seasons for Three George's are Easter and Christmas. Easter is when they make, sell, and ship thousands of nugget eggs, dipped in chocolate and personalized (it takes three days to make an Easter egg), and molded chocolate rabbits. Christmas is when they make lots of George's Heavenly Hash.

Other specialties include pralines, divinity, and Jordan almonds (a Greek candy always served at weddings). Don't overlook the chocolate-covered crystallized ginger or the old-fashioned cinnamon and lemon drops, which are stored in huge glass jars of sugar (to combat the Alabama humidity).

Three George's Candy Shop will ship candy anywhere. While you can call, it is much more fun to stop by for a sweet treat. The shop is located in downtown Mobile, at 226 Dauphin Street. Hours are from 9:00 A.M. until 6:00 P.M., Monday through Friday, and from 11:00 A.M. until 11:00 P.M. on Saturday. The telephone number is (334) 433-6725.

To add a particular note of cheer to the redevelopment of downtown Mobile, Bill Casto and Mike Wojciechowski had a special vision for the refurbishing of a stately old building at 225 Dauphin Street—the first "brewpub" since prohibition. The term *brewpub* tells it all—**Port City Brewery** is brewing its own beer and selling it on the premises.

From the street, you'll enter the largest seating bar in the area— 35 stools for customers to enjoy their concoctions. You may choose from Middle Bay Light, Gulf Coast Gold, Azalea City Steamer, or Admiral Semmes Stout (other labels will be available). Overhead, glass windows expose huge copper fermenting vats and stainless-steel serving tanks. The second floor houses a 300-seat restaurant; specialties include barbecue shrimp and oak-fired pizzas. The telephone number is (334) 438-BREW.

If you are young and resilient, or at least feel that way, take in the night spots on Dauphin Street. This historic, old street in downtown Mobile is alive with music and all kinds of restaurants and bars are open until the wee hours of the morning.

Grand Central (256 Dauphin Street) has live music every night and **Southside** (455 Dauphin Street) is always packed—if you can't fit in there, go to **Iberville's** next door.

For a flavor of the Causeway on Dauphin Street, try **Red's Downtown** (266 Dauphin Street), where you can hear Hank Williams' music most nights.

Monsoon's (210 Dauphin Street) offers live entertainment on Sunday and **Derry's** is cooking up good food and serving up cold beverages. All of these places are just a stone's throw away from each other.

Art lovers will delight in **Cathedral Square Gallery and Coffee Bar,** a vital, attractive art gallery located at 260 Dauphin Street. It is a 3,000-square-foot, co-op gallery of 40 of the top artists from the Mobile-Baldwin County area.

An added attraction is the coffee-lunch bar, where you can enjoy a light lunch while taking in some of the finest of the local paintings and sculpture. Try the Italian Pannini sandwiches with homemade soup or salad or just have a coffee or tea with pastries. It is a pleasant, quiet lunch stop. The works are changed every few months and the hours are from 10:00 A.M. to 5:00 P.M. daily, except Sunday. The telephone number is (334) 694-0278.

If you're strolling down Dauphin Street at lunchtime, you might want to drop in at number 306, **Spot of Tea.** It started out as a tiny tearoom in 1994, but the wonderful strawberry tea and tasty potato soup, loaded with chives, sour cream, or bacon, were so popular that Spot of Tea has expanded several times.

Owner Ruby Moore and son Tony first enclosed the next-door 1836 carriageway, which still shows the scars of carriage wheels and horses' hooves on the colorful tile floor. The Moores then expanded to include a banquet room that seats 200 and is available for parties. Moore also offers an etiquette class and elegant children's birthday teas, complete with candles and music. A small gift shop carries local authors' and artists' works as well as souvenirs and everything pertaining to tea drinking.

The Spot of Tea is alcohol- and smoke-free and is open from 7:00 A.M. to 2:00 P.M., seven days a week. You might want to try one of the dessert specialties, fresh Fruit Pizza. The telephone number is (334) 433-9009.

The bill of fare at the **Bienville Bistro,** 358 Dauphin Street, includes fine food and spirits, earthly and otherwise. In 1852, this historic building was constructed accidentally over an 18th-century Spanish and Indian graveyard. Perhaps for this reason, it is said that a few of the graveyard inhabitants occasionally appear for dinner. The staff prefer to call them "spiritual guests."

The restaurant is loaded with old-world charm. Murals and old brick walls add to the atmosphere of the separate dining and lounge areas. Each level is different: the Bistro with elegant continental cuisine; the Rendezvous with a more casual menu of sandwiches, pasta, and gourmet pizza; and the third floor for private dining parties. The Speakeasy is a cozy lounge with a martini bar and the temperature-controlled wine and cigar chamber can be reserved for special events. The Bistro prices are moderate to expensive and the Rendezvous prices are inexpensive to moderate.

The Bistro is open Tuesday through Saturday from 6:00 P.M. until. The Rendezvous is open Monday through Friday for lunch from 11:00 A.M. to 2:00 P.M. The Speakeasy is open Tuesday through Saturday from 4:30 P.M. until. The telephone number is (334) 694-0040.

When construction began on the **Basilica of the Immaculate Conception** in 1834, the Roman Catholic Diocese extended from St. Augustine, Florida, to the banks of the Mississippi River.

The original plan for the building was drawn by Claude Beroujon, who also designed the original structures of Springhill College and the Visitation Convent. A 1963 restoration revealed that the walls at ground level are 10 feet thick and interior wall foundations are six feet thick. In 1962, Pope John XXIII elevated the cathedral to a minor basilica. It is located downtown on Dauphin and Claiborne streets, with visiting hours from 9:00 A.M. until 12:00 noon and from 1:00 P.M. until 3:00 P.M. on weekdays.

In the shadow of the Basilica of the Immaculate Conception is **Cathedral Square Park.** The park was completed in 1996 with the aid of private citizens and local businesses who purchased personalized bricks and granite pavers. Fountains, benches, and planters add to the landscape with columns in the background. Concerts are held here periodically.

Take the time to look at several other beautiful churches in the downtown area, all on Government Street: the Government Street Presbyterian Church at 300 Government, the First Baptist Church at 806 Government, and the Government Street Methodist Church at Broad Street.

One of the best loved hotels in Mobile is **Radisson's Admiral Semmes,** a member of the Historic Hotels of America. A popular

Mardi Gras hotel, it is ideally situated on the parade route in the heart of downtown Mobile at 251 Government Street. The hotel is named for Admiral Raphael Semmes who was born in 1807 in Mobile and became the South's greatest naval hero. The Admiral Semmes, opened in 1940, has recently undergone an $18-million restoration. The small but elegant lobby with marble floors and tranquil water lily paintings has a cool, welcoming atmosphere. Of interest here are the Art Deco elevator doors. For reservations, call (800) 333-3333 or (334) 432-8000.

Oliver's Restaurant is one of "The Admiral's" best assets. Oliver's is known for excellent buffets with a Cajun-Creole buffet every Friday night and an Italian buffet on Saturday night. A luncheon buffet is also quite popular and some of the entrées served include the chef's famous Blackened Shark with White Wine Butter Sauce. Prices are moderate to expensive. Oliver's opens its doors at 5:45 P.M. and closes at 10:00 P.M. daily. For reservations, call (334) 432-8000.

Mardi Gras in Mobile

"Mobile celebrates Mardi Gras with glittering street parades and masked costume balls. The city is lighted with flares and flambeaux from the parades. Costumed marshals on horseback lead floats carrying masked riders who throw candy, trinkets, and doubloons. Navy ships are in port and there is gaiety and revelry everywhere. For a little while, the city forgets its cares and joins in the celebration.

"Carnival Season and mystic societies have been a dominant part of the social life of Mobile and the entire Gulf Coast ever since the French and Spanish colonists brought to the Christian world the custom of celebrating the period between January 6 (Twelfth Night) and Ash Wednesday (the beginning of Lent)." (Emily Staples Hearin, *Let the Good Times Roll* [Mobile, Ala., 1991], 13-14. Permission to reprint by Emily Staples Hearin.)

Contrary to the fact that many Americans believe Mardi Gras originated in New Orleans, the mystic societies began along the Alabama Gulf Coast in 1704 and were in existence off and on until 1830, when a mystic society was founded that held a parade on New Year's Eve. Out of this group grew the Strikers, the oldest surviving mystic society in America.

Mardi Gras, as we know it today, began in 1842, when the Order of Myths paraded. Many societies have since been formed and the days prior to Lent are as lively as they are memorable. In Mobile, Mardi Gras officially begins the day after Thanksgiving, but the majority of the parades roll the streets at night starting 10 days prior to Ash Wednesday, with parades all day on "Fat Tuesday," which is Mardi Gras.

Somewhere around January 1, both of the Mardi Gras Associations' offices open and you can call for information. The Mobile Carnival Association's telephone number is (334) 432-3324 and the Mobile Area Mardi Gras Association's telephone number is (334) 432-3050.

If you are in town during another season, you can see a wonderful Mardi Gras exhibit in the **Alfred Lewis Staples Mardi Gras Gallery** at the **Museum of the City of Mobile** (355 Government Street). For other Mardi Gras information in Mobile, write or call the office of Tourism and Travel, 150 South Royal Street, Mobile, Alabama, 36602; (800) 252-3862. Even better, pick up a copy of *Coasting Through Mardi Gras: A Guide to Carnival Along the Gulf Coast.*

The **Malaga Inn,** circa 1862, is located in the Historic District of Mobile. Two brothers-in-law built these two townhouses next to each other during the Civil War period. The inn has been beautifully restored and made into 40 suites surrounding a gas-lit courtyard and swimming pool. The rooms in the inn are decorated in the spirit of the times and many have the original hardwood floors.

If you are lucky enough to obtain a room during the Mardi Gras season, the Malaga Inn will put you in the middle of things but far from the maddening crowd. However, this treasure is a good place to stay anytime of the year with very moderate prices. The inn is privately owned and gracious service is always provided as well as a full restaurant and jazz brunch on Sundays. It is located at 359 Church Street and the telephone number is (334) 438-4701.

Most people do not realize that Mobile has more sources for historical and genealogical research than any city in the South—and the records are better preserved.

According to Jay Higginbotham, Director of Mobile Municipal Archives, "We have had people from 350 cities come to Mobile for the sole purpose of genealogical and historical research. We are extraordinarily rich in this respect." About 15 repositories house these records, which include the City Museum, the Archives, and Mobile Public Library.

Greeting visitors in the **Mobile Municipal Archives,** 457 Church Street, are eight statuesque iron maidens who have quite a past. They were discovered in an old, flooded storage shed in 1990 by Jay Higginbotham. He rescued them and, with the help of Dr. Sam Eichold, restored the ladies (who weigh about half a ton each) and traced their origins to Paris. It was learned that they were created for the first Paris International Exposition in 1855, after which they spent many happy years in the garden at Versailles.

In 1940, they were acquired by Walter Chrysler for his gardens on Long Island. After his death, the ladies were purchased by Mobile art collector Jay Altmayer for the opening of Bel Air Mall, where they welcomed shoppers.

In 1982, they were donated to the City of Mobile. The slow wheels of bureaucracy isolated them in the flood plain of Magnolia Cemetery where the maidens languished in the storage shed until spotted by their "white knight," Jay Higginbotham. The telephone number of the Archives is (334) 434-7740 and it is open from 8:00 A.M. to 5:00 P.M., Monday through Friday.

Wildland Expeditions

Nature lovers take note: There is a wildland expedition of the Mobile-Tensaw Delta, the largest inland delta in the country. Capt. Gene Burrell conducts these tours on his 22-passenger boat, which takes you into the marshlands for more than two hours. You'll see Indian shell mounds and Andrew Jackson's dock, which he used in his military campaigns. Yes, it's still there.

Gator Bait is U.S. Coast Guard-certified and Cap'n Gene is a U.S. Coast Guard-licensed master captain. Located at the Chickasaw Marina, the tours embark at 8:00 A.M., 10:00 A.M., and 12:00 noon, Tuesday through Saturday. The telephone number is (334) 460-8206.

Adjacent to the Mobile Public Library on Government Street is the **Church Street Graveyard,** the city's oldest existing cemetery. The first burials occurred here in 1819 in the wake of a yellow fever epidemic.

Headstones include the names of early French and Spanish residents whose burial sites were moved from a Catholic cemetery located on the present site of the Basilica of the Immaculate Conception.

Among the many buried here are Don Miguel Eslava, Spanish colonial treasurer, and Joe Cain, father of Mobile's Mardi Gras.

J. O. Wintzell opened Wintzell's Oyster House in 1938 with $100; the rent on the building was $8 per month. He bought oysters, opened oysters, and answered questions about oysters. After a few hundred questions, he began writing down oyster information on the wall behind the oyster bar. These notes evolved into small signs, and today there are several thousand signs on the restaurant's walls. Some answer oyster lore questions but most just comment on life.

After being closed for a few years, **Wintzell's Oyster House** reopened in 1994 when Wendall Quimby and Par Benstrom bought the name rights and renovated the landmark restaurant. Thankfully, they were able to locate Willie, Miss Doris, and Jo Jo (with a combined total of 58 working years). They returned behind the oyster bar and, on a good day, they might shuck 90 to 100 *dozen* oysters.

A big sign outside announces Oysters: Fried, Stewed, or Nude. But that's not the whole story. Shrimp, flounder, and succulent catfish can be fried or broiled. The po' boys are outstanding (try the Crab Omelet) and be sure to order the West Indies Salad, a Mobile tradition. There is always gumbo and a fresh catch and, with a little notice, they will package you almost anything to go. A small children's menu is titled "For Those Too Young To Vote."

Wintzell's is a delicious and entertaining place. Open Monday through Saturday, 11:00 A.M. to 10:00 P.M., and Sunday from 12:00 noon to 8:00 P.M., it is located at 605 Dauphin Street. The telephone number is (334) 432-4605.

Eat, drink, and be merry . . . for tomorrow you may run out of money.

The **Decorators Market,** 709 Dauphin Street, is a worthy stop even if you're not in the decorating mode. The spacious, old brick building, built in 1866, served as the local carriage works and also housed the horses for a nearby fire station. Massive beams and antique woodwork add to the character of this 10,000-square-foot structure, which is brimming with all manner and style of furniture, rugs, lamps, and unique accessories. It is open Monday through Saturday from 9:30 A.M. to 5:30 P.M. The telephone number is (334) 438-2020.

A neat cocktail spot is the handsome bar at **Gus's Azalea Manor Restaurant and Courtyard,** 751 Dauphin Street. A jazz band performs Wednesday and Saturday evenings and the courtyard is the lively scene of many private parties and receptions.

This attractive restaurant was constructed in 1995 from five storefront buildings from the 1920s. The style is modern but reminiscent of Old Mobile with lots of old brick and the original walls and skylights. The stunning murals in the bar and front of the building are by local artist Mark Davis. Mediterranean cuisine is the menu feature. For reservations, call (334) 433-4877.

Mobile is blessed with many lovely old homes of historical significance that are open to the public. Four of these homes are available on a single tour ticket, at a bargain rate, which can be purchased at any of the four homes and used at your leisure. All are open for tours (on the half-hour), Monday through Saturday, from 10:00 A.M. to 3:30 P.M.

Oakleigh (350 Oakleigh Place at Savannah Street), built before the Civil War, is a graceful old plantation home surrounded by ancient oak trees and furnished and maintained by Historic Mobile Preservation Society. The telephone number is (334) 432-1281.

Conde-Charlotte House (104 Theater Street) was Mobile's first jail and courthouse. Rooms are furnished in the styles of the five nations that have occupied the city during its history. The house is owned and was restored by the National Society of Colonial Dames of America. The telephone number is (334) 432-4722.

Bragg-Mitchell Home (1906 Springhill Avenue), a Greek Revival plantation home, is located in a beautiful setting and filled with elegant antiques. It was built by Judge John Bragg in 1855. The telephone number is (334) 471-6365.

Richards-Dar House (256 North Joachim Street) was a cotton merchant's townhouse and features restored Italian architecture with incredible ironwork and suspended staircase. The telephone number is (334) 434-7320.

Since 1914 when it really was a bakery, the building at 1104 Dauphin has provided good eats to the good citizens of Mobile. Carrying on the tradition today is **The Bakery Cafe** (1104 Dauphin Street). You'll find an open, casual atmosphere where you can be comfortable in jeans or a black tie.

The menu is sophisticated and imaginative. Have you ever had Crawfish Smoked Sausage Strudel with Tiger Shrimp Sauce? Or how about Caribbean Chicken Pizza? (The chicken is "jerk" seasoned—Caribbean style, with fresh lime juice and smoked.) It is open for lunch, Monday through Friday, and for dinner, Monday through Saturday. Brunch is served on Sunday. The telephone number is (334) 433-2253.

In an old, brick, 1907 warehouse set far back from the street is **Atchison Imports** at 921 Dauphin Street. Owners Sylvia and Tony Atchison seek out wonderful country antique pine cupboards, armoires, and chests in England, France, and Belgium. In addition to antiques, there are reproductions as well as comfortable overstuffed sofas and chairs with washable slipcovers. It is open from 9:00 A.M. to 5:00 P.M., Monday through Friday, and closed on Saturday during the summer months. The telephone number is (334) 438-4800.

Near the historic Oakleigh plantation is **La Pizzaria** . . . "Quality Italian cuisine for your table via carry out," says owner Bill Faircloth.

"We can prepare one dish for lunch or a full-course dinner for six, including prosciutto for your melon in the morning."

Bill, a metallurgist by profession, became interested in Italian food when he lived in Italy for two years with his business. He returned in 1992 and opened La Pizzaria as a "serious hobby."

As always, seven types of pizza are available and a great Caesar salad is a favorite among customers. The Rotisserie Chicken stuffed with garlic and fresh herbs, accompanied by fresh baked bread and oven-roasted potatoes, is a mainstay; the Fettucini Gamberi and Cannelloni-Vitello are new to the menu. Prices are moderate with three courses under 20 dollars.

La Pizzaria, located at 351 George Street, is open from 11:00 A.M. to 2:00 P.M. for lunch and from 5:00 P.M. to 9:00 P.M. for dinner, Tuesday through Sunday. It is open all day on weekends. Please call ahead for takeout. The telephone number is (334) 478-0033.

The great sprawling live oaks, trailing tendrils of Spanish moss, are a prominent feature on the landscape of the Gulf Coast. If you look closely up into these trees, you may see a thick, green plant covering the limbs, which is more noticeable after a rain. This is the "resurrection fern," so named because it dies in dry weather and is "resurrected" during a rain. Under drought conditions, it is more of a brown fuzz.

The Loop

The area in Mobile where Government Street and Airport Boulevard merge is called "The Loop." The Loop is aptly named, since in the early 1900s the streetcars looped around here on the return route to

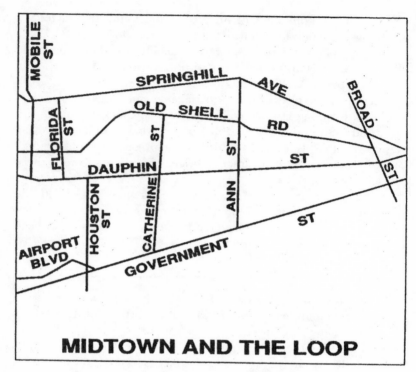

MIDTOWN AND THE LOOP

Permission to reprint map granted by Keith Map Service, Inc.

downtown Mobile. Now an active business district, this was once a residential section and many of the old homes have been converted into shops.

The setting for a meal at **The Pillars** is enchanting: an old and spacious stone residence that is now the home of one of Mobile's most renowned restaurants. When The Pillars first opened in 1976, it was primarily known for exceptional steaks, but has since expanded its repertoire to include a variety of epicurean delights. The crabmeat and eggplant appetizer is a local favorite. The steaks are exceptional.

Chef Filippo Miloney offers elegant dining, excellent service, and superb food, all complemented by an extensive selection of fine wines at affordable prices. For starters, consider the house wine. Prices are moderate to very expensive. The Pillars is located at 1757 Government Street at "the Cannon" and is open from 5:00 P.M. until 10:00 P.M., Monday through Saturday. The telephone number is (334) 478-6341.

The oak trees in Mobile, along its main thoroughfare of Government Street, are 130 to 200 years old. The British planted these trees when they occupied Mobile from 1736 to 1780. During the Civil War, many of them were cut down and then replanted by property owners after the war in 1865.

Live oaks are the largest and live longer than any other variety of tree in the South. They are hardy; their roots grow deep, so they manage to survive storms and hurricanes. Since they do not tolerate long, intense cold, these wonderful trees are found no farther north than the Carolinas.

Just at the cannon on Government Street, veer right to old Government Street. A short distance down, in the fork of the road known as Four Points, is **Hemingway's** (1850 Airport Boulevard). This country buffet has the best fried chicken in town, fresh vegetables, corn bread, and hot miniature muffins (Banana Pudding is served on Thursday and Sunday). If you're in the mood for something light, try the Crabmeat, Egg, and Caper Salad. It is delicious. Prices are moderate. It is open from 11:00 A.M. until 2:30 P.M., Monday through Thursday, and from 4:30 P.M. until 9:30 P.M., Monday through Saturday. The telephone number is (334) 479-3514.

The Loop Area is fast becoming an antique mecca. If you are looking for fine antiques or just bargain hunting for a great deal, you will find shops to suit both your pocketbook and your taste. Yellow House Antiques and Crown & Colony Antiques offer fine American and imported items. Cotton City Antique Mall and Red Barn Antique Mall have wall-to-wall dealers waiting to strike a deal with bargain hunters.

Look for **Yellow House Antiques & Lampshades, Etc.** (1902 Government Street). The owners, James Louden and Gregory Riley, keep this two-story house full of interesting furnishings. The first-floor rooms are filled with 18th- and 19th-century American, English, and Continental furniture; silver; porcelains; Oriental rugs; and accessories. On the second floor, you will find all the ingredients for creating your very own original lamp. There are many colors, sizes, and shapes of lampshades, plus an extensive selection of unique finials. This store is open Monday through Saturday from 10:00 A.M. until 5:00 P.M. The telephone number is (334) 476-7382.

Just behind Yellow House Antiques at 1854 Airport Boulevard is **Expressions.** Owner Gary Arnold collected old silver as a hobby for 15 years before he took the plunge and opened his own shop. Gary had been the buyer for another shop in Mobile and decided to follow his heart's desire by opening Expressions. Old silver is his love and he specializes in estate silver. You will find spoons, forks, and knives in many old patterns for as little as 10 dollars each. There are some coin silver and many beautiful serving pieces in sterling, and he does carry a limited amount of silver plate.

Nearby is **Dogwood Antiques** at 2010 Airport Boulevard, which specializes in Victorian jewelry, cut glass, silver, and furniture. Owner Buddy Ray also stocks a varied line of reproduction antique hardware for furniture. Dogwood Antiques is open from 10:00 A.M. to 5:00 P.M., Monday through Saturday. The telephone number is (334) 479-9960.

If you collect anything at all, you will surely add to your collection at the **Cotton City Antique Mall,** 2012 Airport Boulevard. Eighty or more dealers display collectibles of every description. It is open from 10:00 A.M. to 5:30 P.M., Monday through Saturday, and from 1:00 P.M. to 5:30 P.M. on Sunday. The telephone number is (334) 479-9747.

Red Barn Antique Mall, at 418 Dauphin Island Parkway, has 15 dealers who specialize in oak and walnut furniture, linens, rugs, depression glass, and collectibles. The mall is open from 10:00 A.M. until 4:30 P.M., Monday through Saturday, and from 12:00 noon until 4:30 P.M. on Sunday. The telephone number is (334) 473-9227.

Crown & Colony, 2041 Airport Boulevard, is the "sister shop" of Fairhope's Crown & Colony and carries the same fine French and English antique furniture and accessories. You'll also find the richly colored Imari and Majolica china as well as local artist Mary Kirk Kelly's popular ceramic fruits and vegetables. These exquisite, realistic pieces are widely collected and have been featured in national decorating magazines.

Oriental rugs and linens are among the large selection at Crown & Colony, where there is also a bridal registry. It is open from 10:00 A.M. to 5:00 P.M., Monday through Saturday; closed on Saturday during the summer months. The telephone number is (334) 471-3335.

If shopping at "the Loop" has left you a bit fatigued, a great place for a little sugar for added energy is **Toni-El Bakery** (2058 Airport Boulevard). The European-style bakery specializes in French pastries, doberge cakes, mousses, and flans. The owner and number-one baker, Tommy Janeroux, serves cappuccino to round out this great little shop. Don't forget to take home some of his New Orleans-style French bread or some croissants. Toni-El Bakery is open from 9:00 A.M. until 3:00 P.M., Tuesday through Friday, and closes at 2:00 P.M. on Saturday. The telephone number (334) 479-8479.

Tanner Mercantile Coffee House and Eatery sits just off the south side of Airport Boulevard in an attractive, gray, board-and-batten building. A wide porch is perfect for outside sitting. Inside there is everything for a coffee lover: an extensive selection of coffees, mugs, mills, and makers. Stop by 2101 Airport Boulevard for a relaxing break, coffee or otherwise. This coffeehouse is open six days a week from 9:30 A.M. until 6:00 P.M.

 In the same block for more than 50 years is the **Tiny Diny.** Beginning as a tiny drive-up with curb service (remember curb service?), it was once billed as the "Tiny Diny on Highway 90." But U.S. 90 moved . . . literally . . . a mile or so away, leaving the Tiny Diny on what is now Halls Mill Road.

In 1984, the restaurant moved to its present location at 2159 Halls Mill Road and, in 1987, was purchased by William Glenos, whose parents had previously owned it. It is in a neat, gray building and is no longer tiny, but the good food and excellent service haven't changed. There's a counter (remember counters?) and two big, bright rooms. Breakfast is served beginning at 6:00 A.M., six days a week. The lunch menu offers specials every day (the Grouper Sandwich is wonderful), but the fresh vegetable plates are hard to beat—turnip greens, black-eyed peas, carrot salad, corn bread, and all that good stuff!

Save room for the livin' end—best-ever Coconut Cream Pie with a meringue that's at least five inches high. Chief pie makers Bea Hill and Shorty Carter have been cooking here since 1949 (remember 1949?). Tiny Diny is open from 6:00 A.M. until 9:00 P.M. You can get takeout, too. The telephone number is (334) 476-3880.

As soon as you step inside the **Delhi Palace** at 3674 Airport Boulevard, you forget that you are in a busy strip shopping center. With dim lighting, hand-painted murals on the walls, and Indian music playing softly, this restaurant invites you to enjoy authentic Indian cuisine. Lunch is served seven days a week and includes a buffet for those who want to taste a variety of dishes. The menu is quite extensive; however the servers are most helpful in explaining the dishes.

The tandoori dishes are especially tasty. The tandoori is a special clay oven imported from India that is heated with mesquite charcoal. The delicious garlic flat bread served here is baked on the side of the oven; the bread alone is worth a visit. Prices are moderate. Beer and wine are available. The Delhi Palace is open from 11:00 A.M. until 2:00 P.M. and again at 5:00 P.M. for dinner. The telephone number is (334) 341-6171.

El Giro Mexican Restaurant is located at 2518 Government Boulevard and is considered to be Mobile's most authentic Mexican restaurant. South-of-the-border music adds to the casual dining atmosphere. Some of the most popular dinners include enchilada supreme, yolanda, burritos deluxe, quesadilla Mexicana, and fajitas mix (beef, chicken, and shrimp). At the bottom of the menu there is a description of Mexican dishes such as tostaquac (toast-a-wak), a flat tortilla with beef, topped with lettuce and guacamole. The margaritas are great and can be ordered by the pitcher if you like. El Giro Mexican Restaurant is open for lunch, Monday through Friday, from 11:00 A.M. until 3:00 P.M.; for dinner, Monday through Friday, from 3:00 P.M. until 10:30 P.M.; and on Saturday and Sunday from 12:00 noon until 10:30 P.M. For takeouts call (334) 478-9886. This restaurant is usually packed at noon, so be prepared for a short wait.

If a "magic flying carpet" is ever found in Mobile, it will be at **Plantation Galleries** at 3750 Government Boulevard. For 20 years, owners Johnny Goulas and Frank Lundell have had the largest stock of Oriental rugs in this city and beyond. Here you will also find a very fine, sizeable selection of 18th- and 19th-century English and French furniture, Oriental porcelain, and silver.

Johnny is the rug specialist and, as partner Frank says, "With his Far Eastern ancestry he has a love and innate feel for Oriental rugs." He goes on to say, "Today the demand is for larger-size rugs since the building trend is toward more palatial homes. They are becoming scarce and therefore more expensive." It is a good bet that, comparatively speaking, rugs are still more reasonable here than elsewhere. It is open Tuesday through Saturday from 10:00 A.M. until 5:00 P.M. The telephone number is (334) 666-7185.

Midtown

In a building that for many years housed a landmark butcher shop, **Michael's Midtown Cafe** is as different as it is delicious. Black-and-white tile flooring, eccentric art on the walls (for sale), and a huge blackboard with menu are the first things you see. Tall, lanky Michael

Ivy greets customers, clears tables, and cooks—one of the few restaurant owners who still cooks a shift. "I'll never give up that job," he says. "Even if I were rich, I'd still cook."

Michael graduated from college as an art major, but then he drifted into cooking. He was with Arnaud's in New Orleans for three years and in 1987 he opened his own restaurant and described it as "café food/fine dining."

Indeed, it is both. Tablecloths change from black to white linen at night and the menu changes often. He calls the whole scene "Gulf Coast ethnic." Which means? Well, in the daytime the menu is Creole-Italian (be sure to try the Pizza Blanca made with goat cheese or the étouffée with smoked chicken) and in the evening the menu is eclectic—coming from his travels. His dishes are a fabulous mixture of Thai, New Orleans, Greek, and Caribbean cuisine. The unusual, crispy corn bread is noteworthy. Good luck getting a refill!

Michael has a reputation as being somewhat eccentric when it comes to seasonings. "We have no catsup," he says, smiling, "no steak sauce, and no salt and pepper shakers on the tables at night." And there are no separate checks. Prices are moderate.

Reservations are for six or more only. Lunch is served Monday through Friday, 11:30 A.M. until 2:00 P.M.; and dinner is served Monday through Thursday, 5:30 P.M. to 9:00 P.M., and until 11:00 P.M. on Friday and Saturday. Michael's Midtown Cafe is located on the corner of Emogene and Florida streets. The telephone number is (334) 473-5908. Don't pass this one by.

The Pastry Shop, at 2560 Dauphin Street, has been charming the taste buds of Mobilians for more than 50 years. Owners Wyley and Lauren Burnett, whose family has owned The Pastry Shop for more than 35 years, have studied pastry making in Paris, Zurich, and Vienna, centers of the world's great pastries.

Lauren's specialty is wedding cakes and "pastiage," or sugar porcelain, which is used to create floral decorations on cakes. "I was a floral designer before I got into pastry," says Lauren, "so I have a feel for flowers. I love working with the 50-year-old techniques of cake decorating that are coming back into vogue today." Try the Raspberry Tart, which is the most popular, and the bite-sized Hazelnut Cheesecake, a close second.

In our humid climate, it is advised that pastries not be picked up until the day before they are to be served. Four or five days' advance notice is appreciated for orders. It is open Tuesday through Saturday from 9:00 A.M. until 5:30 P.M. The telephone number is (334) 479-2629.

World Famous Dew Drop Inn Hot Dog

Toast the bun. Put the sauerkraut on the bottom. On top of that, put the chili (secret recipe), then the onions and the pickles. Then put the wiener on top of everything. This is the reverse of the way it would be if it were a regular hot dog.

A tradition in these parts for nearly 70 years, the **Dew Drop Inn** (1808 Old Shell Road) is famous for more than its World Famous Dew Drop Inn Hot Dog. It is famous for some of its other dishes as well: onion rings, oyster loaves, shrimp loaves, and the indescribable Crabmeat Omelet Sandwich. The Dew Drop Inn is also well known for its parking (scarce), its prices (reasonable), and its service (seemingly haphazard but excellent).

The Dew Drop Inn, which moved to the present location in 1937 and was remodeled in 1966, still looks like 1957 with orange Formica plastic tables in brown booths and a linoleum floor. The walls are lined with local art that is for sale, along with some black-and-white photos of early Dew Drop days—a newspaper ad from 1937 announces a five-cent drink. "Back then," says owner Powell Hamlin, "you could get a dog and a drink and a piece of celery for 25 cents." Prices today are still way in line.

Powell, who inherited the place, was just a youngster in 1968 when Jimmy Edgar (former owner) sold the Dew Drop Inn to Powell's dad, George. "Now don't change nuthin'," Mr. Edgar said. "Don't change the dining room, don't change the help, don't change the hot dog. Nuthin." Good advice, obviously. Dew Drop Inn is located at Old Shell

Road and Kenneth Street and is open six days a week, from 11:00 A.M. until 8:30 P.M. The telephone number is (334) 473-7872. Right next door, 1810 Old Shell Road, is the **R. E. Templeton Gallery & Framing.** Beverly Templeton opened the gallery in 1994 as a way of preserving the spirit of her husband, an acclaimed and prolific architect/artist for many years. Today the gallery features his refreshingly unique works, which depict the leisure times of coastal people. Along with Templeton's flamboyant watercolors and prints, the gallery showcases local and nonlocal artists—all noteworthy. A good frame shop is in back. The gallery is open from 10:00 A.M. until 6:00 P.M., Monday through Friday, and from 10:00 A.M. until 3:00 P.M. on Saturday. The telephone number is (334) 476-0966.

Next door again is **Piazza** (1812 Old Shell Road). Co-owner Emily Smilie along with her other "co," her sister, Shannon Luce, made a trip to Savannah, Georgia. After visiting several gift shops, they asked each other, "Why don't we try?"

That was 'nuff said. They opened in 1995 and have a bright and airy shop. Diverse is the password. Here you can find gifts for babies, mothers, gardeners, and best friends. In other words, it is one-stop shopping with great selections from jewelry to fireplace screens. Piazza is open Monday through Friday from 10:00 A.M. to 5:00 P.M. and Saturday from 11:00 A.M. to 4:00 P.M. The telephone number is (334) 478-0093.

The Gallery Old Shell is a jewel of an antique shop specializing in English and Continental-period furniture, plus an eclectic selection of decorative arts and accessories. Owner Jim Johnson's collection is elegant and varied. There is everything from an antique beaureplait (a flat-top French desk usually with ormolu) to a 19th-century Italian abattant (a drop-front secretary). It is located at 1803-B Old Shell Road and open Monday through Saturday from 10:00 A.M. until 5:00 P.M. The telephone number is (334) 478-1822.

Continue west on Old Shell Road. At Upham Street, turn right for a few feet to **Gallery 54.** Once upon a time this was a barbershop, but for 18 years there have been a number of successful galleries here. Gallery 54 is there now and, although it is small, it packs a punch. There is an impressive collection in two roomy-feeling rooms: paintings, framed and unframed, pottery, jewelry, some great wood pieces, and an occasional piece of sculpture—all local. Owners Leila Hollowell and Kathy Dunning opened in 1992. It is open from 11:00 A.M. to 4:30 P.M., Tuesday through Saturday. The telephone number is (334) 473-7995.

When husband-and-wife team Robbie Wolff and Cathy Collins first looked at the 1920s Ashland Garage building, they knew immediately it could become home to **Ashland Gallery.** The walls are the original old brick; and while some of the concrete flooring has been resurfaced, some is original. The front two rooms, which housed the business end of the garage, are fabulous showrooms where treasures abound. In the center of the front room is an old wooden skiff filled with gift items. Watch for Lizard Breath Ranch designs—Jany Katz's tiny animal "sculptures" made using metal from cars and trucks found in New Mexico scrapyards.

In the second room is a marvelous display of handmade jewelry (some by Robbie himself). Yossi from Israel offers colored enamel pins, while Angie Olami's jewelry contains fragments of old Roman glass. On the walls is a small but excellent display of art that changes every six weeks. Some of it is local—be sure to see Stig Marcussen's pieces—but much comes from "away."

In an enormous back room (remember four or five ailing autos at the time) with a 30-foot ceiling, is the frame shop. On and along the walls are mirrors, screens, lanterns, an occasional odd chair, or a wooden trunk. High above, amid a labyrinth of track lighting, more artwork hangs.

This fascinating shop is located at 2321 Old Shell Road. Hours are from 10:00 A.M. to 6:00 P.M., Monday through Friday, and from 10:00 A.M. to 3:00 P.M. on Saturday. The telephone number is (334) 479-3548.

If gallery browsing has given you an appetite, you're in luck because **Queen G's Cafe** is nearby. A neighborhood fixture for years, Queen G's Cafe was formerly a Rebel Queen and served as an afternoon refreshment center for nearby schools.

Located at 2518 Old Shell Road near Florida Street, Queen G's serves regular and special lunch entrées and salads five days a week. Regular, mouth-watering entrées include fried oysters, chicken and dumplings, shrimp Creole, and fried shrimp; all include veggies, bread, tea, and ice cream. If you'd like to know when they'll be serving what or order takeouts, call (334) 344-2220, extension 3361; otherwise, just appear and be pleasantly surprised. Seating is very limited, prices are very reasonable, and there is always a crowd.

One loyal, local patron said, "My favorite day is when they have fried chicken, coleslaw, and deviled eggs topped off with banana pudding. I could eat it every day!" It is open Monday through Friday from 11:00 A.M. to 2:00 P.M.

Billed as "Midtown's Favorite Spot!" **Butch Cassidy's** menu also describes the restaurant as "Soon To Be Famous." It shouldn't take long. Now look sharply or you might miss it—it is just a few feet south of Old Shell Road on Florida Street. Hungry? You'll be at the right place. Offered are appetizers, salads, sandwiches, and burgers. A good house specialty is the Hole in the Wall Chili. The Jesse James Burger on sourdough bread with grilled onions is hard to beat. In contention, however, is the Train Robber Philly (spicy roast beef with onions and peppers).

It is an unpretentious, homey kind of place. There is a nice bar and the Western music is not too loud. On the walls are cowboy pictures and the tables are lighted with "over the pool table" lights. Although there is no pool table, there is a dartboard. It is open Monday through Saturday from 11:00 A.M. to 10:00 P.M. The restaurant offers dine in or takeout and is located at 60 North Florida Street. The telephone number is (334) 450-0690.

Go north on Florida Street to Spring Hill Avenue, then turn east for a couple of blocks. On the north side of the road is the **Visitation Convent** and connected with it is the beautiful little **Visitation Gift Shop** (2300-A Spring Hill Avenue).

The Convent of Visitation was founded by the Most Reverend Michael Portier, the first bishop of Mobile, in 1833 and operated as a convent and a school for girls until 1952. Since then, the monastery has been used for a variety of retreats. Most of the present buildings have

Visitation Monastery & Retreat House
Mobile, Alabama

been in existence since 1855. The cornerstone of the chapel was laid in 1894. Covering 27 acres, the magnificent grounds with huge live oaks also feature a gift and book shop in a building that was erected in 1900 as the chaplain's residence. Begun and operated by the Visitation Auxiliary in 1981, the Visitation Monastery Gift Shop sells inspirational books, framed prayers and blessings, linens, and handmade jewelry.

In 1967, the Convent was marked by the Mobile Historic Preservation Society. Don't miss going behind the beautiful old walls of this historic place. It is located at 2300 Springhill Avenue and open Monday through Saturday, from 10:00 A.M. until 5:00 P.M. The telephone number is (334) 471-4106.

Spring Hill

Once on the outskirts of town, Spring Hill is an exclusive residential area west of downtown Mobile. A direct route to the Spring Hill shopping area is Old Shell Road. In the midst of this popular residential area, you will find interesting shops and several nice cafés—all with convenient parking.

Two specialty shops share quarters in a pretty pink building at the bottom of "the hill." Here at 3615 Old Shell Road, you will find **Three Stitches,** a monogram shop, owned by Jane Dukes, and **The Original Creation,** a personalized stationery shop owned by DeAnne Tollison.

Three Stitches started out with monograms, and that is still the main business, but it has expanded to include lovely linens for bed, bath, and table; soft luggage; and baby gifts. All of the items in the shop are suitable for monogramming, but you may bring in your own things for monogramming, too.

DeAnne Tollison has done an unbelievable job of collecting things to help you with a special party—most importantly the invitations. Whether it is to be a formal wedding, a child's birthday, or a casual graduation party, there are many choices here, or you may create your own invitation. Along with a complete stock of stationery needs, DeAnne has added some special gifts, especially for men and children. Stop in before your next party for some great ideas and most capable and pleasant assistance.

Both shops are open from 10:00 A.M. until 5:00 P.M., Monday through Friday, and on Saturday during the holidays. The telephone number is (334) 342-4008.

If you *really* like exclusive shops, you must see **Debra's,** located at 4068 Old Shell Road in an old house that was once a boardinghouse for girls attending Spring Hill College. Debra Newman provides fine clothes and distinctive accessories and shoes for women. Her shop is open from 10:00 A.M. to 5:00 P.M., Monday through Saturday. The telephone number is (334) 343-7463.

Across the street from Debra's is the beautiful campus of **Spring Hill College,** the oldest Jesuit college in the South, founded in 1830. Be sure to notice the "Avenue of Oaks" that leads to Stewartfield, the former presidents' mansion.

Tommi Rustling, owner of **Carpe Diem,** has turned one of the oldest houses in the area into a fine coffeehouse that is a favorite spot for residents of Spring Hill. Besides having good, fresh coffees, Carpe Diem has quiches, sandwiches, muffins, and desserts. The two favorite coffee drinks are Old House Blend and the Granite Latte, which is frozen espresso. Soft jazz or classical quartets play on weekends at the coffeehouse and an art exhibit is always on display.

Carpe Diem is much more than a coffeehouse—it is more of a gathering place for young and old to enjoy. It is located at 4072 Old Shell Road. It is open Monday through Thursday from 7:00 A.M. to 10:00 P.M. and Saturday from 8:00 A.M. to 11:00 P.M. The telephone number is (334) 304-0448.

The Spring Hill Shopping Center has many worthy shops for browsing, such as **Charley's** for great outdoor and casual wear and **Carwie Hardware** for colorful plants and chimney pots.

Chandler's Cafe, located in Spring Hill Shopping Center (4366 Old Shell Road), is a neat spot, crisply decorated in black and white. It is a busy place but the service is excellent and so is the chicken salad. Chandler's also offers a great variety of frozen casseroles and soups to take home. The stuffed baked potatoes are super and the gumbo is super-plus. It is open Monday through Saturday from 10:00 A.M. until 3:30 P.M. Lunch is served until 2:30 P.M. The telephone number is (334) 344-7999.

At **Elizabeth Adams Incorporated,** Lee Adams and Betsy McCafferty have found just the right niche to show off their unique jewelry; the shop is located at 4407 Old Shell Road. Besides lovely estate jewelry, they have beautiful pearls and some unusual hand-wrought items plus cuff links and studs for men. Betsy says, "We have something for everyone and at affordable prices." This is a great place for special-occasion shopping. Fall and winter hours are from 10:00 A.M. until 5:00 P.M., Monday through Friday, and by appointment. The telephone number is (334) 476-1995.

Gillette's with **Antoinette's Antiques** is located at 4401 Old Shell Road. It is an upscale gift shop with European antiques.

At 4404 Old Shell Road is **Chilton's Fine Art & Framing.** Owner Chip Powell's father, Chilton, began the business in 1940. The Spring Hill shop opened in 1976 and specializes in custom framing and restoration of old frames and paintings, but it is best known for its outstanding selection of antique Audubon bird prints.

If you are interested in shopping for the men in your life, be sure to stop in at **Barnett Simmons** (4413 Old Shell Road). Just a few doors west is one of the area's most popular shoe stores, **Gallery Shoe Boutique** (4456-A Old Shell Road). This shop has an unbelievable inventory of ladies' shoes.

Gudran's is a small, upscale fabric shop located at 4456-C Old Shell Road. With bolts of imported fabrics, laces, and trims, Gudran Russell has created a dream for the seamstress or the lady who demands one-of-a-kind, custom-made creations. Gudran studied fashion design for three years in Frankfort, Germany, and says that tailoring is her specialty. Her custom-made buttons will make any outfit, old or new, into something special. To sign up for one of the sewing classes offered at the shop, call (334) 343-9771.

The Giving Tree is an elegant, upscale shop in Spring Hill with exquisite linens for bed, bath, table, and even kitchen. There are soaps, bath fragrances, accessories for baby's room, fine French and Italian sheets, and beds to put them on. This linen shop will make anyone feel good, with soft music playing and a lovely fragrance in the air. It is located at 4504 Old Shell Road and open from 10:00 A.M. until 5:00 P.M., Monday through Saturday. The telephone number is (334) 342-5265.

Martha Rutledge's **Bobtown Store** is located at 4507 Old Shell Road. Martha has created a sharp, upbeat feeling with clean, white walls as a backdrop to display her gourmet masterpieces. In the back room are freezers stocked with wonderful gourmet dishes such as Oyster and Artichoke Soup, Crawfish Etouffée, and Blackberry and Passion Fruit Sorbet.

Martha says that the most popular frozen entrée is homemade Chicken Pie. She also has a great selection of breads and desserts. In other words, the entire meal is waiting for you in the freezer at the Bobtown Store. The hours of the store are from 10:00 A.M. until 5:00

P.M., Monday through Friday, and 9:00 A.M. until 1:00 P.M. on Saturday. The telephone number is (334) 342-4700.

Holiday Place (4513 Old Shell Road) is located on the south side of Old Shell Road. There are several separate buildings in this mini-shopping center. You can find an extensive collection of jewelry in the back of a small old house at **Private Collection, Inc.** Across the way, in another little cottage, is **What A Stitch,** a shop that does monogramming and has a nice selection of personal gifts. **Hyland's on the Hill** is in yet another building, as is **Gwin's,** a stationery shop. And finally, the main building in Holiday Place holds three very special shops for this area:

> **The Holiday,** a shop for ladies and children, has been in Spring Hill since 1955. The present owners, Perry Stewart, Cornelia Feore, and Nancy Brock, have put a lot of effort into developing a shop with clothing for a wide range of ages, personalities, and pocketbooks. Besides ladies' and children's clothes, The Holiday has a great selection of accessories to meet all of your wardrobe needs.
>
> **The Pavilion,** owned by sisters Joan Christmas and Diana Parker, has an outstanding selection of gifts as well as a most impressive collection of pottery and paintings by local artists. Catering to brides, The Pavilion has a special room displaying many lovely patterns in china and crystal. The most significant asset of The Pavilion is the personal service extended to its customers—everyone feels important here!
>
> As you walk out the doors of The Pavilion, you walk into a tiny shop called **Gold Art,** where you may enjoy browsing through the cases of an unexpected jewelry shop tucked in between The Holiday and The Pavilion. If you have a creative soul, you may want to talk to one of the Clark brothers about your own jewelry design; designing jewelry is a specialty here.

Stop! Don't drive by the **Food Pak** on Old Shell Road without stopping to go inside. Unless you already know one of the best-kept secrets in the city, one might just assume it to be another convenience store; but, in fact, an international foods market is in disguise here. Regardless of your favorite cuisine, anyone who appreciates unusual food items will enjoy browsing the shelves filled with long-grain brown rice, giant

Canadian wild rice, basmati, fava beans, lentils, sesame seeds, and water-melon seeds—just for starters. An abundant selection of exotic spices and condiments are for your perusal. The coolers are filled with hand-made pita bread, spring roll pastry, cheeses, and goat meat. Bags of fruits and nuts, imported cookies, olive oils, vinegars, mustards, and marinades are lined up to tempt any cook. In case you are not a cook, there is a wonderful deli with mouth-watering sandwiches or salads. Try the popular Muffaletta or the Vegetarian Sandwich. A most unusual and varied stock of wines adds to the wonders one can find at the Food Pak at 5150 Old Shell Road. It is open from 8:00 A.M. to 8:00 P.M., Monday through Friday, and from 9:00 A.M. to 8:00 P.M., Saturday and Sunday. The telephone number is (334) 341-1497.

If you are serious about barbecue, you might become a regular at **The Brick Pit,** "home of serious barbecue," located at 5456 Old Shell Road in Spring Hill.

Owner Bill Armbrecht opened the restaurant as an answer to his own question—where to go for good Alabama-style barbecue. He says, "I want to become the Dew Drop Inn of barbecue." Bill is smoking up moist and tender morsels of chicken, ribs, and pulled pork on a huge custom-built smoker. (There's no beef here!)

Everything is made right in the kitchen except for Smith's sour-dough bread and Blue Bell ice cream. Be sure to order the sauces on the side, because you will want to enjoy several bites "au naturel"—it is great. One of the sauces is called "Mama Dot's" (Grandmother Taylor's recipe) and is a surprisingly light citrus and onion-based sauce served with the chicken.

The Brick Pit will smoke your wild game and poultry, but call ahead to reserve space on the smoker. The telephone number is (334) 343-0001. Takeouts are available. The Brick Pit is open from 11:00 A.M. until 8:00 P.M., Tuesday, Wednesday, and Thursday, and until 9:00 P.M., Friday and Saturday.

There are lots or reasons not to cook, but **Loretta's To Go Go** (5552-B Old Shell Road) is just about the best. Located in a small shopping area across the street from the Springhill Post Office, this specialty food shop has everything for a complete meal. Fresh chicken, pasta, and shrimp salads are ready to eat on the spot along with an assortment of delicious breads. However, for a special dinner, whether for family or guests, the Chicken Pie or the Shrimp, Chicken, and Artichoke Casserole along with a bag of fresh baby salad greens with one of Loretta's dressings and a key lime pie will make life simple for any hostess. The fresh dishes vary from day to day, but a variety of frozen appetizers, soups, main entrées, vegetables, breads, and desserts are available. A book of party foods is handy for catering orders and special-request recipes can be prepared with proper notice. The shop hours are from 11:00 A.M. to 6:00 P.M., Monday through Friday, and from 11:00 A.M. to 3:00 P.M. on Saturday. The telephone number is (334) 342-1270.

Should you have a craving for a New York-style bagel, then head west on Old Shell Road until you come to the intersection of University Boulevard and Old Shell Road. On the right you will find **Broadway Bagels Cafe** (5660 Old Shell Road). After Chip and Esther Alexander moved to Mobile from New York, they got tired of having to go back for bagels, so they opened their own shop. Their bagels, baked daily, are fat-free and contain no preservatives. There are literally dozens of different varieties with many choices of cream cheese to put inside them. The two favorite cream cheeses are "lite" veggie (nice and crunchy) and honey nut. The Chicken Salad is made with all-white meat and is great. Chip and Esther also serve New York-style deli sandwiches and have the very freshest bagel chips in town. Broadway Bagels Cafe is open from 7:00 A.M. until 6:00 P.M., Monday through Friday, and from 7:00 A.M. until 3:00 P.M., Saturday and Sunday. Order the chicken soup during the winter! The telephone number is (334) 344-2144.

If you happen to be in the neighborhood of the University of South Alabama, make a point to look for a small, red house with green shutters at 5901 Old Shell Road. Inside, more than likely, you will find Chatman Ellis in the kitchen preparing each dish served at **Guido's Restaurant.** The fact that he is always there is why you will not be disappointed with whatever you choose from the menu, which is posted on a large blackboard. The menu changes daily to allow everything to be as fresh as possible. On most days, a veal dish, soups, and a variety of pasta dishes are offered. The Veal Sienna-style is a local favorite. There is limited seating inside, but a covered patio also allows outside seating. The hours are from 11:30 A.M. until 2:00 P.M., Monday through Friday, and from 6:00 P.M. until 10:00 P.M., Friday and Saturday. The telephone number is (334) 342-3677.

(Sketches courtesy Gulf Islands National Seashore)

A perfect family picnic area is **Mobile Municipal Park** in West Mobile. You'll find playground equipment, picnic tables, and barbecue pits as well as a small lake populated with bream, bass, ducks, and geese—and even a few alligators.

The City of Mobile began acquiring this land as far back as 1890 and people gradually began using this picturesque area as a park. It was a natural with a lake and 720 acres of gently rolling hills. In 1953 it was officially deemed a municipal park. One of the attractions of the park is an 18-hole disc golf course tucked away among pine trees with azalea bushes on either side of the fairway. It is played with a high-tech frisbee instead of a golf ball and a chain basket rather than a hole.

While in the area of Langan Park, across the lake from Municipal Park, you can also slide in a little culture at the **Mobile Museum of Art,** where among other outdoor sculpture is a bronze figure of an artist by Seward Johnson.

The art gallery contains more than 5,000 artworks in the permanent collection as well as traveling exhibits from museums and collections throughout the United States. The permanent collection includes Southern, European, and American contemporary paintings, sculpture and furniture.

The Mobile Museum of Art is accredited with the American Association of Museums and art classes are offered for children and adults. The museum and gift shop are open Tuesday through Sunday from 10:00 A.M. to 5:00 P.M. Admission is free. The telephone number is (334) 343-2667.

For anyone interested in horticulture, a visit to the **Mobile Botanical Gardens** in Langan Park is a rewarding experience. However, keep in mind that the gardens are primarily a living plant museum or a garden collection rather than a display.

One of the gardens in the 64 acres is the area's longest stand of Alabama's state tree, the longleaf pine. Another is the picturesque collection of herbs, broken down into beds of use: culinary, fragrance, medicinal, historical, and spiritual, which includes all herbs mentioned in the Bible, Koran, or Talmud.

Of significance is a nature trail that won the Helen Keller Award for the handicapped because of the raised, accessible beds of fragrant and textural flora and fauna. Other collections include the camellia, fern, rose, and, of course, native azalea and rhododendron. The spacious activity building is available to rent for social events or meetings. It is open year-round, seven days a week. Office hours are from 9:00 A.M. to 5:00 P.M., Monday through Friday. Admission is free. The telephone number is (334) 342-0555.

A handsome and impressive building at 3700 Dauphin Street is home to **Hannon and Williams.** The look of the building gives a clue to what is inside this upscale menswear shop. Hannon and Williams can literally dress a man from head to toe with such lines as Tilley and Filson hats and H. S. Trask shoes. What goes on in between can range from Southwick and Hickey Freeman suits to Sidewalkers khakis and sport shirts. If you need a gift, everything from cigar accoutrements to the best selection of ties in town is attractively displayed here. The telephone number is (334) 343-5740 and the shop is open from 9:00 A.M. to 6:00 P.M., Monday through Friday, and until 5:00 P.M. on Saturday.

More than 60 years ago, Norma Thames started Azalea Brand Pecans. Today the business, renamed **The Nuthouse Too,** features freshly made confections as well as a large selection of gifts and accessories for the home. Everyone loves to receive a gourmet gift basket, and The Nuthouse Too is running over with goodies to make an enviable basket. Don't overlook the best cheese straws in town or the Godiva chocolates.

Located in the Pinebrook Shopping Center, the shop is enhanced by silk floral designs and selective wines and coffees. The Nuthouse Too is best known for its homemade cakes and pies. A pecan pie at Thanksgiving or a fruit cake at Christmas is a most appreciated holiday gift. Shipping is available. It is open at 10:00 A.M., Monday through Saturday, and on Sunday afternoons in December. You can call the toll-free number (800) 633-1306 or (334) 343-5469.

In the Pinebrook Shopping Center is a good combination place: **Naturally Yours Health Food** and **Eats of Eden** health café. The wares in the health food store are quite extensive—everything you would expect and then some. After shopping, go on past shelves of pretty onions and fresh veggies in a refrigerated case to the café. Soups, salads, and sandwiches are the main fare and the fresh baked bread is outstanding. The health food store is open from 9:00 A.M. to 8:00 P.M., Monday through Saturday, and the café is open from 11:00 A.M. to 3:00 P.M. The telephone number is (334) 380-9488.

(Sketch courtesy Gulf Islands National Seashore)

Wild birds in and around Mobile are indeed fortunate to have a store to cater to people who cater to them. When owners Tom and Judi Quimby moved to Mobile, they turned their hobby into **Wild Birds Unlimited,** a full-time business.

In this fascinating shop, you will find everything you've ever wanted to know about or buy for the birds in your life. There are bird feeders of lucite, wire, wood, and metal; bird houses of all shapes and sizes; and birdseed of every variety. There is even a "Squirrel Corner" with squirrel feeding items as well as baffles to keep them from eating your birdseed. Wild Birds Unlimited is located at 6345 Airport Boulevard and open Monday through Saturday and Sunday afternoons. The telephone number is (334) 380-0280.

No matter where you live in Mobile, you must go to the **Red Brick Cafe** at 1248 Hillcrest on the west side of the city. The café is only open for the "lunch bunch" from 11:00 A.M. to 2:30 P.M., Monday through Saturday, but you can pick up prepared food from 11:00 A.M. to 4:30 P.M. Fred and Susan Whitlock own the café; Susan is the chef and her husband, Fred, the manager.

On The Go Bistro, the takeout part of the café, is unrivaled for prepared dishes that you can pick up 30 minutes before your guests arrive—voila! King Ranch Chicken, Chicken Tetrazzini, chicken and wild rice, and jambalaya are just a few of the entrées available. Good side dishes of twice-baked potatoes, sherried mushrooms, and Spinach Madelaine are mainstays. Call ahead for takeouts at (334) 639-1012.

If you go to the Red Brick Cafe for lunch, the Chicken Caesar Pita will be your favorite until you try the Stromboli Sandwich (ham, pepperoni, and cheese baked with marinara sauce on homemade bread). French onion soup and gumbo are always on the menu with a special soup du jour. The list of desserts is a litany of homemade, fluffy cakes and crusty pies so fresh they can hardly be picked up with a fork—Tin Roof Fudge Pie and Hummingbird Cake are two of the favorites.

> Providence Hospital is very close to the Red Brick Cafe and is a welcome treat for those who have to keep long vigils.

Nobody outgrows ice cream and good ice cream can be found everywhere from filling stations to grocery stores; however, Tom Webb's **Gourmet Cream and Bean Shop** at 1432 Hillcrest will have you screamin' for more. Perhaps it is the all-fresh natural ingredients with no salt or preservatives that make Cream and Bean better than most—or maybe it is the secret recipe. Whatever the reason, there is something in the ingredients of this ice cream and yogurt that you will find superior.

Favorite flavors of ice cream at the shop are Butter Pecan and Peppermint, while old faithful flavors of strawberry, vanilla, and chocolate are best for yogurt lovers. Cream and Bean also carries the complete line of Passport coffees as well as cookies, muffins, croissants, and exotic desserts. It is open 8:00 A.M. to 9:00 P.M., Monday through Thursday; from 8:00 A.M. to 11:00 P.M., Friday and Saturday; and from 1:30 P.M. to 9:00 P.M. on Sunday. The telephone number is (334) 633-8001.

Get ready for a treat. On the corner of Schillinger Road and Airport Boulevard (one of the busiest intersections in the area) is a small, very pleasant, very quiet Japanese restaurant, **Banzai.** Inside, bamboo blinds shield you from sun and traffic, ceiling fans turn slowly, and you begin to wind down the minute you enter.

Most Japanese restaurants in the South are steakhouses, but this one is authentic Japanese. Owners Shigeaki and Hiromi Oki say that if you're new to the cuisine, you will probably do well to begin with the soup, clear or the miso (bean), the tempura (oh, so lightly battered, fried veggies and shrimp), and the harumaki (the most wonderful, crisp egg rolls). But you really should get adventurous and try the sushi—incidentally, all sushi does not contain raw fish—there's a marvelous dish called a California Roll, which is greens, rice, cooked crab, and avocado all pressed into little "rolls" that you dip into a sauce.

There are some other lovely dishes, too. The sesame chicken is quite wonderful and then there are gyoza (ground pork wrapped in Japanese pasta) and yokitori (skewered chicken and onion) and . . . well, you just need to go. The menu is translated. Prices are moderate. Located at 450-C Schillinger Road, the restaurant is open from 11:00 A.M. until 2:00 P.M., Tuesday through Friday, and from 5:30 P.M. until 10:00 P.M., Tuesday through Sunday. The telephone number is (334) 633-9077.

Although it is off the beaten path, **Bangkok Thai Cuisine Restaurant** is not hard to find. In Tillman's Corner not far from Interstate 10, this distinctive restaurant sits unobtrusively in the middle of businesses on U.S. 90 (located behind it is a fascinating Thai market).

In a small, white building that you might miss if you're not alert, are two elegant dining rooms with beautiful posters of Thailand on the walls; the quiet waitresses in their beautiful silk skirts make for a very serene atmosphere.

The food? It is great! The Tum Yum Goong (spicy shrimp soup with lemon grass), the Som Tam (papaya salad with hot and sour sauce), and the baby corn chicken (stir-fried with straw mushrooms) are just a few items on the extensive menu. Extensive, too, are the portions. Each item is so generous that it will serve at least two.

You can get beer or wine. A cold beer is good because a great many of the dishes are spicy hot. The spiciness is marked on the menu from one to three stars. The restaurant itself gets four stars! It is located at 5345-A Government Boulevard (U.S. 90). Reservations are accepted, (334) 666-7788. Hours are 11:30 A.M. until 9:30 P.M., Monday through Saturday, and takeout is available.

It is a little out of the way, but it is worth it! Four miles south of Interstate 10 and about one mile east on Terrill Road, under two enormous oak trees, is **Nan Seas,** a seafood restaurant "par excel-

lence." This neat, blue-and-white place sits right on Mobile Bay, with a bay view for almost all of the tables. Outside are a covered deck and swings in an oak tree, for waiting or just for swinging.

Owner Willis Robinson has a menu that is not extensive, but is more than satisfying. Be sure to try the refreshing seafood salad of shrimp and lump crabmeat with a very delicate dressing (it is not assembled until you order, which makes it especially delicious). Fish, oysters, shrimp, and soft-shelled crab are available fried (wonderfully light) or broiled. In addition, a steak, a burger, and a children's plate are on the menu. Combine all this with excellent service and you've got a winner.

Reservations are recommended for both lunch and dinner. The telephone number is (334) 479-9132. This is a neat getaway sort of place. The restaurant has been in business under various owners since the 1940s and it has a quiet, permanent feel to it. You'll like it. It is open seven days a week; call for hours.

Ellen's Place is located four miles south of the Fowl River Bridge on Dauphin Island Parkway. Ellen Gustafson, the attractive, red-headed owner, calls her purchase of this restaurant "an accident." One day she simply was filling in and the former owner never returned! Although she is not from this area and had never made gumbo before she started the business, you can be sure that she knows how to create some tasty dishes now. You will be delighted with her lightly fried seafood dishes, the Flounder Florentine, or the Seafood Pastry (sautéed shrimp, oysters, scallops, or crabmeat, served in a puff pastry and topped with Hollandaise sauce). If Sunday brunch is to your liking, try one of Ellen's seafood omelets served with her special cheese sauce. The side dishes are wonderful, too—stuffed baked potatoes, angel hair pasta, or, on Sunday, O'Brien potatoes. This restaurant is open seven days a week: from 11:00 A.M. until 10:00

P.M., Monday through Thursday, and until 11:00 P.M., Friday through Sunday. The dining area is small, so call for reservations on weekends. The telephone number is (334) 873-4612.

Visitors to Mobile should find the *Mobile Traveler* helpful for special annual events and accommodations. For more information, call (800) 566-2453 or (334) 433-6951 (Mobile Chamber of Commerce); e-mail at judy@mobcham.org.

Dauphin Island

It is worth the trip to Dauphin Island if only to cross the magnificent bridge from the mainland to the island. The view is breathtaking and, on a clear day, you can see across Mississippi Sound on one side, and Mobile Bay on the other. Dauphin Island, a barrier island, is 14 miles long and 2 ½ miles wide with a year-round population of 1,200.

There are Indian burial mounds and, according to documents, 200 soldiers were buried on the island during the British occupation of Mobile. This burial site has not yet been found.

Head toward the west end of the Island and you will find several interesting restaurants, shops, and the public beach with its popular fishing pier. However, according to the sign, Swimming Is Not Allowed Due to Erosion.

The **Audubon Bird Sanctuary** is on the south side of Bienville Boulevard. There is a trail leading to a marsh and a lake, complete with alligators. Three hundred species of birds have been counted in this 160-acre woodland, which is most popular during the migration periods of October and April.

At the island's east end, the **Mobile Bay Ferry** docks hourly and runs back and forth from Fort Morgan to Fort Gaines. For schedule and ticket information, call (334) 540-7787. (Information provided by Jimmie Morris, director of Dauphin Island Development.)

There are extensive oyster reefs in this area of Mobile Bay and Mississippi Sound. Not too far off shore on either side of the Dauphin Island bridge, you might see oystermen in their flat-bottom boats "tonging" for oysters. They bring up oysters with tongs and cull them by hand in the bottom of the boat to separate the undersized shells. Most of the oystermen live in the nearby fishing villages of Bayou La Batre and Coden.

Although there were fortifications built on Dauphin Island by the French before 1717, **Fort Gaines,** located on the east end of Dauphin Island, was built just before the Civil War. Along with its companion, **Fort Morgan,** located across the mouth of Mobile Bay, Fort Gaines

was a stronghold in the Battle of Mobile Bay. For more information, call (334) 861-6992. (Information provided by Jimmie Morris, director of Dauphin Island Development.)

Dauphin Island has a colorful history. Before Columbus's voyage, the island was called *Zamo* (meaning "white island") by the Indians. In the early 1700s, for a short time, it was the capital of the Louisiana Territory and, in 1710, pirates burned the French island village. In 1815, after the Battle of New Orleans, the British camped on the island and buried their dead before sailing home to England in defeat. (Dianne Bryars, "Don't Know Much about History," *Mobile Bay Monthly* (June 1997): 38)

The 25-year-old Dauphin Island Sea Lab recently opened its long-anticipated **Estuarium.** This 10,000-square-foot exhibit hall and outdoor living marsh boardwalk are located next to Fort Gaines. Featured here are a 9,000-gallon aquarium simulating the underwater environment of Mobile Bay, a 16,000-gallon tank filled with exotic sea life from the Gulf of Mexico, and exhibits recreating the Mobile-Tensaw River Delta and explaining the fragile environment of this area. With a view of the open water where the bay meets the Gulf, the 100-yard boardwalk weaves through a replanted marsh.

The Estuarium is open Tuesday through Sunday, 11:00 A.M. to 5:00

P.M. (9:00 A.M. to 6:00 P.M. in the summer). There is a small admission fee. For information about groups, call (334) 861-2141.

Bird Watching on Dauphin Island

The president of the Friends of Dauphin Island Audubon Sanctuary, John Porter, says, "This barrier island is a 'migratory trap' for that class of birds that winter in the tropics. Each April, hundreds of birds migrate from the Yucatán Peninsula and Central and South America and Dauphin Island is their first landfall. Because some of these birds fly as far as 800 miles, Dauphin Island is critical for their survival."

This organization, along with the Dauphin Island Sea Lab, manages and maintains the sanctuary—a beautiful, 164-acre area along the road to Fort Gaines. Within sight of the offshore oil drilling rigs, warblers, orioles, thrushes, tanagers, and painted buntings pause briefly to visit from late March until mid-May. The island is truly a haven for birds and a heaven for bird watchers!

In addition to the sanctuary, the birds are particularly attracted to the shell mounds—ancient ceremonial mounds built by the early Indians of Alabama. These mounds were formed of oyster shells and on them grow many live oaks and deciduous shrubs that attract the feathered visitors.

There is also an autumn migration from mid-August through early November, but the spring migration brings record numbers of birds. Due to the efforts of the Friends of Dauphin Island, who are working hard to ensure that the sanctuary will continue as a refuge for both wildlife and man, their stopovers will continue.

One could write an entire book about **Bellingrath Gardens** (and many people have), but this "charm spot of the Deep South" is not to be missed. There are 800 acres of woodlands and seasonal flowering gardens on the Isle-Aux-Oies (Fowl) River, plus a beautiful home and the world's largest collection of Boehm porcelain on public display.

After touring Europe's gardens in 1927, Mr. and Mrs. Bellingrath were inspired to create their own gardens at the fishing camp. This proved to be a more absorbing hobby than fishing for Mr. Bellingrath and the gardens flourished and expanded over the years. In 1932, they were opened to the public. (Jay Higginbotham, *Mobile: City by the Bay* [Mobile, Ala., 1968], 163-68)

Since then there have been ups and downs, including the devastation of Hurricane Frederick in 1979 and several damaging freezes, but Bellingrath Gardens has always survived and is a sight to behold.

Located on Bellingrath Highway near Theodore, 20 miles west of Mobile, the gardens are open seven days a week, from 8:00 A.M. until dusk. The museum is open from 9:00 A.M. to 5:00 P.M. A snack bar is available for breakfast and lunch. Narrative river cruises are offered all year except in December and January. Call for hours at (334) 973-2217.

Coden

Located on Alabama 188 (The Coden-Bayou La Batre Highway), Coden and Bayou La Batre, known as Alabama's French Coast, were first claimed for France in 1786 by Joseph Bosarge, a native of Poitiers.

The name "Coden" comes from the French words *Cog d' Inde,* which means "Indian turkey." A great number of these wild birds were found in this area. Coden was once a popular place where many Mobilians summered and there was a train to bring families and supplies to this lovely coastal community. Due to the devastating destruction of hurricanes, little evidence remains of those days.

An eating establishment with a rich history that does remain is **Mary's Place.** Opened in 1935 by Mary Hunter, it is nestled under large moss-draped oaks at 5075 Alabama 188 (at the intersection of County Road 59-Bellingrath Road and Alabama 188). According to local historian Vincent Bosarge, "When asked who was the most memorable person she had served in her restaurant, Mary paused and answered, 'Greta Garbo.'" Word of the excellent Creole cooking at Mary's Place has been reported by the *New York Times,* as well as *Look* and *Life* magazines. After Mary's death, the restaurant closed and was reopened in 1990 by Betty Nelson Gunnels, who used to work as a waitress for Mary.

Today you can enjoy seafood po' boys, crab claws, Cajun shrimp "spiders," and gumbo made fresh with locally caught seafood. The restaurant is open at 11:00 A.M., seven days a week, but is closed for dinner on Sunday and Monday. The telephone number is (334) 873-4514.

Be sure to stop at the **Catalina Restaurant** for a taste of such delicacies as fried crab claws and West Indies Salad. Owner Ora Johnson owns his own boat, so you know the seafood is fresh. It is open seven days a week at 11:00 A.M. The telephone number is (334) 824-2104.

Bayou La Batre

The town of Bayou La Batre is truly a melting pot of many cultures. First the French arrived, followed by Italians, Germans, American Indians, and later the Asians. Vincent Bosarge, a descendant of Bayou La Batre's founding family, likens the town to a gumbo pot with each culture adding its flavor to the unique recipe.

Because of the easy access to the Gulf from Bayou La Batre, fishing and ships' stores were its main industry in the early days. In the late 1800s until the mid-1900s, canneries were big business, but all of this changed with the advent of refrigeration. Shipbuilding was a natural development as the shrimpers and fishermen needed vessels to take them out to sea. Today, shipbuilding and seafood processing rival each other as the primary industries here.

When you cross the J. A. Wintzell Memorial Bridge from the north on Alabama 188, notice the picturesque shrimp boats tied to the docks all along the water's edge. Some of the old family names are still in evidence as street names, such as Robby and Gerard. Shipyards and seafood plants still carry the names of their ancestors, such as Steiner and Ladnier.

There are two annual events in the "Bayou." One is the Taste of the Bayou, which is sponsored by the Chamber of Commerce as a way to "show off Bayou La Batre," says Tara Steiner, a past chairman. Seafood is the feature. Restaurants and well-known cooks are invited to prepare their special dishes for the public to taste. The telephone number for the Chamber of Commerce is (334) 824-4088.

The other event is the Blessing of the Fleet, which is a custom that comes from the Mediterranean and was begun in Bayou La Batre in 1950. The celebration is usually held on the second Sunday in May. It gives people of the Bayou an opportunity to acknowledge the skill and tradition of those who harvest the sea and to ask God's blessing for safety and success. The shrimp boats, decorated with colored paper and flags, are anchored in the harbor.

Before the parade of boats begins, the archbishop, dressed in his alb and cope and holding a crozier, blesses each boat with water collected from the bayou in a special bucket. After the prayer, the archbishop lowers a wreath into the water to commemorate deceased fishermen.

Fleet Blessing Prayer

May God in heaven fulfill abundantly the prayers which are pronounced over you and your boats and your equipment on the occasion of the blessing of your fleet. God bless your going out and your coming in; The Lord be with you at home and on the water. May He accompany you when you start on your many journeys; may He fill your nets abundantly as a reward for your labor; and may He bring you all safely in, when you turn your boats homeward to shore.

On your way out of the Bayou, you can eat at the **Lighthouse Restaurant** on Padgett-Switch Road. Fried seafood is the specialty. Fish and grits have been the Wednesday night special for many years. It is open from 11:00 A.M. until 9:00 P.M., Monday through Saturday. The telephone number is (334) 824-2500.

Mobile Bay

(Information was obtained from the NOAA Seminar Series, courtesy of the Dauphin Island Sea Lab.)

The first ship's log that identifies Mobile Bay is dated 1517. In 1519, Captain Alonzo Pineda actually sailed into Mobile Bay and named it "The Bay of the Holy Spirit," because it was a refuge from the stormy Gulf.

Mobile Bay is a submerged river valley, about 31 miles long, and varies in width from 10 miles to 23 miles. The Mobile Bay estuary system drains the sixth largest watershed in the country (five major rivers discharge into Mobile Bay). It is separated from the Gulf of Mexico by the Dauphin Island complex and by the westward spit that forms Fort Morgan Peninsula.

The Mobile Bay Delta is artificially separated from Mobile Bay by Battleship Parkway. Besides being an integral part of the estuary system, the delta provides numerous opportunities for waterfowl hunters. The combined areas of the bay and the delta contain 285,000 acres of open water (most of the delta is fresh or brackish and the bay is saltwater), which are capable of supporting more than one million fishing occasions per year.

Boating is also an important recreational activity. The bay provides excellent sailing, wind surfing, power boating, and canoeing, with public access provided by 35 boat ramps.

The first ship channel was dredged in 1830. Today a 45-foot deep, 400-foot wide channel exists on the west side of the bay, which allows commercial vessels access to the Port of Mobile. This is one of the 10 most active ports in the nation. It is served by the 36-mile channel and is the terminating point to the Gulf of Mexico for the Tennessee-Tombigbee Waterway, which connects Mobile to about 16,000 miles of the nation's inland waterways.

Recently, Mobile Bay was cited as one of 20 "Class A" Civil War sites deserving the highest priority in preservation efforts. In addition, the

Mobile Bay Estuary is a very complex and important system as it is one of the last virtually untouched delta systems in the nation.

Battleship Parkway

Back in 1964, schoolchildren from all over Alabama brought their pennies from home to do their part in the fund-raising efforts to bring the **Battleship U.S.S.** *Alabama* to its final resting place on Mobile Bay. The Battleship U.S.S. *Alabama* (BB-60), one of the most decorated warships of World War II, arrived that year and opened officially to the public in 1965. All of the contributing schoolchildren received honorary passes to board the battleship.

In addition to the battleship, which was commissioned in 1942 and offers wonderful exploration inside and out, berthed here is the Submarine U.S.S. *Drum* (SS-228). There are displays from all branches of the service, including more than 20 aircraft, artillery, and a Redstone rocket. There is a gazebo at the southwest end of the park that offers an excellent opportunity to look over the marsh and watch the shorebirds. **Battleship Memorial Park** is open daily except Christmas. The telephone number is (334) 433-2703.

A notable eating establishment on Battleship Parkway that is not very noticeable is **Argiro's Grocery Store.** Argiro's, about two miles east of the Bankhead Tunnel, began as a grocery store in Mobile in 1939 and moved to the Parkway in the late 1950s, where it has been flourishing ever since. To say that one can buy a myriad of picnic items here is an understatement. There is everything one could want, up to and including straw hats and fishing licenses.

But please go on through to the deli, which has a small but not crowded dining room. The decor consists mainly of vintage decanters and toy trains. You will need to place your order at the counter, where sandwiches (Reubens, po' boys, and barbecues) are ordered by number and nothing is prepared ahead of time. Sandwiches are wrapped in white butcher paper, ready for you to sit down and eat or take with you. Owner Donnie Buckalew says that the most popular item is the Muffaletta (number 3). Argiro's also has gumbo and hamburgers for the kids. Deli hours are from 8:00 A.M. until 8:00 P.M. and the grocery hours are from 6:00 A.M. until 10:30 P.M. The telephone number is (334) 626-1060.

There are quite a few restaurants along this unusual piece of road (before the arrival of the Battleship U.S.S. *Alabama,* it was simply "the causeway"). Built in 1927 as the first alternative to steamboat travel across the bay, the causeway was severely damaged by Hurricane Frederick in 1979.

While at the **Original Oyster House,** sit outside or in, upstairs or down, right on the water at the west end of the Parkway. Specialties include scrumptious gumbo and grilled fish sandwiches. Hours are from 11:00 A.M. until 10:00 P.M. on weekdays and from 11:00 A.M. until 11:00 P.M. on Friday and Saturday. The telephone number is (334) 626-2188.

The **Captain's Table,** located at 2106 Battleship Parkway, overlooks the battleship. Not only can you get great seafood here, but you can also get the best steak in town. If you like West Indies Salad, this is the place. It is open at 6:00 A.M., seven days a week. The telephone number is (334) 433-3790.

At **Pier 4,** you have an unrivaled view of Mobile Bay. Here you find a wide variety of seafood dishes and an excellent Greek salad. Pier 4 is open from 11:00 A.M. until 10:00 P.M., Sunday through Thursday, and until 11:00 P.M. on Friday and Saturday. The telephone number is (334) 626-6710.

Mack's Bait and Tackle Shop is one-stop shopping at its best. There is everything here you could possibly need for fishing—including cane poles. Bubble gum and fireworks are also available.

In the same building, the Delta Deli serves wonderful, hot lunches with crowder peas, pole beans, and sliced tomatoes on the side. The Delta Deli also has a mouth-watering sandwich menu. Owner Virgil ("Mack") McCullough says that the best item on the menu is the burger, but the lemon pepper chicken is hard to beat. And although it is not on the menu, if the Delta Deli is serving lima beans on the day you visit, they'll make you a lima bean sandwich.

Decorations are strictly Southern—a few ducks on the wall, a couple of hornets' nests, and a huge map of the Mobile Bay delta area. The dining room is semidivided and business is steady, with a mixture of fishermen, businesspeople from Mobile, and driveovers from the Eastern Shore (of Mobile Bay). Ceiling fans turn slowly, the windows are shuttered against the sun, and there is not much clatter from the kitchen. It is a good place to go.

The hours are 5:30 A.M. until 8:30 P.M., seven days a week, for the shop, and from 6:30 A.M. until 2:00 P.M., six days a week, for the deli. Takeouts are available and only breakfast and lunch are served. The telephone number is (334) 626-9769. In addition, there is a boat ramp and planned dry boat storage.

Margaret Myers' West Indies Salad

$^3/_4$ c. Wesson oil
$^1/_3$ c. vinegar
Salt and pepper to taste
1 tsp. celery seed
$^1/_8$ tsp. Tabasco sauce
4-5 tbsp. capers
2-3 bay leaves, broken
1-2 medium onions (Vidalia, if possible), chopped fine
1 lb. crabmeat
1 lb. shrimp, cooked and peeled (optional)

Combine oil, vinegar, salt and pepper, celery seed, Tabasco
sauce, capers, and bay leaves. Gently toss onions and seafood
together. Pour the marinade over all. Cover and refrigerate for
several hours.

Watch carefully or you might miss the understated sign that
announces **Meaher State Park.** But do stop at this beautiful park,
which is open all year from 8:00 A.M. until dusk. Meaher Park has
boat launches, a fishing pier, a picnic pavilion for large gatherings,
and paddleboats for rent. Campsites are planned for the future.

There are a 1,200-foot nature boardwalk and two hiking trails, which
overlook one of the small bodies of water that comprise the Mobile Bay
Delta. Here you can see mullet jumping, and herons, egrets, and ducks
abound. The bird watching is fabulous. Among the many beautiful trees
in the park are two champions recognized by the Forestry Department—a youpon and a wax myrtle, which are the largest in the state.

All of this is available for an entrance fee of $1.00 per adult and
50 cents if you are younger than 12 years or older than 62 years. For
more information, call (334) 626-5529 or (800) ALA-PARK.

Gaillard Island

There is one local spot that is hard to see—and you don't want
to visit—but it is a unique and most noteworthy place. Out in
the middle of Mobile Bay is **Gaillard Island,** a triangular island
(continued)

(about two miles long on every side) that has no facilities at all, not even any trees. It is, in fact, almost a wasteland since nearly all of the island is baked mud inhabited by mosquitoes and flies. The remaining rim of this island is home to thousands of birds, and their home is a dredge disposal.

It was created with dredging materials when the Theodore ship channel was dredged in the late 1970s. The creation of the island provided a place for about 30 million cubic yards of matter, while creating a habitat for attracting shore-nesting birds to Mobile Bay. At that time, the brown pelican was making a comeback after nearly becoming extinct from the use of DDT, and it was hoped that the bird could be enticed to this barren spot.

Pelicans have always needed remote places to nest. Because these huge birds build huge nests on the ground, they are easy prey for raccoons or even small dogs. By 1983, there were three pelican nests on Gaillard Island. Today, the number of nests has swelled to 4,000, with a population of around 10,000 pelicans, along with hundreds of terns, mottled ducks, and other shorebirds. These inhabitants don't seem to mind that the island is not particularly beautiful!

Although the island is hard to see, you can see these ungainly pelicans—almost majestic in flight—flying and diving before returning to their own private island. (Information provided by Roger Clay, Nongame Wildlife Biologist for the State Conservation Department.)

What's for Dinner?

Along with a large year-round population (10,000) of brown pelicans, Mobile Bay is also winter grounds to nearly 1,000 white pelicans (not to be confused with the nonbreeding brown pelican that has a white head). The brown pelican feeds individually by diving—an ungainly, almost comical accomplishment—but the white pelican often gets its meals in an entirely different manner. Small groups of these birds will float buoyantly on the water's surface, their heads and bills partially submerged. At the same time, they are actually herding the fish in front of them so that they can use their wide, flat bills to scoop up supper!

Boat Launching

The following map shows state and county launches. Tensaw and Chacaloochee are on the north side of Battleship Parkway; one is just east of Battleship Park and the other is just west of the on and off ramps to Interstate 10. The launch at Meaher Park is on the south side of the Parkway. There are also a few private launches, some that are free and some that charge a nominal fee. Most sell bait and tackle. Among these are **Shirley's, Autrey's Fishing Camp, Chocolatta,** and Mack's. At the east end of the Parkway is **Mizell's Fishing Camp,** where you can also rent boats.

If you prefer to launch farther up in the delta, you have a couple of alternatives. There are two county launches off Alabama 225. From U.S 31, take Alabama 225 for 9 ½ miles to the Byrne's Lake sign (4 ½ miles north of Blakeley Park). You will have to turn off onto a good dirt road for about two miles. **Byrne's Lake** is a beautiful spot to launch with ample parking but no facilities; you do pass **Tensaw Lodge** ("Fine Food—Friendly Folks") if you are hungry.

Also on Alabama 225, 4 ½ miles north of the Byrne's Lake sign, you will see a sign for Carpenter Station—Cliff's Landing. Again, two miles off the road (this one is paved), you will find very convenient launching and parking with an ample landing. You will also find **Cliff's Bait and Tackle,** which, besides selling the obvious, sells drinks, snacks, ice, and fishing licenses. Cliff's Bait and Tackle is open seven days a week from 4:30 A.M. until 8:30 P.M.

If you keep on heading north on Alabama 225 and cross Interstate 65, you'll be close to Stockton and the beautiful **Live Oak Landing,**

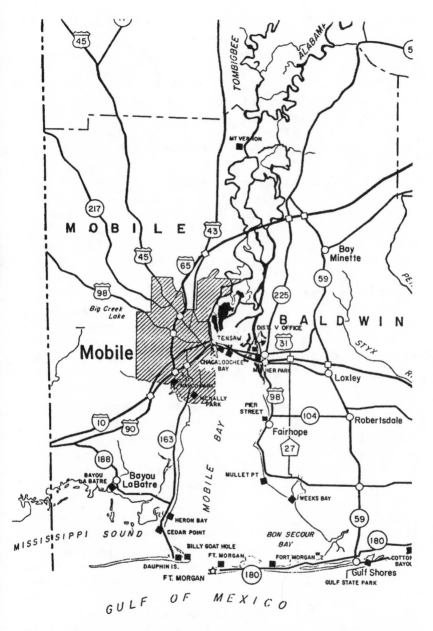

Courtesy of Fisheries Division of Alabama Department of Conservation.

the "Gateway to the Delta." Two main things draw folks here—the beauty and the fishing.

Live Oak Landing has been used by local fishermen for hundreds of years; about 15 years ago, it was developed into a public establishment. The 63-acre landing is on the Tensaw River, within 10 minutes of Middle River and 15 minutes of the Mobile River. These are good fishing waters with lots of bass, crappie, and bream.

Here you will find a boat launch, picnic facilities, overnight camping, gas pump, boat sheds, and the **Live Oak Emporium,** a "convenience" store with atmosphere and necessities from bait to Oreo cookies!

There are fishing tournaments practically every weekend from March to November. A beautiful fishing pond surrounded by cypress trees and huge live oaks lend to the serenity and beauty of this untouched place. There are nominal launch and camping fees. For information, call (334) 937-9542. Follow Alabama 225 North ½ mile north of Interstate 65; turn left onto Live Oak Road.

The remaining launches on the map are clearly marked, the one exception being **Mullet Point** launch, which is actually on County Road 1 (continue south on County Road 1 after U.S. 98 turns east).

Freshwater and saltwater fishing licenses are required and there are visitors' licenses. Borders between fresh and salt waters are confusing, so before you begin to fish, be sure you have the correct license, which can be obtained at courthouses, sporting goods stores, and most bait shops.

Blakeley Park is located six miles north of Interstate 10 or 16 ½ miles south of Interstate 65 on Alabama 225. Site of the last major battle of the Civil War, this magnificent 3,800-acre park sits along the eastern edge of the Mobile Bay Delta and has something of interest for almost everyone. History buffs will thrill at the remnants of earthen forts and battery sites and especially the Civil War breastworks, among the best in the country.

Marked hiking and nature trails of various distances abound or you can go down to the ¼-mile waterfront boardwalk. Two observation decks on the Tensaw River will afford you places to simply sit and meditate . . . or fish. Park rangers are on hand and there are facilities and campsites, although there is no electricity. There is no food court either, so bring your own picnic. A pavilion may be reserved for large groups on special occasions. Historic Blakeley Park is open from 9:30 A.M. until dusk, seven days a week. For more information about this lush, hushed park, call (334) 626-0798.

Spanish Fort

The site of **Spanish Fort** is in the residential area of the town of Spanish Fort and is on private property. Nearby are historic markers describing **Fort McDermott** (the highest point along two miles of Confederate battle lines) but, unfortunately, there is nothing you can see. You will have to imagine.

There are conflicting schools of thought about the origin of Spanish Fort: one is that it was constructed by the Spanish in 1780-81 under the direction of a young Spanish governor, Galvez. However, in Craighead's *Mobile: Fact and Tradition,* there is a reference stating that "the fort was possibly of Indian origin and was old even at that early day." Those who disagree contend that the Indian fort was at the mouth of D'Olive Creek and is still undiscovered. Whatever is true, the Confederates established defensive positions high on the bluffs from Spanish Fort to Blakeley and it was in this beautiful upper-bay region that the last important battle of the Civil War took place.

To fully appreciate the scope that these bay batteries had, you might want to drive up to the **Larry Dee Cawyer Overlook** at the intersection of Interstate 10 and U.S. Route 98. Here you can see that the defensive positions of the Confederacy (which stretched for more than 15 miles) had a spectacular view of the upper bay and the lower delta as well as the city of Mobile.

An unexpected vision of a neo-Byzantine structure looms up in the midst of vast Baldwin County farmland—**Malbis Greek Orthodox Church.** Located just east of Daphne, only a few minutes from Interstate 10 at the Malbis exit, it is an exact copy of a church in Athens, Greece. The church was built in memory of Greek immigrant Jason Malbis, who founded a colony here in 1906. The building of the church was begun in 1960 and took five years to complete. The marble came from the same quarry in Greece that provided stone for the Parthenon. The walls and 75-foot ceiling are covered with magnificent paintings. The work was done by artists brought over from Greece. The brilliant colors and golden detail are highlighted by the sunlight pouring into the sanctuary through the stained-glass windows. All of this gives an ethereal feeling to the church and it is well worth the trip to see it. Visitors are welcome from 9:00 A.M. until 12:00 P.M. and from 2:00 P.M. until 5:00 P.M. daily.

Daphne

Interstate 10 Area

Located on the west side of U.S. 98, less than a mile south of Interstate 10 in Daphne, is a most unexpected delight for those who like authentic Italian food—**Papa's Place.** As you might expect, the tables are covered with red-and-white checkered tablecloths, but wait until the first basket of garlic bread is placed in front of you—then the unexpected begins! The menu includes a variety of appetizers and one specialty is the Crab Claws Alfredo. The entrées are as mouth-watering to taste as they sound: petite peppered Filet Mignon (this is really good), Shrimp Diablo, Seafood Pasta, and Chicken Marsala, often served with oven-roasted vegetables. Don't fill up on all of these goodies because the best is yet to come. The desserts are heavenly. Try the Banana Cream Pastry or the Double Chocolate Fudge Cake served with Papa's special Italian Cream. Another unexpected surprise—the price. Enjoy!

No reservations are accepted, but don't be put off if there is a line; there are benches outside for waiting. No alcohol is sold at Papa's Place, but you can bring your own. If you don't have any to bring, not to worry: **Kathy's Package Store** is just next door and has an extensive selection of wines; some whites are even chilled.

Papa's Place is open for lunch Monday through Saturday from 11:00 A.M. until 4:00 P.M., and dinner Monday through Saturday from 4:00 P.M. until 10:00 P.M. The telephone number is (334) 626-1999. Not open for lunch during the summer.

It seems that the most successful restaurants and businesses are those that are owned and operated by the same person. **Catering to You** at 28623 North Main Street (two short blocks north of U.S. 98) is no exception. Kathy Buckson's love for cooking was developed by her mother. She first began catering small affairs out of her home and, in 1993, she moved her business to its present location in Daphne. Soon after opening, she began serving soup and sandwiches at lunch. The business grew and prompted Kathy to expand her menu as well as the table space.

The dining area has the feel of an attractive patio with clay pots of brightly colored flowers painted around the walls. The menu consists mostly of man-sized hot or cold sandwiches and salads, with chicken being the specialty. It is all delicious and Kathy is usually present to be sure each plate looks pretty. To phone in your order for takeout, call (334) 626-1744. Lunch is served from 11:00 A.M. until 2:00 P.M., Monday through Friday.

Riley's Gourmet Market, at 2101 U.S. 98 in the Fountain Square Shopping Center, is owned by Clint and Kim Riley. The market carries specialty items for the ethnic or gourmet cook, including fresh pasta, ostrich steaks, imported and micro brews, wines, teas, and coffees. In the freezer are entrées prepared in the Market Kitchen and there are some from Pinhook Seafood Market of Lafayette, Louisiana. A good selection of cheeses and a variety of sausages from Gerhard's Napa Gourmet Sausage, such as chicken with basil and pinenuts and smoked turkey and duck with fennel, are in the cooler.

Riley's also offers an entire dinner to go. If you call by 2:00 P.M., you can choose a frozen entrée and a side dish that will be heated, with a salad and bread, and ready to eat by 5:00 P.M. While you are there, you can pick up a bottle of wine and some cheese and crackers and—voilà—your dinner is done. Riley's telephone number is (334) 621-CATER.

An art gallery that sells clothing, **Spirit Works,** 2102 U.S. 98, has colorful, casual jackets, vests, and shirts that are delightful conversational subjects without being too far out.

Artist/owner Marilyn Gordon has won many awards and her artwear has been exhibited in galleries and museums around the country. In addition to displaying her wearable art in shows, Marilyn is skilled in custom couture work. Her gallery is open from 10:00 A.M. until 4:00 P.M., Wednesday through Saturday, and by appointment on other days. The telephone number is (334) 626-1366. Don't fall over the big, friendly cat in the doorway.

Old Daphne

Daphne is a quaint and quiet little town along Mobile Bay between Spanish Fort and Fairhope. More than a hundred years ago it was settled by Italian immigrants who knew that a more rewarding life could be had in rural Daphne than in the busy northern cities. Settling began in 1889 and later that same year the Trione family and the Castognolli brothers arrived. They began farming and, as the colony grew, sweet potatoes and green corn became the main crops, with wheat being introduced later. The Italian farmers of today grow Irish potatoes, soy beans, pecans, and sweet white corn, while others are still leaders in the production of beef and dairy cattle.

The descendants of these early families are still here. Casually thumb through the white pages of the telephone book and you will find such names as Boni, Corte, Trione, Guarisco, Lazzari, Allegri, Marco, Pintarelli, Bertolotti, and Manci.

Although Daphne has grown considerably during the last few years due to annexation, the original tiny town has not changed much. Dominated by a pretty City Hall surrounded by grass and trees, Daphne contains a beautiful little park and a small number of shops.

 Tommy Nix, owner of **Nix Florist,** has been demonstrating his artistic talent in this area for a number of years. His creative arrangements have graced many a table for special occasions. The shop is a combination of flowers and gifts. Once again, Tommy's eye for style shows up in his selection of unusual and decorative accent pieces. Containers for fresh flowers or permanent arrangements are surrounded by pretty, little boxes and vases for a single blossom, along with the best selection of candles in a vast array of colors and sizes. The shop is located at 1800 Main Street and the telephone number is (334) 626-6323. It is open from 8:00 A.M. to 5:30 P.M., Monday through Friday, and from 8:00 A.M. to 12:00 noon on Saturday.

Manci's Antique Club (1715 Main Street) is actually a bar/museum whose walls are covered with antique tools, cowbells, and political campaign buttons. On shelves everywhere are Jim Beam decanters,

the biggest assemblage outside the distillery's own collection. In the late 1890s, the building was a warehouse for storing fruit that came to Baldwin County on the ferry boats. Later, it was a service station and auto parts store.

In addition to being a landmark that you can't miss, Manci's (run by Alex and Gwen Manci) now serves lunch and dinner, seven days a week. The po' boys are outstanding (oyster, shrimp, and combo), the Veggie Sub is super, and they have the best Steak Sandwich near or far. Burgers and seafood baskets are delicious. If you're going home late and hunger attacks you—stop by—and they'll fix you an after-midnight snack of a Bacon, Egg, and Cheese Sandwich. It is open from 10:00 A.M. until 2:00 A.M. Lunch is served from 11:00 A.M. until 2:00 P.M. and dinner is served from 6:00 P.M. until 10:00 P.M. The telephone number is (334) 626-9917.

Guido's, which is on Main Street in Old Daphne, offers a welcome alternative to travelers and locals alike. Serving authentic Italian cuisine, Chef Chris Conlon uses farmer's market produce and the freshest of local seafood. The daily specials are posted on the big blackboard that greets you as you enter the restaurant. Some of the specials include eggplant sandwiches and Roasted Corn and Tomato Soup. The seafood dishes depend upon what is available and the pasta dishes depend on the chef's mood. The prices are moderate, the atmosphere relaxed, and wine and beer are served. The telephone number is (334) 626-6082 and the restaurant is open from 11:30 A.M.

to 2:00 P.M., Monday through Friday, and from 5:30 P.M. to 10:00 P.M., Tuesday through Saturday.

The Main Street Cafe, 1716 Main Street, is a local favorite. Everybody talks to everybody while enjoying the popular Corn and Crab Soup, the shrimp salad sandwiches, or the old-fashioned meat loaf. Every bite is fresh and flavorful and guaranteed to bring you back to Main Street.

At night a chalkboard menu displays about six entrées in addition to the daily specials. Service is fast and will brighten your day. Prices are moderate. Main Street Cafe is open for lunch, Monday through Saturday, from 11:00 A.M. to 3:00 P.M., and for dinner on Thursday, Friday, and Saturday, from 5:00 P.M. to 10:00 P.M. Takeouts are available. The telephone number is (334) 626-0040.

If a home-cooked breakfast is what it takes to get you up and out in the morning, look for the **Camellia Cafe** at 810 Manci Avenue in the heart of downtown Daphne. Besides the staples of eggs, bacon, and toast, the café offers a delicious breakfast casserole made with layers of hickory-smoked bacon and fluffy eggs combined with rich cheeses. The pecan waffle is another favorite.

Owners Rhonda Brinsfield and Debbie Crigler discovered this quaint, wooden house with an overgrown garden filled with old camellia bushes and have turned it into a great place for breakfast or lunch. Inside the ceilings have been removed to expose the beams and give a feeling of openness to the rooms, which have been decorated with old kitchen utensils. Along with a variety of salads and sandwiches, a daily hot plate is served at lunch. The pot roast on Tuesday is a local favorite. It is open from 7:30 A.M. to 3:00 P.M., Monday through Friday. For takeouts, call (334) 621-1146.

The Custard Cottage is across the street from a school on Main Street; way back in 1897 this building was once a schoolhouse.

In a yellow clapboard house, across the street from Christ the King School, Lisa Frayer has been sweetening the town for a good while.

She began serving floats, sundaes, sodas, ice-cream cones, and to-die-for banana splits. Recently, she added frozen custard to her menu. "This is the first frozen custard spot south of Nashville," she says. "It is made fresh every day and it is wonderful."

Service is from a window on the deck, with comfy seating outside under a giant pecan tree. The Custard Cottage is located on Main Street. Summer hours are from 12:00 noon until 8:00 P.M., Tuesday through Saturday, and from 12:00 noon until 5:00 P.M. when school starts—but call ahead to be sure. The telephone number is (334) 621-8316.

About one-half block south of the Custard Cottage is a small, circa-1940 filling station that has been remodeled and now houses **The Frame Corner.** Owners Howard and Ceanne Wachter have been in business since 1981, doing custom framing and selling original, mainly local art.

Ceanne has recently updated her shop to include invitations (yes, she does printing) and gift items. She has a great display of framed mirrors, some beveled—all ready to be taken home. She also has some nice baby gifts—tiny frames, nighties, and quilted, soft angel dolls. Don't miss her selection of birth and marriage certificates, which are lovely reproductions of early 1900s lithographs.

It is worth the trip to see the wonderfully painted floor. Artist Janet Reid-Dover painted the filling station concrete to resemble the sky, so that when you walk into The Frame Corner, you feel as though you are literally walking on clouds! Hours are 9:00 A.M. until 5:00 P.M., Monday through Friday, and 9:00 A.M. until 12:00 noon on Saturday. It is located at 1411 Main Street.

South of downtown Daphne on Scenic U.S. 98 is **Judge Roy Bean's,** a gray-roofed building that entrepreneur Jack West bought in 1976 as an investment. "The Bean" has unusual seating, a volleyball court, a basketball goal, and a shish-kebab bar. In other words, something for everyone—"everyone," for the most part, meaning young (between the ages of 21 and 40) and professional or college upperclassmen.

On the outside bandstand, West has presented some great entertainment over the years, starting with Jimmy Buffet, who came to the area to visit his family and gave a few impromptu performances. Good music continues on a regular basis. The Fall and Spring Concert Series, always benefiting a charity, has attracted such musicians as Emmy Lou Harris, Leon Russell, Dr. John, Stephen Sills, and, of course, Alabama. There is live music every weekend.

Every week, in addition to listening and playing, you can avail yourself of a large variety of "eats." Roving chefs cook up crawfish, quesadillas (their version is black bean with chicken), pizzas, hamburgers, fish, and "Corte" corn (when in season). In season, too, another house specialty: oysters on the half-shell, either raw or steamed, at 25 cents a piece!

Out in the swept-dirt yard, there's a resident goat (of course, his name is Billy) to greet you. This is truly a one-of-a-kind place. Says Butler Sheldon, longtime part-time bartender, "This is the best bar in the world, bar none!" Case closed. Judge Roy Bean's is open Tuesday through Sunday from 4:30 P.M. until.

Jubilees

Along the Eastern Shore, the almost-annual cry of "Jubilee!" signals a strange phenomenon when fish, crabs, shrimp, and other bay inhabitants passively swim into the shallow waters in an apparent attempt to escape their natural habitat. The fish come quite close to the shore and are lethargic enough that they are easily caught. It is a scene rarely encountered anywhere else in the world.

The usual season for Jubilees is from June through September. Natives of the area know the signs to watch for—the moon, the tides, and the wind. But in reality, Jubilees are notoriously unpredictable. Some years there may be as many as 10 and other years there are none. Jubilees usually begin anywhere from midnight to dawn and can last a few minutes or a few hours. They mainly occur along the Eastern Shore from Mullet Point to Spanish Fort.

When the cry of "Jubilee!" is heard, visitors and natives alike rush to the water's edge with nets, pails, gigs, floundering lights, and buckets—anything with which to snare a bounty of seafood. The dictionary defines Jubilee as "an occasion of joyful celebration." How true!

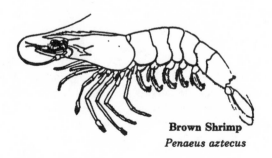

Brown Shrimp
Penaeus aztecus

Jubilee Stuffed Flounder

1 large founder
½ cup chopped green onions
½ stick butter
2 tbsp. chopped parsley
½ cup bread crumbs
2 hard-boiled eggs, chopped
½ to 1 lb. crabmeat
1 tsp. salt
½ tsp. pepper
Dash Tabasco sauce
Paprika
Some additional melted butter

Prepare flounder for cooking. Slit a pocket for stuffing in the back of the flounder, using a sharp knife. Lightly brown onion in butter; add parsley, bread crumbs, eggs, crabmeat, and seasonings. Mix well and stuff into pocket. Brush flounder with melted butter. Sprinkle with paprika and bake for 30 minutes in a 375-degree oven. Makes 6 medium servings.

(Recipe courtesy of *Recipe Jubilee!* cookbook of the Junior League of Mobile.)

Harry & Co., County Road 64 and Friendship Road, is truly a family enterprise. Every two weeks, Harry and his three sons drive three trucks down to Mexico and load up with wrought-iron furniture, wooden cabinets, chests, pottery, glassware, and anything that grabs them. They then return to Daphne to unload in a mob scene of eager customers. The prices are great and the choices are abundant. If they are out of an item, come back in two weeks. It is open from 9:00 A.M. to 5:00 P.M., Monday through Saturday. The telephone number is (334) 626-7080.

Antique collectors can have a field day browsing the open, spacious 25,000-square-foot **Gallery Antique Mall** at 1302 U.S. 98, Daphne. One hundred dealers display everything from tin to Tiffany as well as a permanent exhibit of antique and classic cars. This mall has a lounge or "Husbands' Recovery Room" and a Kiddie Korner. A large parking lot is convenient for RVs and they are open seven days a week: from 10:00 A.M. to 6:00 P.M., Monday through Saturday, and from 1:00 P.M. to 6:00 P.M. on Sunday. During winter months, closing time is 5:00 P.M. The telephone number is (334) 626-0353.

It is "garonteed" authentic Cajun food, already prepared and ready to take home, from the **Cajun Connection.** Delicious seafood gumbo, crawfish étouffée, jambalaya, and boudin are but a few of the Cajun specialties Bob Lopez cooks for you to heat, eat, and take all accolades. The Cajun Connection also has the Tur-Duc-Ken, which is a boneless turkey stuffed with duck, then stuffed with chicken, with a fabulous cornbread dressing of pork or shrimp—great for the holidays.

In these busy times, entertaining is difficult. The Cajun Connection makes it possible to serve genuine Cajun meals to guests, including bread pudding for dessert. Call for pickups or drop by 697 U.S. 98, Monday through Friday, from 10:00 A.M. to 7:00 P.M., and Saturday from 10:00 A.M. to 4:00 P.M. The telephone number is (334) 621-2262.

Live Oak

(Sketch courtesy Gulf Islands National Seashore)

Gulf Coast residents love trees—so much that, enthused by a dynamic volunteer corp called Corridor 98, they accomplished the largest private landscaping project along public rights-of-way in the entire United States. On either side of Highway 98, south from Interstate 10 for eleven miles, 1,200 live oaks, 1,700 crape myrtles, hundreds of maples, red oaks, red buds, cypresses, birches and pines and thousands of shrubs were planted. In addition, the Montrose Garden Club planted over 200 live oaks along Scenic Highway 98—all through private donations.

The Arbor is a garden center that makes up a part of Jubilee Landscaping Company on U.S. 98. The big, white arbors and beautiful landscaping of the center makes it hard to pass up. Kim Jovings and Whitney Allen manage the garden center and have come up with some innovations of their own. Kim has found a wonderful source for fine, custom-made arbors. Whitney makes up miniature gardens in clay pots, such as plants from Monet's Giverny—a beautiful gift that lasts and lasts.

Gardening is becoming America's best pastime and The Arbor is "right on" with the latest innovations in this ever-changing industry. The Arbor can make a topiary out of anything: juniper, holly, blooming hibiscus, azalea, and lantana—to name just a few. The center also has first-step plans for you to test your skill at water gardening or bogs. Hours are from 9:00 A.M. to 5:00 P.M., Monday through Saturday, and (according to the season) from 10:00 A.M. to 4:00 P.M. on Sunday. The telephone number is (334) 626-3900.

Montrose

Situated between Daphne and Fairhope, quiet **Montrose** predates both of them. In 1847, the founder, Cyrus Sibley, laid out this charming village in large parcels and long lots stretching to Mobile Bay. As early as 1768, there was a settlement here near the unique red clay bluffs. This point boasts the highest elevation of any of the eastern coastlines from Maine to Mexico. An historic marker on Scenic U.S. 98, just north of this property, describes "Ecor Rouge," the Red Bluff.

The Red Bluff, site of British camp "Croftown" in 1771. (Sketch courtesy of Richard Scott, Jr., from *Montrose* by Florence and Richard Scott.)

Montrose is almost entirely residential and much of the community has been designated as a Historic District. Listed on the National Register of Historic Places is the original Montrose Post Office, constructed in 1890 and still standing on Adams Street.

Modern-day Montrose is a blend of historic structures and newer homes of Creole and Greek Revival architecture, together with attractive cottages and smaller homes. (Prepared for *Coasting* July 23, 1994, by Richard J. Scott, Jr.)

The Old Postoffice on Adams Street
From a photograph taken about 1907

The Old Post Office on Adams Street, from a photograph taken about 1907. (Sketch courtesy of Richard Scott, Jr., from *Montrose* by Florence and Richard Scott.)

The Northern Gulf Coast has two growing seasons, which is great for annuals. Azaleas thrive in the moist, sandy soil and some of the large varieties grow up to 10 feet in diameter and six feet in height. However, weeds thrive too—just look at the healthy kudzu vine that you will see flourishing in the gullies, covering vacant houses, and enveloping trees in Baldwin County.

According to Fairhope's Green's Nurseries, kudzu was brought to this country from Asia after the Civil War for the prevention of soil erosion and for cattle fodder. Unfortunately, at that time, no one anticipated the kudzu's rampant growth potential in the South. It was indeed successful in controlling soil erosion and, briefly, as cattle fodder, but the farmers claimed that their cows didn't eat fast enough to prevent the kudzu from eating them! It has a growth rate of a foot a day!

Pier, Wharf, Dock—What?

In many parts of the country, the word *dock* is used to signify a type of loose structure built out over the water. Along the Eastern Shore, however, the words used are *pier, wharf,* and/or *landing*. Which is which? A *landing* is simply a site for landing (as in ferryboat landing); while a *wharf* is a landing place at which vessels may tie up to load or unload (as in the Grand Hotel Wharf); and a *pier* is a platform extending from a shore over water and supported by piles that is used to secure, protect, and provide access to boats and used predominantly for entertainment (as in "Let's have a party on the pier!").

Silverhill

The timeless village of Silverhill, on Alabama 104 near Alabama 59, was founded in 1897 primarily by Scandinavian and Bohemian settlers. Today there are about 400 families in the immediate district, many of them descended from these early colonists.

Silverhill was named for one of these settlers, who lived on a hill in the area and was known for dealing solely in silver. Although his name was not Silver, he was nicknamed Silver and therefore today the town bears his name.

A jewel of a building is the **Silverhill Library,** which is the second structure built in the village in 1897 by the first mayor and founding father, Oscar Johnson. This historic, white-frame building served as the Land Company Office, the first school, and the Lutheran Church and is on the National Register of Historic Places.

Today it is known as "the old building bursting with new books" and, as a library, has been under the leadership of Elsie Chandler since 1947. The library is open Monday through Friday from 2:00 P.M. to 4:00 P.M., Thursday from 10:00 A.M. to 5:00 P.M., and Saturday from 1:00 P.M. to 4:00 P.M. The telephone number is (334) 945-5201.

Somewhat tucked away, the **Peoples Supply Company,** corner of Alabama 104 and Alabama 55 in Silverhill, is a fascinating antique shop and worth whatever detour is necessary. It appeals to men as well as women with a spectacular collection of antique tools and lovely old linens and quilts.

Perhaps most outstanding are the handcrafted reproduction Windsor chairs made in New Hampshire exactly as they were in the 1700s. Peoples Supply Co. is the only dealer in the state for these chairs and benches, which are so beautifully constructed they are destined to be tomorrow's heirlooms. The building is of historical interest since it was built in 1902 and served as a general store under the same name. It has recently been placed on the National Register of Historic Places. Then the merchandise included groceries, clothing, fabric, and tools and the proprietors lived upstairs. It is open from 10:00 A.M. to 5:00 P.M., Wednesday through Saturday. The telephone number is (334) 945-5168.

SILVERHILL, ALABAMA
EST. 1902

Fairhope

Nestled on a bluff under sprawling live oak trees and overlooking Mobile Bay is Fairhope—a pretty little town of 10,000 souls and a colorful array of seasonal flower beds, boxes, and hanging baskets that line the streets. Fairhope's mayor, James Nix, and its talented landscape director, Tim Kant, have created a clean, neat, and picturesque community that is reminiscent of an English village.

Fairhope is unique in its origin, for as local historian John Sledge says, "Fairhope was an idea before it became a place." The idea was that land should be leased, not individually owned, with rent for 99

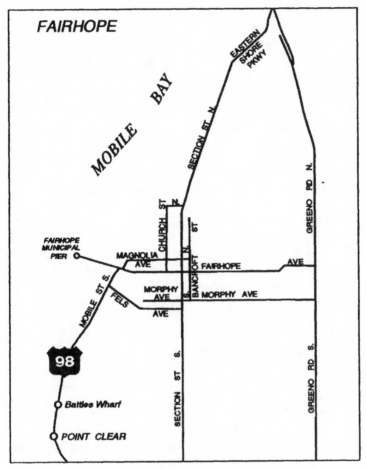

Permission to reprint map granted by Keith Map Service, Inc.

years to be used to pay ad valorem taxes and expenses of the Single Tax Corporation. Today, with its 4,000 acres, Fairhope functions as the only single tax community in the nation.

In 1894, the founding fathers (mainly from the Midwest) named the town "Fairhope," noting that their utopian settlement had "a fair hope of success." The fact that there is no individual land ownership has helped control land speculation and has prevented Fairhope from becoming a typical waterfront tourist town. Growth here is viewed with a jaundiced eye.

Fairhope is located eight miles south of Interstate 10 on the Eastern Shore. From Interstate 10, exit onto U.S. 98 (Exit 35) and travel south for approximately seven miles; take a right onto Scenic U.S. 98 at the Welcome to Fairhope sign and travel two miles farther to downtown Fairhope.

The best way to enjoy Fairhope is to drive to the center of town, park, and walk along the tree-lined streets to the many shops and restaurants. Looking in any direction is pleasing to the eye—Fairhope is a city where flower boxes and hanging baskets abound and pretty mini-parks have been created to allow people to rest or eat outside if they wish. Even the trash receptacles have flowers planted on top of them. Just strike out on foot and take in all the pleasures this little city affords.

Begin at the **Fairhope Welcome Center,** about a block north of the center of town on Section Street. This beautiful building was completed in 1993. Volunteers staff the building and there are restrooms here.

Crown & Colony, 15 North Section Street, is one of the most irresistible antique shops in the area, specializing in French and English furniture. Proprietors Ann and Peter Fargason journey to these countries quarterly to search out and discover the finest and most well-priced chests, linen presses, tables, chairs, and decorative accessories. Collectors will delight in the large and lively selection of English tea caddies, tortoise items, and Imari and Majolica china. It is open from 10:00 A.M. to 5:00 P.M., Monday through Saturday. The telephone number is (334) 928-4808.

The Obvious Place, 12 North Section Street, is indeed an obvious place for a wide variety of arts and crafts, many of them by local artisans. There are gifts for all ages, including handmade jewelry, handblown glassware, pottery, baskets, and interior decorative fountains. It is an entertaining shop. It is open Monday through Saturday from 9:30 A.M. to 5:00 P.M. and on Sunday from 1:30 P.M. to 5:00 P.M. The telephone number is (334) 928-1111.

Also on North Section Street is the **Renaissance Cafe,** which has an outdoor balcony for dining in good weather. The menu consists of specialty seafood dishes and French Caribbean cuisine. Try the Barbados Glazed Shrimp, the Redfish Calypso, or the Shrimp Grand Terre. The Seafood Bisque is also a house specialty. A live jazz band plays on weekends. It is open at 11:00 A.M. Tuesday through Saturday and again at 5:00 P.M. for dinner. A champagne brunch is served on Sunday from 11:00 A.M. until 3:00 P.M. It is recommended that you call (334) 990-6221 for reservations.

Just around the corner on Fairhope Avenue is **Andree's Wine and Cheese and Things** (403 Fairhope Avenue). Andree's is well known for its fine wines and deli. Try the latest in the shop's specialty foods, such as the famous Catfish Pâté, or one of "Andy's" gourmet recipes—creamy Stilton Soup. While Andree's has inside seating for tea or luncheon, takeouts are fun for a picnic-style lunch in one of the parks scattered throughout the town (the Muffaletta is hard to beat).

While brother, Jim Ketchum, and wife, Stacy, have come into the business and added a new bakery, Andree is beefing up her culinary skills at the Johnson and Wales Institute in Charleston. She will return on a consulting basis. Everything is business as usual: fine wine section, great lunch menu, all kinds of prepared foods to take out, beautiful gourmet gift baskets, a new cocktail spread and cracker section, delicious homemade breads, and, of course, the Godiva chocolates. Andree's is open from 7:00 A.M. to 6:00 P.M., Monday through Friday, and from 7:00 A.M. to 5:00 P.M. on Saturday. The telephone number is (334) 928-8863.

When Pam Klarman moved to Fairhope from Atlanta, she found a real need for a place to obtain educational supplies for teachers. She opened **Teacher's Tools** (407 Fairhope Avenue), a small store with a big red apple on the front, next door to Andree's. The purpose of Teacher's Tools is to supply not only teachers, but parents with creative materials for children to have fun, while getting a "leg up" on their studies.

Pam offers moderately priced aids such as resource books and "manipulatives" for preschoolers to eighth graders—all geared to enrich the subjects the child is already learning in school. If you are planning a car trip with children and want to keep your sanity, pick up some of the Wonderboard games at Teacher's Tools. Grandparents would do well to snatch up some of these stimulating materials for visits from the little darlings. Pam has regular business hours from 10:00 A.M. to 5:00 P.M., Monday through Friday. The telephone number is (334) 928-2020.

A few doors down is Fairhope's oldest restaurant—**Julwin's** (411 Fairhope Avenue). Since 1945, Julwin's has been a favorite of local politicians and is also a place in town where you can get breakfast on

Sunday morning. Fairhope has long been a haven for creative folks and local authors meet at Julwin's for literary chitchat while enjoying Julwin's country fare and homemade banana pudding. It is open seven days a week at 6:00 A.M. The telephone number is (334) 990-9372.

Grandmothers, close your eyes when you pass **Stitch in Tyme.** Whether you smock or not, you won't be able to resist these children's clothes. Here is all you need to create beautifully smocked items or you can purchase outfits already finished.

Owner Nancy Little also has a great variety of novelty fabrics for children's clothes and, if you are a quilter, you'll love her cottons. Call her about classes. Stitch in Tyme is located at 6-A South Bancroft and is open Monday through Saturday from 10:00 A.M. to 5:00 P.M. The telephone number is (334) 928-5321.

The **Village Peddler** is a sharp and shiny cookware shop at 412 Fairhope Avenue owned by Suzi Eleventh and husband Mike. When Mike took a food manager's job at a local hotel, he and Suzi decided to open up because "we couldn't find quality cookware merchandise in the area."

As well as the basics that any bride would need, Suzi offers cooking classes and many unique items. (It is worth a stop just to see her cookie cutter collection). But the signature here is quality. "When you buy a garlic press, it should last forever," she says.

Stop by for a sample of her "Zo" bread. She makes it every day in the fabulous Zojirushi bread maker. The Village Peddler is open from 10:00 A.M. to 5:00 P.M., Monday through Saturday. The telephone number is (334) 928-4850.

Fairhope jumped for joy when owner Anne Freeland decided to open a branch of **Christine's**—a fabulous gift shop that has "lived" in Birmingham for more than 20 years. In a cozy, fragrant shop at 408 Fairhope Avenue, Anne has assembled a dazzling array of gifts.

One of the signature items is the distinctive MacKenzie-Childs china, glassware, and enamelware. Beautiful linens abound too—Anachini, Palais Royale, and Peacock Alley sheets, coverlets, and shams will entice you. Please note the line of unusual picture frames. Christine's is open from 10:00 A.M. until 5:00 P.M., Monday through Saturday. The telephone number is (334) 990-0588.

One of many outstanding shops you will see on your trek through Fairhope is **Uptown** (400 Fairhope Avenue). Clothes in Uptown are easy and casual, just right for life on the Eastern Shore; the store also carries "Mobile casual," which is a line of clothes a bit more formal.

The belts are the piéce de résistance and will last through many seasons in your wardrobe.

Owner Mary Ann Corte has a flair for buying contemporary clothing. She also loves to order beautiful formals and cocktail dresses for the special times in your life. Whether it is Mardi Gras, the Polo matches, or the Grand Summer Ball, you can be sure that Mary Ann has had a hand in outfitting many of the people attending these functions. When you go to the shop, you will hear George the canary sing his heart out for you. Uptown is open from 10:00 A.M. until 5:00 P.M., Monday through Saturday. The telephone number is (334) 928-7664.

Next door to the **Frame Shop** (31 South Section Street) is **The Colony Shop** (27 South Section Street), an up-to-date, sophisticated, classic clothing store that's a family affair. More than 35 years ago, Verona Beiser started out working in The Colony and ended up buying it. Her granddaughters, Debbie and Kim, have joined her in creating a shop with clothes for all ages.

Across on the corner (32 South Section Street) you will find **The Lyons Share** (long before, however, the stunning window displays will "find" you). Owners Kelly and Mike Lyons stock some of the very best local art as well as great vintage furniture. They are also the exclusive dealer in Fairhope for Walter Anderson silkscreens.

Upstairs is an excellent frame shop specializing in shadow boxes and French matting. As well as being the largest dealer of custom and ready-made frames on the coast, Lyons Share has an unusual selection of hand-carved and hand-painted moldings. Kelly says, "If you can dream it up, we can frame it!" The Lyons Share is open from 9:30 A.M. until 5:30 P.M., Tuesday through Saturday. The telephone number is (334) 928-2507.

Next door is **Page and Palette** (32 South Section Street), a book and art shop founded in 1972. Besides best sellers, the shop carries a good supply of backlist books, classics, poetry, and nonfiction. For the children, there is a bright, fun room filled with books, games, and educational kits and, for the artist, there is an ultracomplete line of art supplies. It is open from 9:00 A.M. to 6:00 P.M., Monday through Saturday, and from 12:00 noon to 5:00 P.M. on Sunday. The telephone number is (334) 928-5295.

Bungalows, Inc., 40 South Section Street, is the only discount store in town. It is worth checking regularly if you are furnishing home or apartment. The stock, from major national department stores, consists of linens, furniture, accessories, and garden accents. Prices are great if you find a long-sought-after item. It is open from 10:00 A.M. to 5:00 P.M., Monday through Saturday. The telephone number is (334) 990-3995.

Just around the corner from Bungalows is **The French Quarter,** an enclosed brick courtyard with a fountain surrounded by small shops. Among them are **Punta Clara II, Watercolors by Willoweise,** and **Benoist's Cafe.**

Antique buffs should press on up Section Street to the **Antique Emporium,** which features 21 dealers and is bulging with collectibles and bric-a-brac. While in the vicinity you should poke into the shops next door.

Three George's Candy Shop has finally come to Fairhope. Located at 58 South Section Street, this long-established Mobile business, famous for its hand-dipped confections, is making it easy for Eastern Shore "sweet tooths" to indulge. For special orders, call (334) 928-9973.

Across the street from Three George's is **Greer's Food Tiger** grocery store, where you can pick up some of the best crispy-fried chicken in town and even a bottle of Dom Pérignon champagne for a wonderful impromptu picnic.

William F. Colburn, Jr., started designing iron furniture in 1987 and what started out as a hobby has turned into a full-time occupation. He has since opened **Iron Age Gallery,** where he displays a few examples of his custom-made beds, tables, chairs, sofas, and occasional pieces.

William can do anything in this difficult medium. He once designed a bed for a young, married couple from Pittsburgh who wanted a piece of art that would remain strong and beautiful through many generations. (Using an old porthole from a revered boat that had been destroyed, William made another client a table around the porthole that would be used and loved every day.)

Iron Age Gallery is located at 107 South Section Street and is open from 10:30 A.M. to 5:00 P.M., Monday through Saturday, and from 1:00 P.M. to 5:00 P.M. on Sunday. The telephone number is (334) 990-5351.

Nancy Scott and her 2,000 teddy bears now reside at 26 South Section Street. According to Nancy, bears are the second most collectible item in the United States (stamps being the first). **Bears By the Bay** has bears from $6.00 to $1,700.00; bears from one inch to five feet tall; as well as bears for the newborn to bears for the serious collector. They are dressed in everything from christening gowns to biker outfits and the bears in the window are always dressed for the season. You need to see it to believe it. It is open Monday through Saturday from 10:00 A.M. to 5:00 P.M. The telephone number is (334) 928-8989.

The Purple Mullet next door is just plain fun! Here you will find painted furniture, faux finishes, and whimsical accessories. Custom painting for furniture is offered to customers. Owner Mike Lyons (of Lyons Share) also has a great selection of iron works—from candleholders to fireplace screens. And if you are looking for a painted fish on a footstool, this could be the place to find it! It is open Monday through Saturday, from 10:00 A.M. to 5:00 P.M. The telephone number is (334) 990-6114.

In **The Friendshoppe** (326 De La Mare) you will find quaint antiques and collectibles and, if you are an angel collector, you will think you have gone to heaven! The telephone number is (334) 928-2800.

A handsome, new restaurant has opened in Fairhope. **Aubergine** (French for eggplant) is located at 315 De La Mare. The building that houses Aubergine is the creation of Walcott, Adams, Verneuille and has received the coveted AIA Award for the best design of a new building in Alabama.

Ann Bridgeman is the owner and operator of Aubergine and is certainly well connected in the business of international cuisine, having studied in Paris and spent some years heading up a cooking school and television show.

Notice how the eggplant theme has been carried through to the delightful eggplant-shaped china in the perfect puce color. Ann also serves a special eggplant dish every day. Hours for Aubergine are from 11:00 A.M. to 2:00 P.M. for lunch and from 6:00 P.M. to 10:00 P.M. for dinner, Tuesday through Saturday. Prices vary from moderate lunches to expensive dinners. Walk-ins at lunch can easily be served, but reservations for dinner are suggested. The telephone number is (334) 928-9541.

You can't (and won't want to) miss the stunning, three-story, wrought-iron staircase climbing to the sky at the entrance of **Joy's Patio** (311 De La Mare Avenue). Recently revamped, Joy's now consists of the usual great plant selection, a Garden Shed Shop, and a fabulous new gift gallery called J. P.'s run by the mother-daughter team, Joy Ward and Leslie Richmond.

As you enter the shop, a gold, concrete block wall (yes, gold and great!) and an 11-by-15-foot framed oil canvas by Eileen Santa Cruz tell you that you're in for a treat. Joy and Leslie have gathered such diverse items as hooked rugs, gazing balls, a twig bench, colored Mercury glass house ornaments, "sun drops," weather vanes, etcetera.

Hours are not rigid. "I usually open up around ten or eleven, Tuesday through Saturday," Joy says, "and close sorta near five." It is worth waiting for if necessary, for where else can you get a tiny iron rocking horse or a copper bowl big enough to bathe in!

Chef Jean Pierre, a baker and French pastry chef, is from Lyon, France, where his family operated a bistro. He settled in Miami where he and his wife, Pat, a Canadian, owned and operated a bakery. After selling the bakery, they moved the shop to 302 De La Mare Avenue and **Jean Pierre's Cafe** opened to rave reviews.

Lunches are the freshest of salads with wonderfully light dressings (try the Chicken Sautéed Salad), linguini with fresh sautéed tomatoes, quiches, and a superb Croissant Crust Pizza. In cool weather, the onion soup is nearly impossible to beat. Breads and dessert pastries are made right here.

If you call ahead, you can order cakes and French bread for takeout. Recently, Pat and Jean Pierre began offering French gourmet dinners at night (preferably on Sunday) by appointment. Call for reservations for six to 20 friends and Jean Pierre and Pat will cook for you. The café is open for lunch, Tuesday through Saturday, from

11:00 A.M. to 2:30 P.M. and for a great Sunday brunch from 11:00 A.M. to 2:00 P.M. The telephone number is (334) 928-4405.

A park is a park is a park, but not necessarily. The **Fairhoper's Community Park** was organized in the Spring of 1994. In a five-day park-build, this beautiful park on Church Street was built by more than 3,000 volunteers.

Lathers and Associates of Ithaca, New York, designed the park using input from the most discerning and influential citizens—the students at the Fairhope Kindergarten and Elementary Center—who, incidentally, came to the meeting with drawings and who, not incidentally, go to school directly across the street from the park. You can see them at recess, hands joined and with teacher leading, crossing the street to enjoy their project.

Volunteers (some skilled) dug and sighted, poured, leveled, raised, hammered, bolted—you name it. Donations were generous and fund raisers were abundant. One favorite was the hand-print wall where, for a donation, your child of choice could imprint his or her hand onto a tile and the resulting tiles were then assembled into a colorful wall. It is wonderful! The play equipment is sturdy and innovative and there are good resting spots for adults.

There are many fine restaurants in Fairhope, but you will find yourself going back again and again to **Mary Ann's Deli** (7 South Church Street) for lunch. Quite apart from the delicious food and family atmosphere, it is a pleasant interlude in a busy day. John and Mary Ann Nelson are there every day, without fail, working hard to serve you.

Nothing seems to deter customers from coming to the deli; while it was being expanded people still crowded in as usual, although hammering and drilling went on around them.

The deli has specials every day, but the Chicken Salad, followed by a piece of Mississippi Mud Pie, is hard to beat. Also take a look at all the little collections John has accumulated over the years, especially the *Gone With the Wind* memorabilia.

You can always tell who the locals are because they clean their tables after they eat. This place is a kick.

Mary Ann's Bacon Chive Potato Salad

8 cups small red potatoes
1 cup mayonnaise
3 tbsp. Dijon mustard
1 bunch of green onions, chopped
10 slices crisp bacon, cooked and cooled

Boil unpeeled potatoes until tender; quarter after boiling. Mix mayonnaise and mustard together. Toss with potatoes, green onions, and bacon. Serves 8.

Hallie Youngblood, with many years in the business, brings you **Chit Chat** (7 South Church Street). What a versatile shop! Here are loads of gifts, rocking horses for children, and fabulous "go anywhere" casual clothes.

At **The Studio** (7 South Church Street), the sign outside says it all: "Art and Other Irresistible Stuff." In this newly enlarged shop, you will find an outstanding array of local and regional art, both fine and folk. One room is full of bright and whimsical selections, including Dr. Jim Poteet's colorful furniture, fun painted china and glassware, Jan Burn's angels, and A. E. Barnes' happy nudes.

A second room is more impressionistic and features such artists as Barbara Gallagher, Tommy Mathis, and Emilee Lyons. There are a lot of fun gift items, too. It is open from 10:00 A.M. to 5:00 P.M., Monday through Saturday. The telephone number is (334) 928-0537.

For fans of homemade Italian Pizza Pie, **Papa's Pizza** is a place for you. Whether you want thick or thin crust, a slice or a whole jumbo, you can satisfy your cravings here. A favorite is the White Veggie Pizza, made with sweet basil pesto, mozzarella and Romano cheeses, broccoli and tomato, and topped with a ricotta cheese sauce. There is only room for a few "eat-ins," so you may choose to call in your order at (334) 990-9600 for a takeout. It is open Monday through Thursday, 11:00 A.M. until 8:00 P.M., and Friday and Saturday from 11:00 A.M. until 9:00 P.M. By the way, Papa's Pizza is owned by the same family that owns Papa's Place in Daphne.

Take a break at **Ye Old Tyme Ice Cream Parlor and Sandwich Shop** and treat yourself to one of its delicious, diverse flavors of ice cream— grape, coconut, or pumpkin in the fall—or go for broke and order a Choco Taco!

Tucked into a neat shop on Church Street is **Mr. Gene's Beans
... Espresso Bar,** home of the "Fairhope Float" (iced mochaccino with
vanilla yogurt topped with whipped cream). This small, fragrant shop
has an astonishing assortment of all kinds of goodies, from Hawaiian
Juleps to Cheesecake On A Stick (a kind of sophisticated popsicle).

Owner Gene Leighty, who bought the shop "sort of by accident,"
also has a fine selection of coffees (Leighty says that Vanilla Hazelnut
is a favorite) and chocolate (Ghiradelli and Lindt, to name a couple).
In addition, you can buy jelly beans, chocolate sand dollars, or truffles.
Leighty says that his "best-selling item is cappuccino—hot in the winter
and iced in the summer." This shop is open from 9:00 A.M. until 8:00
P.M., Monday through Saturday, and from 1:00 P.M. until 6:00 P.M. on
Sunday. Right outside are delightful sidewalk tables and chairs.

Want some lunch before your chocolate? You're in luck! Right next
door to Mr. Gene's Beans is **Jus' Gumbo** . . . yep . . . gumbo, New
Orleans style (they also have great red beans and rice). You can eat
in or take out. You can buy a bowl or a gallon. It is open from 11:00
A.M. until 8:00 P.M., Monday through Saturday. The telephone
number is (334) 928-4100 if you want to call in an order.

Gumbo

The word *gumbo* is African, meaning "okra," which is used as a thick-
ening agent in stew or soup. Actually, at one time, gumbo was a
poor man's food brought to the Western Hemisphere by slaves in
the 18th century. There are several types of gumbo—chicken or
turkey with sausage or fish—however, the great favorite of the Northern Gulf Coast is created with crabmeat, shrimp, and sometimes oysters (among other ingredients). A Gulf Coast chef, Cortlandt Inge,
points out that there is a difference between New Orleans Seafood
Gumbo and gumbo of the Northern Gulf Coast region. "The major
difference," he explained, "is that in New Orleans the soup is usually cooked to a dark or what they call a 'black roux.' This takes
four to five hours of constant stirring, which thins out the gumbo."

Alabama Seafood Gumbo

3 tbsp. Crisco oil
4 tbsp. flour
2 large onions, chopped
6 celery stalks, chopped
1 large green pepper, chopped
2 #2 cans tomatoes, undrained
2 lb. okra, sliced
4-6 crabs, cleaned (optional)
4 qt. water
1/2 tsp.garlic salt
2-3 crumbled bay leaves
1 tbsp. salt
Black or red pepper to taste
Tabasco sauce to taste
1 1/2 tbsp. Worcestershire sauce
1 1/2 lb. raw peeled shrimp
1 lb. crabmeat and/or crab claws

Make a dark golden roux in heavy skillet of oil and flour. Stir in onions, celery, and green pepper and simmer a few minutes, stirring constantly. Add undrained tomatoes and okra. Simmer until okra is tender. Place in large soup pot the crab bodies and four quarts of water. Add seasonings and cook very slowly over low heat for several hours, stirring frequently. Add crabmeat, crab claws, and shrimp during last 15 minutes of cooking time. Adjust seasoning. Serve in soup bowls over hot rice. Serves 10-12.

M. Rivers and Co., 8 South Church, is an interesting store of international flavor and is described in *Southern Living* magazine as "a shop not to be missed in Alabama." The shop is also listed as a source in a multitude of cookbooks for rare, varied, and worldwide selections of hot sauces.

Owner Rivers French takes off several times a year for the far corners of the world to purchase African masks, unique musical instruments, the popular Filly hat from Canada, the durable Aussie outback coat, and other items unusual and exotic.

There are 50 different product lines, including bath gels and a great line of bush teas. Rivers explains, "Bush teas are curative teas—

among the many I have are Passion Fruit Tea for arthritis and Sour-sop Tea for insomnia." In addition, there is a mail-order catalog. This shop is open from 10:00 A.M. to 5:00 P.M., Monday through Saturday. The telephone number is (334) 990-6088.

New to Church Street but not Fairhope is **Cathi Ginder,** a talented young artist who crafts a brightly happy and whimsical line of ceramic dinnerware and accessories. Her pieces compliment the casual Eastern Shore life-style and add a fun touch to the dinner table. A bonus is that her pieces are all microwaveable.

Cathi also does faux finishes, murals, and furniture. She custom designs and makes dishes or tiles to match your wallpaper or "anything else." Her newest line is a happy Mardi Gras design. Cathi says, "I love doing this!" You can tell. Her shop is located at 2 South Church Street and is open from 11:00 A.M. until 5:00 P.M., Tuesday through Saturday. The telephone number is (334) 928-2324.

On the corner of Fairhope Avenue and Church Street is **Sandra's Place,** a tiny café with inside and outside patio tables and a delectable chicken salad. Good takeout sandwiches and soups are also available. Sandra's Place is open from 10:00 A.M. to 5:00 P.M., Monday through Saturday. The telephone number is (334) 990-3344.

Beginning at the intersection of Church Street and Fairhope Avenue, merchants have coined the term "West End of Fairhope Avenue" to describe their location. Yellow flags fly in front of most shops to distinguish this area.

Martha Fuchs, owner of **The Brown Pelican,** located at 212 Fairhope Avenue, has used her artistic talents to creatively display an unusual collection of jewelry and gifts for your perusal. The Pelican proffers pottery, paintings, picture frames, pillows, purses, place mats, and pewter pulls. Be sure to notice Betsy Fowler's animal prints (Betsy is the wife of Jim Fowler of "Animal Kingdom"). The Pelican's telephone number is (334) 928-8022.

Good quality is hard to come by these days, but it can be found—excellence is another thing. **East Bay Clothiers** is an excellent store for men and is owned and operated by Genie McCown. The interior of East Bay is its best advertisement. Scored cement floors stained in muted shades of gray and black with saddle-colored trim sets the tone of the place. The track lighting is cleverly suspended on tiny wires across the ceiling that illuminate the heavy metal and glass racks of men's clothes.

Genie McCown is the "can-do" gal that can ease men into the look they want by coordinating the clothes to look perfectly uncoordinated. Genie is fabric driven, which is the real difference in her clothes. She keeps the classic look but uses wonderful cashmere and blended silks, cottons, and the lightest wools and linens for the mild Gulf climate. She is a master of the dress-sport look, taking the clothes from the boardroom to the boardwalk.

Men's clothes have gone through an evolutionary period where the same classic styles have taken a contemporary mode. East Bay Clothiers makes the new statement better than anyone on the Gulf Coast. The shop is expensive, but the staff will help build your wardrobe painlessly. It is located at 225 Fairhope Avenue. The telephone number is (334) 928-6848.

The walls of **Plate and Platter,** 217 Fairhope Avenue, are alive with bright, fun, handmade plates designed by artists from all over the country. Each piece is an original work and no two are alike. Children's pottery can be personalized. In addition, there is hand-painted furniture, great accent pieces, as well as hand-painted table linens. It is open from 10:00 A.M. to 5:00 P.M., Monday through Saturday. The telephone number is (334) 928-0400.

Antique aficionados will enjoy **The Interiors Mart,** 122 Fairhope Avenue. This extensive, varied collection of antiques by multiple, regional dealers includes porcelains, furniture, rugs, and some special museum pieces, as well as reproductions and works by local artists. It is open from 10:00 A.M. to 6:00 P.M., Monday through Saturday. The telephone number is (334) 928-1819.

North of Fairhope Avenue on Church Street is another small collection of shops. On each side of the banana trees, you will find a shop that carries "art wear" and on the corner of the building is **Corner-Copia** with birdhouses, garden accessories, and a great selection of flags.

The decor of the newly renovated **Church Street Cafe** at 9 North Church Street is still a collage of Southern remnants with hand-painted walls of oak trees and Spanish moss. The menu is still Southern Creole and the famous Artichoke and Crab Bisque is still served.

Owners Martha and Fred Watkins have added three dining rooms that can also be used for private parties. In the main room, the 25-foot bar is still in place; shiny copper-topped tables are opposite. The bar is open from 11:00 A.M. until, six days a week. Lunch begins at 11:00 A.M. and dinner at 5:00 P.M. At least once a week there is live music—often it is jazz piano. For reservations, call (334) 928-6611.

Past Pleasures Antiques, 19-D North Church Street, has an amazing array of American coin silver. The proprietor, Ted Stickney, inherited some antique silver, researched it, and became passionately interested in the subject.

Southern silver is his specialty, but it is rare and expensive, he says, with South Carolina silver the most valuable and Alabama silver so rare that most of it is in museums. The shop is closed several times a month when he travels to antique shows, so it is best to call ahead. The shop telephone number is (334) 928-8484 and his home telephone number is (334) 626-0176.

Enchanted Cottage

For a unique selection of children's clothing and accessories, stop by the **Enchanted Cottage,** located at the north end of Church Street. Owner Jacqueline Thomas manufactures many of her own designs and also imports clothing from Europe and South America. If you are looking for a handmade outfit for a special occasion, Jacqueline offers hand-smocked and French hand-sewn designs. Sizes range from infant to size 14 for girls and up to size five for boys. The telephone number is (334) 928-0000.

Royal Oaks is a snug English pub patterned after the ones you might see in the Cotswolds of England. The menu at the pub is provincial English fare—Cottage Pie, fish and chips, Steak and Mushroom Pie, good lamb chops, steaks, and everyday specials that are not on the menu. English and Irish draft beers top off a very pleasant dining experience.

Lisa and Jim Fields own the pub and have fair prices. The hours are 11:00 A.M. to 3:00 P.M. and from 5:00 P.M. to 9:30 P.M., Monday through Friday; and from 11:00 A.M. to 10:00 P.M. on Saturday and Sunday, serving brunch from 11:00 A.M. to 2:00 P.M. The telephone number is (334) 928-1714.

A recent light and airy addition is a new dining room that resembles a greenhouse. Part of the ceiling is glass too so you can enjoy looking up into the branches of an enormous live oak.

If you'd prefer something lighter than the traditional pub fare, order several appetizers. The smoked salmon is fresh and good, the eggrolls are delicious, and the coconut shrimp rates four stars!

At the corner of Church Street and up Fairhope Avenue, you'll have a hard time deciding where to stop. There are restaurants where you can get everything from steamed seafood to a chilled margarita on a balcony, and there is an excellent selection of clothing shops (some have been here for years; others are remodeled bicycle shops and filling stations filled with snappy collections and great gifts).

You can also buy crab traps, china, kites, and lace. **The Picture Show** has Edna Nelson's wonderful River Expressions ceramics and **Jubilee Music Store** has a cat that sleeps in the window. **Wilkins** (395 Fairhope Avenue) is a great small department store; **Brenny's** (333 Fairhope Avenue) and **Stowe's** (393 Fairhope Avenue) both have exceptionally different jewelry; and **Fantasy Island** (335 Fairhope Avenue) will delight every adult and child. If you are looking for casual sportswear, **Charley's** carries Patagonia, along with other well-known brands.

Believe it or not, you can get a terrific haircut at **Ken and Vernon's** for $6.00. Go to the middle of Fairhope Avenue, but go before 5:00 P.M. There will probably be a line.

When you walk into **CK Collection,** you get the feeling that something is different—it feels soft and quietly subdued. Perhaps it is because the walls are beautifully draped with fabric. Owners Lisa and Tom White explain that the walls had been decorated with original paintings by a previous tenant and the owner did not want them disturbed; therefore, the idea of using fabric as a wall covering came into play as they began to decorate the full-line shoe shop. CK's not only has beautiful footwear, but also belts, purses, hats, jewelry, and even sunglasses. According to Lisa, she can accessorize any outfit and offers shoe dying for that dyed-to-match look. This great little shop is located on Fairhope Avenue in the middle of town and the telephone number is (334) 928-9006.

John Collette Fine Arts, at 332 Fairhope Avenue, is the ideal spot to search for that major art find for home or office. John Collette, who also has a gallery in Highlands, North Carolina, has assembled a varied, world-class collection of paintings and sculpture for his Fairhope gallery.

The artists whom he represents are professional living artists from all over the United States and Europe. Among them are Don Hatfield, considered by many to be the most important working artist today, and Frank Jauca, who grinds his own pigments for his beautiful still-lifes, which are similar to the Old Masters' technique.

John Collette and director Alice Taylor of Montrose see a trend in the art world today toward three-dimensional art, such as sculpture, pottery, and art glass. This gallery is open from 10:00 A.M. to 5:00 P.M., Monday through Saturday. The telephone number is (334) 990-9575.

M & F Casuals, 380 Fairhope Avenue, established in 1930, is the oldest clothing retail business in Baldwin County and its tradition goes back four generations. Marc and Ann Miller are carrying on this tradition. You'll find casual to dressy ladies' wear, accessories, and the ever-popular Birkenstocks and Clarks shoes. It is open from 10:00 A.M. to 5:30 P.M., Monday through Saturday. The telephone number is (334) 928-5564.

Kathy Lambert's clothing store is a dream come true for her. Originally from Athens, Greece, Kathy came to this country in 1955 when she was a young woman, only intending to spend a week. She ended up spending a lifetime. The interior of the shop is beautifully decorated and the stock is artistically displayed. Clothing and accessories are feminine, romantic, and very often one-of-a-kind. Kathy claims she can literally dress you from head to toe now that there is a shoe boutique within the shop—and she can even do your makeup. It is located at 382 Fairhope Avenue. The telephone number is (334) 928-4454. Call for hours.

Dock Of The Bay, 386 Fairhope Avenue, has the distinction of being Fairhope's only clothing manufacturer. Designed here on the spot and shipped to specialty shops and catalogs throughout the United States, Dock Of The Bay is a relaxed resort shop. Along with other sports lines and accessories, the store is an authentic outlet for bright, snappy, cotton print casuals that are very reasonably priced. It is open from 10:00 A.M. to 5:00 P.M., Monday through Saturday. The telephone number is (334) 928-3325.

Fly Creek Cafe, located at 831 Section Street North at the Fair Harbor Marina, has an open-air pavilion where you can feel the bay breeze while you watch the sailboats sway. Fish sandwiches and fried shrimp, and oyster po' boys are the standard along with an ice cold beer. It is open from 11:00 A.M. to 9:00 P.M. every day except Monday. The telephone number is (334) 990-0902.

El Giro Mexican Restaurant has come across the bay to allow amigos along the Eastern Shore a chance to enjoy the same great menu as in Mobile. Food and drink specials are offered every day. Located at 800 Section Street North, El Giro is open for lunch and dinner from 11:00 A.M. to 10:00 P.M., Monday through Saturday, and from 12:00 noon to 10:00 P.M. on Sunday. The telephone number is (334) 990-0783.

Don't leave Fairhope without checking the exhibits at the **Eastern Shore Art Center,** a 15,000-square-foot visual arts exhibition and teaching facility, which is located on the corner of Oak Street and Section Street.

If you're hungry head south on Section Street to **The Wine Merchant,** a popular luncheon spot for many of the locals.

Owners Mike and Robert Renz have planted flowers outside to welcome you. Inside, beyond a wide windowsill of happy African violets, is a pleasant and serene room. There is always a daily special (the Shrimp Stuffed Eggplant is outstanding) and a nice selection of light dishes will leave you feeling virtuously well fed and healthy.

Along with light sandwiches such as the "Sweet Lavender" (sliced turkey, fresh pear slices, Gouda cheese, sprouts, and Russian dressing on pumpernickel), you will find chicken salad made with yogurt and a variety of quiches. For dessert, try their delicious lemon bars or a giant oatmeal cookie. You can also take out if you wish. The Wine Merchant is open Monday through Friday from 11:00 A.M. until 6:00 P.M. The telephone number is (334) 928-7777.

In a whitewashed house with a rose arbor at the entrance is **Canarela's Cottage Cafe.** Its clipped lawn and patio are so inviting that you will want to partake of whatever is inside and you will not be disappointed.

The menu has universal appeal with leanings to a light Italian fare. The pizza dough is homemade with your favorite topping and the

Funilli Tricolore is a favorite with corkscrew pasta gently folded with sun-dried tomatoes, artichoke hearts, ripe olives, fire-roasted pimentos, fresh scallions, and dill—all tossed with the Canarela Classic Dressing.

Canarela's is excellent for lunch or dinner and the child's menu is so appealing to the young (dessert is ice cream with chocolate syrup and rainbow sprinkles), what child will not ask for it every time! Canarela's Cottage Cafe is located at the corner of Pine and Bancroft and is open Monday through Thursday from 11:00 A.M. to 9:00 P.M., Friday and Saturday from 11:00 A.M. to 10:00 P.M., and Sunday from 11:00 A.M. to 2:00 P.M. The telephone number is (334) 990-0807.

Most days, Pete and Kay Taylor are doing what they love best—working in their rose garden. Their passion for roses led them to shows and seminars all over the country and eventually led to their business, **Taylor's Roses.**

Miniature and heirloom roses are the specialty at Taylor's Roses, located at 3450 Gayfer Avenue Extension. All of the miniatures are hybridized by the Taylors and are registered with the American Rose Society. The Eastern Shore Collection includes Fairhope (creamy, light yellow), which was rated the number-one exhibition rose in the United States by the American Rose Society and the number-one garden rose. The nursery also features Old Garden roses and unusual varieties from Europe.

Taylor's Roses is also an extensive mail-order business. The roses come in all forms: bushes, topiaries, hanging baskets, climbing, and cascading. The nursery hours are flexible, so call ahead (334) 928-5008. This hobby turned business keeps Pete and Kay busy year-round and Kay says, "You can plant a rose any time of year in our climate although spring is optimum."

If you are a biscuit lover and want to try something really different, stop by **Biscuit King Cafe** at 19605 Greeno Road (U.S. 98). Owners Nancy and Willie Foster have come up with a new twist on biscuits. You may be overwhelmed with the varieties, but you won't go wrong with the combo or the cinnamon and raisin biscuit. For large orders, call ahead at (334) 928-2424. The café is open for breakfast at 5:00 A.M. daily and if you want more than biscuits, there is an extensive buffet. Lunch is also served.

In small towns, the town square is a place where people usually tend to gather, visit, and gossip, but not in Fairhope. Here, the **Fairhope Pier,** located at the foot of Fairhope Avenue, is the place to go. Take a stroll on this large, 1,425-foot concrete pier. There are benches and clean restrooms and it is fun to watch the fishermen and netters and check out the catches.

Just at the entrance to the Fairhope Pier is the locally famous Rose Garden, which surrounds a lively fountain and the flag pole. Truly, it is worth a trip just to view these magnificent roses.

On the shore north of the pier is a pretty little park with tables, benches, and barbecue pits. It is pleasant for all ages to be under the trees along the lovely creek and to watch the antics of the ever-growing duck and goose population. It is certainly a happy haven for all species of ducks. In fact, there is a sign at the entrance declaring Caution— Mating Season—Drive with Care—Watch for Our Ducks. They May Not Be Paying Attention to Traffic. There is a fee for enjoying the park.

The Fairhope Pier, in one form or another, seems to have always been there. At one time, before the causeway linked Mobile to Baldwin County, it was one of many ferry landings along the Eastern Shore.

Bed and Breakfast Inns

The Fairhope area has a fascinating collection of Bed and Breakfast Inns—each with its own personality and charm. They are conveniently located and should each be a happy home away from home.

Church Street Inn is a restored 1921 house that is on the National Register of Historic Places and is located on the corner of Church Street and DeLaMare in "uptown Fairhope." It has three guest rooms with private baths. The telephone numbers are (334) 928-5144 and (334) 928-8976. It is wheelchair accessible.

At **Villa Whimsy on Mobile Bay** (360 South Mobile Street), you will find two bright, colorful cottages—Blue Crab Cottage and Pelican Cottage—as well as a main-residence accommodation (with a private entrance) called the Conch Shell Suite.

The cottages are roomy, with kitchen and dining room space, and the decor has the added charm of owner Stevi Gaston's whimsical paintings on the walls, inside and out. There is a wharf with a beckoning hammock, a nice view of Mobile Bay, and families of ducks. The telephone number is (334) 928-0226.

The Guest House (63 South Church Street) is located in a vintage 1900s house that was restored in 1990. The telephone number is (334) 928-6226 or (334) 928-0720.

On historic Mobile Bay, the **Bay Breeze Guest House** (742 South Mobile Street) has two guest rooms with private baths and glassed-in "Bay Room," plus access to a nice, 462-foot private pier. There are also two Garden Cottages with bed, bath, and living area, plus an equipped minikitchen. One guest room is wheelchair accessible. The telephone number is (334) 928-8976.

Just two doors down at 19493 Scenic U.S. 98 is **Point of View.** Set in the midst of a wonderful garden behind the circa-1900 main house

is the smoke-free guest cottage. The "Jubilee" suite, located downstairs, houses two bedrooms, living room, dining room, and full kitchen. The "Magnolia" suite, upstairs, has two bedrooms, living room, and break-fast-area kitchen. Enjoy access to a wharf and beach, and a bike path connecting Fairhope and Point Clear at the rear of the property. The telephone number is (334) 928-1809. Call for a brochure.

Marcella's (114 Fairhope Avenue) is an attractive, conveniently located home midway between Mobile Bay and downtown shops. Built in 1914, the house is called an American Four Square and has two rooms with private baths, plus a cozy cottage. The telephone number is (334) 990-8520.

Mandevilla (6 and 8 Fels Avenue) is a pair of pretty, pastel, two-story houses with a bay view and is attractively furnished. These short-term apartments are within walking distance of the popular Fairhope Pier and beach and are fully equipped, including washer and dryer. The telephone number is (334) 990-8653.

Dr. and Mrs. Joseph Gravlee have one of the best views of Mobile Bay. They are way up on a bluff, in a rich woodland setting with a bird's-eye view of sailing regattas during the day and a display of twinkling lights from the western shore at night. **Away at the Bay** (557 North Mobile Street) is billed as short-stay apartments. Winding steps lead down to the beach and swimming. The telephone number is (334) 928-9725.

Best Places to Watch the Sunset

Sunset watching is serious business on the Eastern Shore in Baldwin County. Local residents tend to be very possessive of the sunsets, referring to them as "our sunsets," but be assured that you, too, are free to watch them. The very best sunsets are not always during the summer, however, because the sun is inclined to slip behind the hazy summer sky. The ideal sunset-watching time is fall, spring, or even winter, when the air is clearer.

The following are a few places for superb sunset watching. Remember, it is not just the setting sun you are watching, but the beautiful shades and colors of the afterglow.

Located at the intersection of Interstate 10 and U.S. 98, near the remains of the old Spanish Fort (the exact location is unknown), Larry Dee Cawyer Overlook offers an unparalleled view of the bay and Mobile. Here, on a clear day, you can really see forever and the sunset watching is spectacular from this high point.

At the foot of Fairhope Avenue is the Fairhope Pier, one of the most ideal spots for serious sunset watching. It is a spacious, substantial concrete pier, 1,425 feet long with benches, restrooms, a marina, and a great little restaurant. The Fairhope Pier is great for sunset watching, but it is also interesting at night to stroll up and down and watch the fishermen pull in their catches.

In the same area of the Fairhope Pier is the **Fairhope Park.** This park is a heavenly sunset-watching area, particularly if you have small children. Here, along this clean and pretty beach, are swings, slides, volleyball nets, benches, picnic tables, and restrooms (entrance fee).

If you want to get some exercise while watching the sunset, there is a pleasant stretch of sidewalk or jogging path along Mobile Street. This is partially along the bluff overlooking the bay and partially along Fairhope Beach, and the view is lovely. At the same time, you can walk, jog, or bicycle and watch the sunset while admiring the seasonal flower beds en route. The path extends to the Grand Hotel—a round trip of about seven miles.

A particularly romantic way to watch the sun go down is to rent a boat and sail out onto the bay and into the sunset. Boats are available from the **Eastern Shore Marina** on Seacliff Drive in Fairhope. Here

you can get a captained day charter (which eliminates liability) on a 30- to 44-foot sailboat. There is also a 34-foot catamaran and a 34-foot air-conditioned traveler. For information, call (334) 928-1283.

The Grand Hotel at Point Clear is probably the most elegant sunset-watching spot in Baldwin County. Besides being rich in history, the spacious grounds of the Grand Hotel are a treat to the eye and beautifully maintained. There is a walk in front of the hotel along the seawall and around what is known as **Julep Point,** where you can see the sunset from several angles. There is also a great wharf.

If you would rather do your sunset watching inside, try the **Bird Cage Lounge** in the Grand Hotel. This is an attractive and comfortably furnished lounge with cozy groupings of chairs and sofas and a broad expanse of bay windows. Here you can sit and sip something cool or hot and watch the sun in utmost comfort and style.

You may even be served by the famous beverage server, Buckey Miller, a long-standing institution at the Grand Hotel. Buckey, who is 75 years young, has worked for the Grand Hotel for 55 years. He knows everybody, far and near, and everyone knows him and his specialty drink, a Hot Mint Toddy, for which he grows his very own mint just outside the Bird Cage Lounge door.

Buckey's Hot Mint Toddy

3-4 medium fresh mint leaves
Boiling water
1/4 oz. Walker Deluxe Bourbon
Honey to taste

Place mint leaves in bottom of cup and pour boiling water to cover leaves. Stir and add bourbon and honey.

(This is just as good cold! Lighten up on the boiling water and add lots of crushed ice.)

Another fashionable (and laid-back) sunset-watching spot is the **Pelican Point Grill** on Mullet Point, located at the end of County Road 1, a few miles after Scenic U.S. 98 turns east. This is a rustic, Caribbean-style restaurant with a nice, enclosed porch, outdoor decks, and a beach for children or adults to roam.

The atmosphere is pure casual and bathing suits are okay. Aluminum buckets on each table contains a roll of paper towels, which you can easily go through since the specialty here is ribs. Seafood is always featured. Pelican Point Grill is open from 5:00 P.M. until 9:00 P.M. on Monday and from 11:30 A.M. until 9:00 P.M. on Tuesday through Sunday. The owner, Harry Johnson, calls the food "Lower Alabama Style." Whatever it means, it is good! The telephone number is (334) 928-1747.

Middle Bay Light

Mobile's famous hexagonal lighthouse, Middle Bay Light, has stood sentinel over the waters of Mobile Bay for more than a century. Flashing a kerosene-fueled light, the lighthouse began operations on December 1, 1885, to aid navigation into the port city. Its hexagonal shape, pyramidal roof, and spiderlike legs make it unique among lighthouses, and it is one of only a few lighthouses that were built as a navigational aid and as a permanent residence.

Middle Bay Light has been restored in several stages, the restoration beginning in 1985 for its centennial year and continuing until the present (underwater repairs were begun in 1993), while routine maintenance is accomplished by the Propeller Club and the Middle Bay Light Commission. (Information courtesy of John Sledge, Architectural Historian for the Mobile Historic Development Commission, and *Landmark Letter,* a publication of the Historic Mobile Preservation Society.)

Battles Wharf Area

Gambino's Restaurant, located on the corner of Laurel and Mobile streets, is fun, casual dining with an Italian flavor. It has the best veal on the Eastern Shore—try the Veal Zingari or the Veal Rocco, which is owner-manager Rick Gambino's own creation.

If you like to sing, try the karaoke lounge in the back where there is dining, dancing, and live entertainment (maybe provided by you, should you be so inspired). The karaoke is on Wednesdays, Fridays, and Saturdays. It is open from 11:00 A.M. to 3:00 P.M. for lunch, Monday through Friday, and nightly from 5:00 P.M. to 10:00 P.M. for dinner.

Owner Rita Higbee is, according to her daughter, "a people person who loves clothes," so what better career for her than her attractive **Bay Boutique** (19440 Scenic 98 at Battles Wharf). This is a clothing store with a relaxed, friendly atmosphere and "fashions that will take you from New York to L.A."—that's Lower Alabama.

Bay Boutique has almost everything, from classic sportswear to Mardi Gras gowns and an extensive line of Ann May suits and jackets with skirts in five different lengths. Rita also has a fine selection of costume jewelry and belts. A local artist's work is featured. Bay Boutique is open from 10:00 A.M. until 5:00 P.M., Tuesday through Saturday.

In 1981, P. J. Bass McAleer opened her successful and beautiful silver shop, **Silver Market,** and it is filled to the brim with estate silver and linens and many unusual pieces. The shop is P. J.'s second career and, since she did extensive traveling in her first career, she has many contacts helping her locate the different and beautiful items she offers for sale.

P. J.'s sister-in-law, Dianne, joined her in 1986 and together they attempt to research every piece of silver they sell. Diane says they are the "ultimate in recycling." Beautiful, handwritten cards are attached to each purchase telling about its age and origin. P. J. says, "As we

pass this knowledge on to our customers, we hope it will stimulate them to have a deeper appreciation of their own family pieces."

Here you may find baby rattles, silver crab-claw crackers, and Victorian glass tiebacks—all displayed in antique cabinets and armoires. The shop is located at 19164 Scenic U.S. 98 and is open from 10:00 A.M. until 4:00 P.M., Tuesday through Saturday. The telephone number is (334) 928-4657 or toll free at (800) 472-8483.

Point Clear

> "Old abstracts disclose that the Spanish government granted to one Eugene LaValle of Pensacola, a tract of land at 'Punta Clara' containing 1,800 arpents (approximately 1,800 acres) and dated May 19, 1800." (Florence and Richard Scott, *Battles Wharf and Point Clear* [Mobile, Ala., 1971], 64. Permission to reprint granted by Richard Scott, Jr.)

Hotels were subsequently built on this beautiful "point" of land, as were summer homes, churches, general stores, and a post office. Point Clear was served by two wharves, one just below Battles Wharf and one at Zundel's, and it was a two-hour trip from Mobile by steamboat.

Today, Point Clear officially embraces **Marriott's Grand Hotel** on each side for about two miles and, except for the hotel, the post office, and a very few small businesses, this gorgeous stretch of land along Mobile Bay looks much as it must have a century ago.

The Grand Hotel

"In 1847, when the settlement of Point Clear was only 20 years old, Mr. F. H. Chamberlain built the Point Clear Hotel, now known as the Grand Hotel. He built the long, rambling, two-storied structure with rooms so situated that each one could benefit from the summer breezes. Once visited, the hotel's desirability as a resort became well known.

"Before the hotel burned in 1869, it served as a base hospital during the Civil War. Unfortunately, lost in the fire were the records of the more than 300 Confederate and Union soldiers who died of wounds and are buried at nearby 'Confederate Rest.'" (Florence and Richard Scott, *Battles Wharf and Point Clear* [Mobile, Ala., 1971], 64, 66. Permission to reprint granted by Richard Scott, Jr.)

Rebuilt in 1875, the Grand Hotel has undergone many changes, both in ownership and in additions to the hotel itself. New buildings fit in beautifully with the old ones on the magnificent grounds, where ancient live oaks and flowers surround a lagoon and border Mobile Bay.

Lakewood Golf Club, located on Scenic U.S. 98 and just across from the Grand Hotel, is actually a part of the hotel. Lakewood's dining room looks out on a picturesque lagoon where occasional alligators provide an entertaining spectacle. The golf course is reputed to be one of the country's finest. It has 36 holes, a championship 18, and an island green. For more information, call (334) 928-9201. The dining room is open seven days a week, from 11:30 A.M. until 3:00 P.M. for lunch.

Ye Olde Post Office Antiques and Militaria is a genuine man's antique shop, but one that women and children will also enjoy. The setting is an old, 1920 gas station, and a varied array of concrete statuary surrounds the entrance.

Inside is a fascinating and largely historical accumulation of firearms, swords, knives, Civil War memorabilia (Confederate and

Union), tools, maps, and old Civil War books. Don't miss the collection of early miniature sewing machines, antique toys, and colorful, authentic police hats from all over the world. Needless to say, it takes a while to see it all so don't try to pop in and pop out. This shop is open from 9:00 A.M. to 5:00 P.M., Monday through Saturday. The telephone number is (334) 928-0108.

Begun in 1952 as a hobby of the present owner's mother, **Punta Clara Candy Kitchen** has grown into a family-owned and -operated business. About a mile south of the Grand Hotel is the sprawling late-Victorian home that was built in 1897 by Edward Brodbeck. The house is listed on the National Register of Historic Places and is furnished as it was at the turn of the century.

The candies are all made from scratch in the kitchen, where you can watch the cooks cooking! Samples are always available and the candy—pralines, heavenly hash, brown sugar-coated pecans, and divinity, to name a few—is all beautifully wrapped and packaged. In addition, the shop offers homemade cakes and a wide variety of toppings, jellies, and pickles (vegetables are locally grown and the nuts come from the family-owned pecan orchard).

Dorothy Brodbeck Pacey, owner, also does a large mail-order business. Take a little time while you're here and visit this lovely old place where you can sit on the shady front porch in a big rocking chair and indulge your sweet tooth. It is open from 9:00 A.M. until 5:00 P.M., Monday through Saturday, and from 12:30 P.M. until 5:00 P.M. on Sunday.

Punta Clara Fudge

2 cups sugar
1/4 cup cocoa
1/2 cup milk
1/2 stick margarine
1 1/2 tbsp. light corn syrup
1 tsp. vanilla
1 cup pecans

In a heavy saucepan, mix all ingredients (except pecans). Cook to 238 degrees. Cool to 170 degrees. Add pecans, then beat until thick. Pour into a greased 8-inch pan. Cool and cut into squares.

To get to the **Wash House Restaurant** from the Candy Kitchen, you walk past a grassy lawn and live oak trees onto a shaded gallery, which leads to a board-and-batten replica of the kitchen and wash house originally built away from the main house.

Once inside, you will find a long, cozy dining room with an immense fireplace. Much of the dining room's seating is located along the extended window that looks out onto a lovely lawn. The acoustics are good—courtesy of the attractive wooden floors and ceilings. With the ceiling fans turning slowly, you will find the Wash House Restaurant an especially pleasant place to dine.

The menu is varied with a selection of beef, poultry, and usually two "catches of the day." Without hesitation, owners Johnny and Wanda Taylor say that the best item on the menu is their center-cut filet (prime Angus). To quote them, "It's the best in the country. And stuffed soft-shell crab (in season) runs a very close second." Reservations are recommended. Prices are moderate to expensive. The Wash House Restaurant is open Sunday through Thursday from 5:00 P.M. to 9:00 P.M. and Friday and Saturday from 5:00 P.M. to 10:00 P.M. The telephone number is (334) 928-1500.

Architectural Tidbits

You may like to know that there is a unique architectural feature that is found only on Mobile Bay at Point Clear. This is the "Rain Roof."

If you walk down the picturesque mile-long boardwalk at Point Clear, look for a roof supported by columns that extend out from the existing porch roof. This rain roof is, of course, to protect happy porch sitters from the blowing rain (before the days of air conditioners, there were a lot of porch sitters).

Another architectural point to ponder is that not all of the 19th-century frame cottages you see along the Gulf Coast are Creole cottages, as is widely believed. Some are called Gulf Coast cottages, the distinction being an interior passageway or breezeway and an exterior chimney. Creole cottages have interior chimneys and no interior passageways, but otherwise the exteriors of these two types of cottages are very similar. Therefore, although it looks like a Creole cottage, it may not be a Creole cottage.

In and around Fairhope, you will see many bumper stickers and T-shirts reading "Polo at the Point." On just about any Sunday, September through November or April through June, you can go to the **Point Clear Polo Club** field, stretch out on a blanket, and spend a great afternoon watching polo.

In the 1970s, Kenny McLean and George Radcliff (both three-goal players), started polo in Point Clear. Today, the Point Clear Polo Club rests on 80 acres of beautiful land on County Road 32 and hosts the finest international polo teams, which come to big charity events throughout the year. Maj. John Ferguson has captained the visiting British team for several years and the highly respected Argentines, as well as the Costa Rican and Nicaraguan teams, also compete.

There is an October benefit match that is a splendid affair with everyone dressed "to the nines," drinking champagne, and lunching under huge tents. On the other side of the polo field, you can wear your grub clothes, eat fried chicken, and drink beer. It is a great day wherever you are and the proceeds go to cancer research.

Okay, nature lovers, **Minamac Wildflower Bog** is for you! Whether you are a wild flower buff or just looking for an interesting outing, you will enjoy this experience. There are more than 300 varieties of wild flowers native to the South in this one small area. What you see depends on the time of year. Here is a host of pitcher plants, wild orchids, blazing star, wild lilies, and black-eyed susans. The bog surrounds a lake and has walking paths to allow you to get close to many of the flowers.

One of the most interesting things about the bog is that the owners discovered it by accident. They were clearing the area around the lake and decided to burn the underbrush. Imagine their excitement at watching these beautiful flowers pop up after being dormant for so many years. Call for an appointment to tour the bog: (334) 945-6157. Minamac Wildflower Bog is open April through September.

Off the beaten path, but not too far (eight miles east of Fairhope in the area known as Clay City), **Tom Jones Pottery** has been in business since 1976. Owner and potter Tom Jones doesn't have to go far for his materials. "You'll find some of the finest clay in the Southeast here," he tells visitors. "Here" is a mile-wide streak of abundant clay veins that extends from the bluffs of Mobile Bay into the heart of Baldwin County.

One hundred years after the first pottery works opened on Fish River and then closed, a "new" building was located close enough to the river to receive coal shipments that were brought upriver on barges to fuel the bee-hive kiln. This building presently houses Tom Jones Pottery and, although no longer in use, the bee-hive kiln is still intact for visitors to see.

Among the usual pottery objects, you will find Tom's white-glazed pottery with irises, which have been a top seller. Do take the time to drive out into beautiful Baldwin County to see this interesting spot.

Take Fairhope Avenue (County Road 48) east for 4 ½ miles to County Road 33, turn south for three miles to Clay City Road, watch for signs to his studio, and then east again for one-half mile. Tom Jones Pottery is open Monday through Saturday, from 9:30 A.M. until 5:00 P.M. The telephone number is (334) 928-2561.

Nanny's Kountry Kitchen (9111 U.S. 98), located in a rustic building with red-checked tablecloths, is named for grandmother Berta

Nolte, known as "Nanny." Most of her children and grandchildren work there. The good fried chicken, seafood, and fried mushrooms have people traveling for miles to munch out on Nanny's food. Wednesday night is "All-you-can-eat catfish" night and Thursday night is mullet night. Nanny's Kountry Kitchen is open from 11:00 A.M. until 9:00 P.M. daily, except Sundays, when they are only open for lunch. The telephone number is (334) 928-0524.

Just next door is a barn called **Paw's High Stepping Country,** here, on Friday and Saturday nights, there is a band and line dancing as well as square dancing and slow dancing. If you'd like to learn line dancing, you can take lessons on Tuesday and Thursday nights. Paw's opens at 8:00 P.M. The telephone number is (334) 990-6260.

The **Weeks Bay Estuarine Research Reserve,** one of 18 in the nation, is a cooperative program of the State of Alabama and the National Oceanic and Atmospheric Administration. There are 3,000 acres here; two marked nature trails lead through the wetlands to the bog via boardwalks.

An estuary is a body of salt and fresh water and here the fresh waters from the Magnolia and Fish rivers combine with the salty

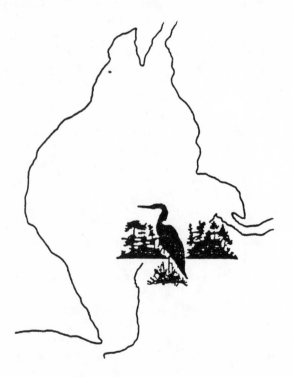

waters from Mobile Bay to make a rich mixture necessary for the spawning and feeding grounds of fish and shellfish. Nearly 90 percent of the fish caught by local fishermen are dependent upon estuaries for at least one phase of their lives. Therefore, no estuaries—no Shrimp Etouffée, no Trout Amandine, no Crab Bisque!

The rich landscape of the reserve includes tidal flats, seagrass meadows, salt marshes, and forested swamps. Look closely and among the species you may see are the Great Blue Heron, alligators, crabs, and shrimp. On the east side of the Fish River Bridge is the New Manatee Park, built on reserve property and providing a handicapped-accessible fishing pier.

Guided tours, observation deck, and outdoor exhibits are all here, on U.S. 98, about 15 miles southeast of the Grand Hotel, just west of the Fish River Bridge. Hours are from 8:00 A.M. until 5:00 P.M., Monday through Saturday, and from 1:00 P.M. to 4:00 P.M. on Sunday. The telephone number is (334) 928-9792.

Magnolia Springs

Magnolia Springs is a pretty, peaceful village just off U.S. 98 on the Magnolia River with a tree-shaded main street aptly named Avenue of Oaks. It was established in the early 1900s from a Spanish Land Grant of 1880 and has been designated as a Historic Preservation Area.

Known as a Creole community, Magnolia Springs was populated by descendants of the Spanish, French, Indian, and even the Irish and English. Today it is famous for having the very last and only mail delivery water-route in the United States. The residents' mail boxes are attached to the end of their wharves.

Former postmistress Kay Manders says, "This water route has been a colorful tradition since 1916, but it is also the most convenient and efficient way to deliver mail here." The route is 22 miles by water, which takes 2 to 2 ½ hours, and 85 miles by land, which takes 6 hours. "Only once," she says, "has weather deterred mail delivery, which was the day after Hurricane Frederic in 1979, and that was because there was no mail to deliver."

That stoic motto of the U.S. Mail, "neither rain, nor sleet, nor snow, etc.," should include in Magnolia Springs, "nor fog, nor wind, nor rough seas."

In a beautiful, old, circa-1898 home on Oak Street is the **Magnolia Springs Bed and Breakfast.** Over the years the house has been used as a community meeting place and was a popular Sunday dining place until the 1950s. A heart-pine porch extends across the front and east side of the house. Walls and ceilings are beaded heart-yellow pine and most of the woodwork is rare curly pine.

The home has five guest rooms plus living quarters. Amenities include private bath, television, and telephone. For reservations, call (800) 965-7321 or (334) 965-7321 between 8:00 A.M. and 8:00 P.M. or write to owner/host David Worthington, P.O. Box 329, Magnolia Springs, Alabama, 36555; or visit their web site at http://www.bbonline.com/al/magnolia.

Alabama Highway 59

Alabama 59 is an important north-south road linking Loxley, Robertsdale, Foley, and Gulf Shores. It can be reached from Interstate 10 and U.S. 98. Nooks and crannies—worthy ones—abound along this road.

Driving south on Alabama 59 you will find **Burris' Farm Market** on the corner of Alabama 59 and County Road 64 in Loxley. This large, busy, open-air produce center has all the charm of an old-world

Scale: 1" = 5½ Miles

market in a foreign land. It is a favorite stopping spot for folks en route to or from vacationing in Gulf Shores and on summer Sunday afternoons it is packed.

People come from miles to poke, prod, and purchase these wonderfully fresh tomatoes, peaches, beans, etc. It couldn't be fresher, since most of the produce is grown in the Burris' nearby farm garden. The peaches are perfect and you will also find the most delicious homemade sourdough bread and peach shortcake in the bakery in the back. Burris' Farm Market is open from 8:00 A.M. until 7:00 P.M., seven days a week.

Miss Kay's Favorite Pecan Pie

3 eggs, beaten
1 cup Karo syrup
1 tsp. Vanilla
2 cups pecans
1 cup sugar
2 tbsp. melted butter
1/8 tsp. salt
1 unbaked pie shell

Mix all ingredients together and pour into pie shell. Bake at 400 degrees for 15 minutes, then 350 degrees for 30 minutes. Cool before serving.

The place for die-hard, dedicated bargain hunters and fabric fans is **The Bargain Barn,** 24480 Alabama 59. From major mills, discontinued patterns, over-runs of designer fabric cording, and foam rubber for furniture are stacked to the ceiling in this unheated, uncooled Quonset hut. Genny Jenkins, manager of The Bargain Barn for more than 20 years, is on the telephone list of most of the local interior decorators who check in regularly. It is open from 8:30 A.M. to 5:00 P.M., Monday through Saturday. The telephone number is (334) 947-5601.

Farther along Alabama 59, you will come to **Succulent World,** on the west side of the road or across from Plunderosa Antiques.

Here you will find an overwhelming, confusing tangle of herbs and perennials. The owners, James and Linda Monroe, have 500 varieties of culinary, aromatic, and medicinal herbs. They also specialize in old-fashioned heirloom and pass-along plants.

James Monroe can regale you for quite some time on herb lore and herb use today. They grow hard-to-find culinary herbs like French tarragon and epazote. In the medicinal line, they have purple cone flowers, Indian ginseng, and gravel root. Then there are lamb's ears, which the Romans used for bandages, garden tansy for keeping fire ants out of the garden, and mullein for arthritic aches and bronchial relief.

The Monroes believe people are becoming more health conscious and herb use represents a more wholesome and natural life-style.

Succulent World is open seven days a week: from 8:00 A.M. until 5:00 P.M., Monday through Saturday, and from 10:00 A.M. until 5:00 P.M. on Sunday, but it is closed during December and January. (*One hint:* in the heat of the summer, choose cooler hours, such as early morning or late afternoon.) The telephone number is (334) 964-5661.

Just across Alabama 59 from Succulent World is **Plunderosa Antiques**, a spacious, 17,000-square-foot, antique-filled warehouse bursting at the seams with tables, chests, chairs, stools, china, glassware—you name it and it is probably here.

The owners, Jim and Betty Ponder, go four or five times a year to England, Scotland, Ireland, Wales, and even Belgium in their search for stock. It is not the most expensive or finest furniture, but most of it has potential and it does make one wonder if the British Isles will ever run out of furniture. The place is always brimful.

The Ponders got into the business by accident. Jim says, "We had an auto parts store that was not doing so well. Just on a whim my wife put some of her antiques in the window and they sold in a flash. So, we went into the antique business!"

The front page of the menu begins with this quote from *Zorba the Greek:* "How simple and frugal a thing is happiness . . . a glass of wine, a roast chestnut . . . the sound of the sea." Although it is not near the sea, **Ivey's Restaurant** has a romantic atmosphere that complements the good food. It is located on Pennsylvania Street in Robertsdale, on the site of Nan's Cafe, a classic dining place in the 1940s. The paintings, antiques, and original furnishings add to the gracious setting.

The veal Marsala is wonderful, as is the filet with crawfish and crab Béarnaise. There is also an excellent mixed grill on the menu. Finish it all with one of the bread puddings. Ivey's is open from 11:00 A.M. until 9:00 P.M., Tuesday through Saturday, and until 3:00 P.M. on Sunday. For reservations, call (334) 947-4000.

How can you pass up a restaurant with "Mama" in the name? Nobody in Robertsdale does—and it is packed everyday with locals and passing-through tourists. **Mama Lou's** is just what you would expect—a buffet of home-style cooking, all you can eat for five bucks.

"I taste every single item every single day," says Lou Polka, owner of Mama Lou's. "If the food isn't good enough for me, it isn't good enough for my customers."

Mama Lou's sits back from the highway at 22288 Pine Street and is open from 11:00 A.M. to 2:00 P.M., Monday through Friday, with brunch on Sunday from 11:00 A.M. to 2:00 P.M. The restaurant turns into a steakhouse on Friday and Saturday evenings, serving hand-cut steaks cooked on a mesquite grill. Check on evening hours by calling (334) 947-1988.

Weekends are the time to go to the **Highway 59 Flea Market,** when dealers from all over the county and beyond set up their booths—from 8:00 A.M. until midafternoon. However, the **Town Square Antique Mall,** located on the premises, is open Monday through

Friday (closed on Tuesday) from 10:00 A.M. to 5:00 P.M. and on Saturday and Sunday from 9:00 A.M. to 5:00 P.M. A touch of charm is added to the enclosed shops on the grounds with whimsical murals painted on the exterior by Gulf Shores artist William Harrison.

If you should be cruising down the highways of Baldwin County in the spring and spot big, beautiful fields of yellow flowers, they are not Wordsworth's "hosts of golden daffodils" but canola. This popular crop in the county is the source of the third-leading cooking oil on the market today.

Happily, canola has substance as well as beauty since it is low in cholesterol and the young leaves are even edible.

Elberta

During the early 1980s, Doug Wolbert and his wife, Alyce Birchenough, were dairy farmers in Michigan (beginning when he gave her a cow for Christmas). After visiting friends several times in Elberta, they decided that the climate and property taxes were more agreeable there, so they moved their operations south. (Because of the mild climate, pasture for the cows grows all year long.)

Sweet Home Farm opened for business in 1987 in, according to Doug, a "pocket of great farmland." He had researched the area and had found a 60-acre spot that had neither the sandy soil nearby to the south nor the red clay nearby to the north. Doug and Alyce intended to have only a mail-order dairy, but were discovered in spite of themselves.

They now sell between 10,000 and 12,000 pounds of 15 varieties of natural cheese each year. Doug says, "Our production is small by any standard, but we are committed to doing our best to keep things natural and wholesome."

While you sample the cheese (don't miss the heart-shaped goat cheese with herbs), you can browse through the tiny shop, whose walls are covered with portraits of . . . cows, of course! They also have local wine and their own brand of honey. Pasta and spices are also available. Sweet Home Farm is located two miles east of Elberta and one-half mile north of U.S. 98 and is open from 10:00 A.M. until 5:00 P.M., Wednesday through Saturday. There are signs showing the way to this lovely place and you'll be glad you stopped.

An interesting nature center and upcoming native nursery is located on County Road 95, a quarter-mile south of U.S. 98 and eight miles east of Foley. The goals of the **Biophilia Nature Center,** which opened in 1992, are to promote conservation and preserve native plants. A black gum swamp and an emerging picture-plant bog are being restored by Carol Lovell-Saas and Fed Saas.

Next to a large wildflower meadow, Carol has lovingly seeded or transplanted such diverse plants as wild poinsettias, morning honeysuckle, evening primrose, cudweed, and sensitive plant—to name a few of the 300 native flowers, grasses, and shrubs that are here. Hummingbird, butterfly, and caterpillar plants are offered for sale—red sage, bee balm, honeysuckle, salvia, and scarlet hibiscus—as well as pond plants, pitcher plants, and Venus's-flytraps.

The 20-acre center is open Wednesday through Sunday from 8:00 A.M. until 12:00 noon (call to confirm; they are often open all day). Admission is free although a $3.00 per person donation is suggested. Private tours can be arranged by calling (334) 987-1200 or (334) 987-1228.

Be sure to get Carol to show you how she painstakingly collects eggs and caterpillars to keep her butterfly conservatory "alive." If you would like to join the Biophilia Nature Association for $10.00 a year, you will receive a newsletter about progress and programs. The mailing address is 6816 South Bayou Drive, Elberta, Alabama, 36530.

About 10 miles south of U.S. 98 on County Road 95 is **Pirate's Cove,** a beautiful little cove of water leading into the Intracoastal Canal. There are parking spaces and a boat launch (for a fee), a few picnic tables, and a tiny beach. There is also a small restaurant. Nautical flags hang over the bar and there is a nice eating area on a deck overlooking the water. Order the hamburger. It is open from 8:00 A.M. until 8:00 P.M.

In 1985, Kit, a barber, and Rose Russo, a dental clinic manager, were visiting the area from Chicago when they spied a marina for sale and, almost as a lark, made an offer. The offer was accepted and **Kit's Marina** opened, quickly becoming (and to this day remaining) a successful dry dock, launch, and marina. Meanwhile Rose needed something else to occupy herself so, in 1991, she opened **Miss Kitty's Restaurant** to "take them through winter."

Miss Kitty's Restaurant, on Perdido Bay, just west of the Lillian Bridge, is a cozy, pine-paneled place. Inside you will find seating at pine trestle tables with real cloth place mats. The comfortable Windsor chairs, soft lighting, and good acoustics make for a very pleasant dining experience. Also available is outside seating on a covered deck overlooking Perdido Bay and the Lillian Bridge.

The menu is wonderfully varied, with selections of Roast Duck with Blackberry Sauce, Crawfish au Gratin, and stuffed eggplant. A superior dish is the Snapper Innerarity. Recently Miss Kitty's was featured in the *Alabama Vacation Guide;* actually, Miss Kitty's was one of only two restaurants mentioned in all of Alabama. Regarding the freshness of the seafood (it comes from local charter fishermen), the article described the selections as "out of the gulf today seafood."

Personable Rose is usually at the door to greet you. Sunday brunch is served from 11:00 A.M. until 2:30 P.M. Miss Kitty's Restaurant is also open for Sunday dinner from 2:30 P.M. until 8:00 P.M. and at night, Wednesday through Saturday from 4:00 P.M. until 9:30 P.M. Reservations are advised during "the season" (Memorial Day through Thanksgiving). The telephone numbers are (800) 844-2701 or (334) 962-2701.

Foley

Although Foley is generally considered to be the "Gateway to the Gulf," it actually has an identity all its own. This prosperous city of about 6,000 permanent residents is a blossoming major antique mecca. You can hardly turn a corner without running into an antique mall, all of which are open seven days a week:

> **The Antique Mini Mall,** consisting of four dealers, which is located at 902 North McKenzie Street (better known as "Highway 59"); **The Gas Works Antique Mall,** consisting of 70 dealers, is in an interesting Art Deco building that is located at 818 North McKenzie Street; **The Old Armory Mall,** located at 812 North McKenzie Street; **The Ole Crush Antique Mall,** which is two floors of an old Orange Crush bottling company, located at 200 South McKenzie Street. The Ole Crush Antique Mall has free coffee and even a husband recovery area, which allows wives to wander freely among the 50 dealers, many of whom are located in colorful, eye-catching booths. **Perdido Antiques,** which has many primitives, old tools, and farm equipment is located at 323 South Alston Street.

At 311 South McKenzie (Alabama 59), **Verbatim** is a bright and cheery bookstore. The books at Verbatim are well displayed so that it is very easy to find what you want and there is an especially excellent selection of Southern authors. There is a nice children's corner and in the back are rare books. Verbatim is open from 10:00 A.M. until 6:00 P.M., Monday through Friday, and from 10:00 A.M. until 5:00 P.M. on Saturday. The telephone number is (334) 943-2280.

If you have worked up an appetite browsing through these miles of antique malls, don't miss an appropriately named eating nook for lunch—**Sweetie Pies,** located on Alabama 59, with pink-and-white awnings on the exterior and, inside, the sweetest pies you will ever eat. Delicious sandwiches on homemade bread and cakes, cookies, and coffee are served in a bright, clean, casual setting. Sweetie Pies is run by three generations of very sweet, smiling ladies and the shop is named for the granddaughters, each one affectionately known as "Sweetie Pie"—what else? Takeout orders are also available. It is open Monday through Friday, closing promptly at 2:00 P.M.

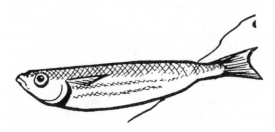

The family-owned **Foley Fish Company,** at 321 South McKenzie Street (Alabama 59), has served fish lovers since 1921. It is a bright, spotless shop where you'll find almost everything pertaining to the sport of fishing, except the boat. There are bait, lures, tackle, and, of course, seasoning for cooking your catch. However, should there be no catch, the beautiful, fresh seafood here is a good substitute and no one will know the difference. The frozen gumbo, stuffed crab, stuffed peppers, and hush puppies will tempt the taste buds. The Foley Fish Co. packs all seafood for travel.

Proprietress Peggy Hesse recommends a simple marinade for broiling or baking fish: "lite" Italian Dressing, lime juice, Worcestershire sauce, and pepper (but no salt as there is a sufficient amount in the dressing, which she prefers because it contains less oil). It is open from 8:00 A.M. to 6:00 P.M., seven days a week. The telephone number is (334) 928-6461.

The **Performing Arts Center** is located in the historic, old Foley Hotel. Built in 1928, the 48-room hotel was a popular place to stay for out-of-town buyers who came to buy South Baldwin's abundant crops.

During World War II, the hotel served as living quarters for servicemen and their wives stationed at Barin Field. The hotel continued to operate until the late 1960s and in 1977 a portion was rented to the Performing Arts Association.

Inside there is a main gallery for shows of area artists, a gallery for member artists, exhibits, sales, and a boutique/craft gallery. Arts and crafts classes are conducted for adults and children. It is open Monday through Friday, 10:00 A.M. until 4:00 P.M., and Saturday, 11:00 A.M. until 2:00 P.M. The center is located at 119 West Laurel (U.S. 98). The telephone number is (334) 943-4381.

If you are the least bit thirsty when you leave the Performing Arts Center, hang a left and, just a few doors down, drop in at **Stacey's Drugstore,** This is a treat from the past with an old-fashioned soda counter serving delicious longtime favorites such as lime rickey, cherry colas, sodas, and banana splits.

In the next block is **The Gift Horse,** a unique and popular restaurant. Here meals are served buffet style on a handsome 1870 table that is as noteworthy as the food upon it is. The table is documented as having graced the White House and was purchased in New Orleans. The specialties are fried chicken, fried biscuits, and Apple Cheese. The telephone number is (334) 943-3663. It is open for lunch at 11:00 A.M., daily, and for dinner at 5:00 P.M., Tuesday through Sunday. Just next door is **The Gift Horse Antique Centre.**

Orange Blossom Tearoom

If you develop beach fatigue or foul weather descends, a brief inland excursion to Orange Blossom Square, 105 West Orange Street, should be a pleasant diversion. **The Orange Blossom Tea Room** is an attractive luncheon location with tables of fresh flowers and a varied collection of antique china and silverware. Favorite specials are the Chicken Salad and Salmon with Cucumber Salad. Luncheon hours are from 11:00 A.M. to 2:00 P.M. and tea is served from 3:00 P.M. to 4:00 P.M., Tuesday through Saturday. Takeouts are available. The telephone number is (334) 943-7077.

Before or after lunch, go upstairs and stroll through the **Cathedral Art Gallery,** which opens into the Old Crush Antique Mall. The gallery hours are from 10:00 A.M. to 5:30 P.M., Monday through Saturday, and from 1:00 P.M. to 5:00 P.M. on Sunday.

Down the street from Orange Blossom Square, at 117 West Orange Street, is a quaint, colorful, small café, **Twisters.** Yogurt and the "Original Beignet" are the major attractions. The beignets are actually better than New Orleans style and melt in your mouth when eaten fresh, warm, and rolled in powdered sugar. A distinctive new twist to these beignets is that the dough is twisted, hence the café's name Twisters.

Breakfast, as well as grilled lunch items and sandwiches, are served all day. Another new twist for dessert is the Sweet Potato Bread Pudding, created with a sweet taste for those who cannot eat sugar. It is open from 6:00 A.M. to 6:00 P.M., Monday through Saturday, and from 12:00 noon to 6:00 P.M. on Sunday. Takeouts are available. The telephone number is (334) 971-1500.

Fried Green Tomato Research

Never mind, it's no contest. The best ever are at **Katy's Barbeque** in Foley. Situated on Alabama 59, about 3 blocks south of U.S. 98, Katy's serves 'em plain, with ranch dressing or in a cornbread sandwich. For a side dish you can order the barbecue! Katy's is open from 11:00 A.M. to 9:00 P.M., Monday through Saturday, and from 11:00 A.M. to 3:00 P.M. on Sunday. The telephone number is (334) 943-7427.

En route to Gulf Shores from Foley, south on Alabama 59, you can hardly miss **The Riviera Center,** a huge outlet shopping mall of more than a hundred shops. It has a very pleasant food court with fast food of virtually every description and nationality. Not a bad place to spend a rainy day!

From the "Show Me" State comes **Lambert's Cafe**—showing Alabama how it is done in Missouri. This gigantic family restaurant is as big as an airplane hanger and has a capacity to seat 350 people at a time.

Lambert's is renowned for its "throwed rolls," a tradition that started in the 1976 original café. Homemade, hot rolls are literally thrown to the customers. Family-style food is served with lots of "pass arounds" consisting of fried potatoes and onions, macaroni and tomatoes, black-eyed peas, and fried okra (all are "freebies" with each entrée). The cinnamon breakfast rolls are so big they are called "hubcaps."

Lambert's must have invented the words "child friendly" and you cannot bring too many kids. In season, it is packed but the wait is short and the prices are reasonable. It is open seven days a week from

7:00 A.M. to 9:30 P.M. The restaurant is hard to miss on Alabama 59 in Foley, but if you do, the telephone number is (334) 943-ROLL (7655).

About two miles south of The Riviera Center on Alabama 59 is **Casa Playa Restaurant and Cantina.** Sitting unobtrusively on the east side of the road in a small, red brick building with aqua awnings, Casa Playa features delicious homemade Mexican food. It is the only Mexican restaurant around offering chile rellenos and, in addition, Cynthia and Nigel Ivory have a really good selection of Mexican beers and margaritas. There are several noteworthy specials (try the Snapper Vera Cruz), a children's menu, and a couple of "Americana" dishes. Prices are reasonable. Casa Playa is open from 11:30 A.M. until 9:00 P.M., Monday through Saturday. The telephone number is (334) 943-3666.

Bon Secour

As you prepare to leave this part of Baldwin County, you most assuredly will want to purchase a cooler and take home some of the area's delicious seafood. The Bon Secour fisheries and seafood markets pack seafood to go (all have coolers for sale) and the seafood is fresh off the boats.

Bon Secour is located between Gulf Shores and Foley. To the west of Alabama 59, at the end of County Road 6, you will find **Plash Seafood.** Just north of Plash, on County Road 10, are **Billy's Seafood, Aquilla Seafood, Safe Harbor,** and **Bon Secour Fisheries.** Some of these places sell wholesale, but all of them sell retail. All are open six days a week beginning at 8:00 A.M.

Most of the markets are directly on the Bon Secour River and you will see the wonderfully colored shrimp boats tied up behind the shops. Equally colorful are some of the boat names: *Lunch Money, Restless, Wahnella Ann,* and *Daddy's Girl.* County Road 10 is well marked with signs, so you should have little difficulty locating these markets. Shrimp, crabs, flounder, trout, red snapper, redfish . . . a real bounty awaits you!

By far the largest industry on the Gulf Coast is fishing, a great part of which is shrimping. According to Jimbo Meador (longtime fisherman), "Boats from the fishing villages of Bon Secour and Bayou La

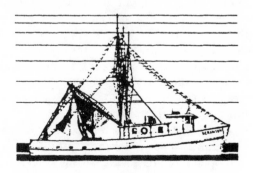

Batre have shrimp boats dragging the waters from Key West to Brownsville, Texas. There are about 1,500 in the Gulf."

The larger boats fish the Gulf and the smaller ones fish the bays and bayous. "The open season depends on the size of the shrimp inshore, but in the Gulf, the season is always open," explains Jimbo. "Periodically, some of the areas will be temporarily closed and some of the estuaries, the all-important nurseries, are permanently off limits."

There are actually two seasons. The brown shrimp are the first out of the estuaries and the white shrimp come out in September and October. If you see shrimp boats dragging close into shore, they are after the large white shrimp, which are more of a shallow-water shrimp. To some, the white tend to be sweeter than the brown.

Another variety of shrimp, not as popular, is the royal red, which is found in extremely deep waters—a hundred fathoms deep! They are quite salty, but this may be due to the salt brine solution used in a necessary quick-freeze method since the boats are so far out at sea.

White shrimp are caught more often in the daytime, while brown shrimp are found usually at night, but if the shrimp are out, it is around the clock!

It may be a minor adventure to find the **Fish Camp Restaurant** at 4297 County Road 6, but it is well worth the effort. Located on the Bay of John next to Plash Island, Fish Camp Restaurant is a casual, rustic spot serving fresh catch-of-the-day (don't even mention the word "frozen"), grouper, snapper, mahi-mahi, or flounder prepared broiled, fried, or panéed.

The signature dish, created by Chef Anthony King, a Gulf Coast native, is Riverbank Catfish, a sautéed filet topped with crawfish, sweet peppers, onion, fresh mushrooms, and a Parmesan cream sauce. The homemade key lime pie is the hands-down favorite dessert.

Sunsets from the restaurant are spectacular and, with temperatures cooperating, the ideal sunset viewing and dining area is a covered screened porch directly on the water. Dolphins are frequent visitors here and since the Fish Camp Restaurant is in a bird sanctuary, there is an abundance of wildlife to observe between mouthfuls.

Three wharves provide adequate docking space so a dinner cruise here is pleasantly appropriate and convenient.

Dinner is first come, first served, even in bathing suits and flip-flops, but for large groups and on busy weekends, call (334) 968-2267. Prices are moderate. It is open seven days a week from 11:00 A.M. to 10:00 P.M.

The Gulf of Mexico

The **Gulf of Mexico** is a great curved arm of the Atlantic Ocean and forms a huge ocean basin. The low-level coastline of the Gulf of Mexico is about 3,000 miles long and contains hundreds of lagoons and many marshes. The Gulf of Mexico also has many shallow places with gently sloping beds formed by the silt poured into the Gulf of Mexico by the rivers. The Mississippi River is the largest river that empties into the Gulf of Mexico, others being the Rio Grande, the Mobile, and the Apalachicola.

Fort Morgan Peninsula

A truly worthwhile day for an excursion on the Gulf Coast is a visit to **Fort Morgan,** on Alabama 180 West. From Alabama 59, it is 22 miles to the fort at the tip of the peninsula, with the Gulf of Mexico located on its south side and Mobile Bay on its north side.

On the way is the **Bon Secour National Wildlife Refuge Headquarters,** about nine miles down Alabama 180 West, on the south side of the road. Inside the neat, gray-framed headquarters is a fascinating assortment of alligator and turtle skulls and skeletons, snake skins, shells, and a rare, perfect hummingbird nest.

Bon Secour means "safe harbor," which is an appropriate name, since the purpose of the refuge is to protect the native flora, fauna, and wildlife. The entire refuge covers 4,000 acres of woodlands, lagoons, sand dunes, and beaches.

The **Pine Beach Nature Trail** is four miles long. The best time for a hike, particularly during summer, is early morning or late afternoon. Always carry a can of bug spray.

After the first mile, you arrive at a bridge over the mouth of picturesque Gator Lake. By the way, a 12-foot alligator has been spotted in the lake, so swimming is not advised. Press on down the trail for another mile to a pretty, quiet stretch of Gulf beach and a cooling swim before heading back. On the lake shore, there is a small row-

(Sketch courtesy Gulf Islands National Seashore)

boat equipped with oars and life jackets. This is available to anyone who might enjoy a pleasant row around the 40-acre Gator Lake.

Spring and fall are ideal times for serious bird watchers to take this trail, since Fort Morgan peninsula is the first landfall for migratory birds en route to and from South America. In October, the monarch butterfly population stops over at the peninsula on the way to its winter quarters. In areas where they are especially profuse, there is the most amazing Disneyland quality. It is really delightful! If you need further information, call (334) 540-7720.

The **Betsy Ross Flag Company,** located between the 3- and 4-mile marker on the south side of the road, is an interesting nook. The exterior is a replica of the Betsy Ross house and inside is the most amazing, colorful assortment of flags, which represent every state and almost every nation. There are party flags, seasonal flags, religious flags, and historical flags.

The founder of Betsy Ross Flag Company, Warren Wilson, retired to the Fort Morgan area. He and his wife decided that they wanted a small, part-time business in their home. "Since my wife's name is Betsy Ross," he says, "the flag business seemed a natural. But it sort of outgrew us. After the first year, we had to move to larger quarters." With more than 500 flags in stock, it is no longer a small, part-time business. It is open at 10:00 A.M. (but call first during the winter months). The telephone number is (334) 540-2246.

The Beach House, 9218 Darcus Lane on Fort Morgan, is a five-bedroom, five-bath bed and breakfast loaded with charm. A bottle of wine and banana nut bread is provided upon arrival. In addition to a full breakfast, you can get all-day snacks and picnic coolers for beach excursions.

The large, handsome exterior is of weathered, gray siding with screened decks overlooking the Gulf from three floors. Many interesting architectural features compliment this contemporary house, which was designed by the owner, Russell Shackelford, from Atlanta.

The Beach House is not set up for small children. Prices are moderate to expensive and fluctuate seasonally. For reservations, call (800) 484-8262, code 3071.

Bird-Banding

For a memorable birding experience, visit the spring and fall bird-banding site at Fort Morgan, which is one of the first landfalls for migratory birds.

Bob and Martha Sargent of Birmingham are licensed bird-banders who lead a small group of dedicated birders here, where they trap the migratory birds in the finest of mesh nets, weigh, band, and record them. The travel-weary little birds are then released to continue their journey.

What a thrill it is to follow along as the volunteer staffer periodically checks the nets and perhaps discovers an exquisite ruby-throated hummingbird, a painted bunting, or even an angry gray catbird.

The banding usually takes place in October and April for about two weeks from dawn until dusk. Morning is the best time since birds are more active then. For information, call Bob and Martha Sargent at (205) 681-2888 or (205) 681-1484. This worthy project is sponsored by The Hummingbird Study Group.

In 1519, Captain Pineda named Mobile Bay *Bahia del Espirito Santo,* meaning "Bay of the Holy Spirit." After Pineda and his crew landed in the Fort Morgan area, a priest said mass, making it the first recorded Christian service in America.
    —Dianne Bryars, "Don't Know Much about History,"
                              Mobile Bay Monthly (June 1997): 38.

If you've forgotten a "Fort Morgan Picnic," do not despair. A few miles before the fort is the **Fort Morgan Marina** (cold beverages, store, telephone, ice, bait, launch, and dry storage) where you can stock up; and the **Oar House,** where you can fill up. Up on the second floor, with a panoramic view of Mobile Bay, the Dauphin Island Bridge, and languishing pelicans, this good restaurant will fill the bill.

It is airy, efficient, and friendly and, of course, is decorated with nets, crab traps, and fake frogs that croak!

Yes, po' boys are available and fried grouper, grilled shrimp, redfish, oysters, gumbo, burgers . . . you get the picture. Just picture it on a great deck overlooking the bay or inside under ceiling fans. The telephone number is (334) 540-7991.

Underneath, on the first floor, is the **Happy Hooker Beach Bar,** a welcoming and colorful spot to sit and sip. The Oar House is open from 11:00 A.M. to 9:00 P.M., Tuesday through Sunday. The Happy Hooker is open from 4:00 P.M. until, Tuesday through Sunday.

On down the road, you come to Fort Morgan and the docking wharf for the ferry *Mobile Bay*. If you have time, don't miss this thoroughly pleasant and scenic trip across the mouth of Mobile Bay to Dauphin Island. The ferry takes about 30 minutes one-way and makes nine round-trips daily, carrying a possible load of 44 vehicles. The ferry *Mobile Bay* takes you past the immense gas and oil drilling platforms and sometimes passengers see dolphins and pelicans as well as the great cargo ships making their port of call at Mobile. For schedule and fees, call (800) 634-4027.

The mouth of Mobile Bay, which empties into the Gulf, was heavily mined with torpedoes during the Civil War and strongly guarded by Fort Gaines on Dauphin Island. This is also a historic spot. It is the site of the Battle of Mobile Bay, which took place during the Civil War and during which the Union Admiral Farragut issued his famous command, "Damn the torpedoes! Full speed ahead!"

A red buoy just west of the fort marks the watery grave of the monitor *Tecumseh*, which was struck by a torpedo and sank with all the crew on board. The exact location has been discovered, but the salvaging operation was determined to be too expensive to undertake and the condition of the vessel too fragile to repair.

Fort Morgan is a wonderful pre-Civil War fort and is an ideal spot for children to explore and run about. They can climb the very steep steps that Confederate soldiers once climbed and swing from cannons that once fired upon Union ships in battle. They may even pick

up some knowledge of history and sleep all the way home. The fort
was completed in 1834 and it has been used, in one way or another,
in four of the major wars in our nation's history.

Be sure to stop at the **Fort Morgan Museum Information Center**
for a self-guide map and information sheet. In the museum are fascinating old photos of the fort and a collection of ancient cannon
balls, as well as interesting letters from the wives of famous military
officers.

Don't miss the blood-stained step at the very top of one of those
steep stairways at the west side of the fort. Children love this! There
is a nominal admission fee. Hours are from 8:00 A.M. until 5:00 P.M.
for the fort and from 9:00 A.M. until 5:00 P.M. for the museum. Cold-
drink machines are available on the grounds, but not much else.

(Sketch courtesy of Gulf Islands National Seashore.)

Gulf Shores

Although most of Gulf Shores is on Pleasure Island, the city limits now span the Intracoastal Waterway. Swimming and fishing are excellent and there are many charter boats available. In addition, the island has a number of freshwater lakes.

Something exciting is happening at **Faulkner Community College** in Gulf Shores. The Culinary Arts and Hospitality Administration is making a splash in Alabama as well as all over the United States.

After only three years, Faulkner's two-year program in the culinary arts is winning medals in Alabama and 14 other states in all kinds of culinary competitions. Although they have met the standards of excellence required by the American Culinary Federation, they never stop trying to reach new goals of accreditation. Chef Ron Koetter heads up the Culinary Arts Division and has been with the program since its inception. Ed Bushaw is the instructor of the Hotel/Restaurant Management part of the program.

The best thing for you is **Frederic's,** an on-campus restaurant operated by the students. Here they prepare and serve beautiful gourmet dinners to the public; they practice on you, but no guinea pig ever had it so good. Frederic's serves five-course dinners on Mondays, six or seven times a year. The cost of dinner runs about $15.00 per person. (Sorry, no wine can be served because Frederic's is on campus.)

Reservations should be made at least two weeks in advance. Tours and other information can be obtained by calling (800) 231-3752. All gratuities at Frederic's go to a fund for scholarships and field trips. You'll love watching these new, young chefs in action.

There are few things more beautiful than looking up at a colorful hot-air balloon gliding over the white beaches and green Gulf waters. Gulf Shores boasts the only hot-air balloon chartering company on the Northern Gulf Coast. This is the **Gulf View Balloon Company,** which sells more hot-air balloon systems than any other company in the United

States. Owners Susan and Bob Shallows are dedicated enthusiasts and Bob has FAA Lighter Than Air certification and has held the Alabama State Championship for hot-air balloon competition since 1989.

Weather is the crucial factor in ballooning. The Baldwin County area is convenient for the sport. There are no immediate military installations and there is ample flat pasture and farmland to serve as the necessary 200-foot-by-200-foot launching site. Should you aspire to a ballooning experience, you might like to know that it takes about three hours: One hour for setting up, one hour in flight, and another hour to take down and join in the traditional champagne celebration. The flight perimeters are generally Mobile Bay, the Gulf of Mexico, and Perdido Bay. Lift-off time is always sunrise and sunset, except during summer months when it is limited to sunrise due to the heat.

The cost is $200.00 per person. The address is P.O. Box 1144, Gulf Shores, Alabama, 36547; and the telephone number is (334) 968-7201.

If you are a cheesecake fan, stop at **Hope's Cheesecakes** (210 East 20th Avenue). Here you will find truly delicious cheesecakes in a variety of flavors such as "Pecan Praline" or "The Original New York" and even designer cheesecakes, all of which can be ordered and shipped anywhere. The telephone number of Hope's shop is (334) 968-5858.

We were not too surprised when Hope declined to give us her cheesecake recipe, but she did offer a recipe for preparing shrimp:

Shrimp

Cover bottom of pot with beer. Add a tablespoon of Old Bay Seasoning. Bring to a boil. Toss in 1-2 pounds of shrimp, in shells with heads. Steam and stir until pink. Serve with melted butter and lemons. Serves 2.

Gulf Coast visitors and residents alike often tend to rise early and walk the beach, thereby working up a fierce early-morning appetite. A great breakfast buffet is at **Hazel's** on the corner of Alabama 59 and Fort Morgan Road. This is a good family restaurant with a children's menu and it is quite reasonably priced. In fact, children under four eat free. This is also the "house of the original biscuits of Alabama," and they are tasty. It is open seven days a week, from 6:00 A.M. until

8:00 P.M. The breakfast buffet opens at 7:00 A.M. and the dinner buffet opens at 5:00 P.M. The telephone number is (334) 968-7065.

In the Paradise Isle Shopping Center on Alabama 59 in Gulf Shores is **Just Books.** This store has a huge assortment of bargain books and something is always on sale. There is a good selection of works by Southern writers. Books on tape are available for the drive back home. This is a great place to relax and browse. It opens at 10:00 A.M. The telephone number is (334) 968-7117.

Nearby, **Zooland Animal Park** has had a big population explosion, particularly among the tiger families. Unlike such an occurrence for the rest of the world, a population explosion is a dream come true for a zoo. Director Troy Peterson explained why Zooland has been so blessed with babies: "We have them on the best diet available and the environment is conducive to breeding. The habitat is as natural as possible and the tigers have a lush landscape with a waterfall, pool, and deck. They seem to like it." (You can't blame them. It sounds like a luxury resort hotel!)

The park has more than 250 exotic and endangered animals on 16 acres currently developed. There are also an aviary and a picturesque pond with swans. It is open daily from 9:00 A.M. until 6:00 P.M., except holidays. The telephone number is (334) 968-5731.

Mikee's, 2nd Avenue East and 1st Street North, two blocks north of McDonalds, is good, casual dining with a country-beach decor of postcards, burlap bags, and nets. Seafood is the specialty and fishermen should know that, for a small fee, Mikee's will cook their very own catch. Fried mullet night is every Tuesday and Friday, all you can eat, and, as tasty as it is, that might be a lot!

Mikee's is owned by two brothers from L.A. (Lower Alabama): Mike Spence, the chef, and Eddie, the manager. The prices are moderate. The telephone number is (334) 948-6452.

MIKEE'S

A PLACE
FOR SEAFOOD

The **Gulf Coast Coffee Merchants of Gulf Shores,** 701 Bayou Village on Alabama 59, is a cozy, colorful spot to sip your favorite brew and watch for fish and fowl in the backyard lagoon. A large puzzle in the corner, magazines, and games add to the homey ambience.

The sandwiches, which are memorable, are grilled on Italian pan bread called foccacia and are served with a fresh salad and a homemade dressing that is so good you will want to buy one of the available bottles for sale, take it home, and share it with no one. Lunch hours are from 10:30 A.M. to 4:00 P.M.

Singer/songwriters entertain during weekends on the deck. It is open from 8:00 A.M. to 10:00 P.M. daily and Sundays during summer months. The telephone number is (334) 948-7878.

Nolan's Restaurant is the place where the locals gather for dinner and dancing. They claim that the food is always good here. You can find Nolan's on the beach highway in Gulf Shores, just east of the Alabama 59 intersection.

If you want a fun evening of old-fashioned dining and dancing, **Shirley & Wayne's** is the place to go. This is one of the few places in the beach area that take reservations (which are recommended). They are open from 6:00 P.M. until, Monday through Saturday. The telephone number is (334) 981-4818.

Live Bait (Beach Road) is a colorful, popular hang-out for the younger crowd. The decor is zany with an inviting back deck overlooking a lagoon where you can sometimes see alligator eyes glittering at night. In fact, alligator is on the menu for starters as "Blackened Gator Strips—spicy perfection."

A lively band commences about 10:00 P.M. and at this time, according to state law, guests under 21 years of age are not allowed. However, kids love it for lunch. Live Bait has moderate prices. The telephone number is (334) 974-1612.

There is a spectacular 360-degree view from **The View Restaurant** on the top floor of the Gulf Shores Surf and Racquet Club. This is undoubtedly the best view in town and the French-American cuisine is just as spectacular. It is only open for dinner and is an ideal spot for a sunset cocktail. It is located on West Beach Boulevard, 3.2 miles west of Alabama 59, and is open from 5:30 P.M. until 10:00 P.M. It is closed on Sunday. Reservations are a good idea. The telephone number is (334) 948-8888.

The Beaches

If you have never seen the beaches along the Northern Gulf Coast, you are in for a treat. According to veteran world travelers, these wide, white, sugarlike beaches are among the world's most beautiful. The sand dunes, with their gracefully swaying sea oats, are the icing on the cake, but don't be tempted to pick them. It's against the law, and you could be booed and hissed. Sea oats protect the dunes, which protect the beach from erosion, which protects the houses.

The public beach, at the main intersection of Gulf Shores, is clean and inviting, with an attractive pavilion and benches along a boardwalk. Beach equipment is available for rent.

Gulf State Park is a good, economical place to hang your sunglasses. It is all here—hotel rooms, cabins, camp sites, boat ramps, picnicking, nature walks, a nature center with planned activities, and even a golf course.

One of the major attractions of the Gulf State Park is the 825-foot concrete fishing pier, one of the longest on the Gulf Coast. Built in 1968, it is in good condition in spite of periodically damaging hurricane winds.

Some sizeable game fish have been landed from this pier such as a 42-pound sailfish and a record 50-pound mackerel. Remember that a fishing license is required for all fishing—and keep an eye on your bait container—a pair of hungry pelicans, Pete and Mabel, regularly graze the pier. There is a small fee for fishing and sight-seeing on the pier.

The entire park contains 6,000 acres, which is, in large part, protected wilderness with two freshwater lakes. In fact, this is one of the few places in the world where fresh water is found a short distance from salt water.

Just across the road from one of these lakes, Lake Shelby (at County Road 2 and North Beach Boulevard), is an amazing colony of marsh rabbits. They appear every morning and evening and one resident told us that he once counted 21 marsh rabbits sitting by the road watching the cars go by.

Given the park's setting, it is no surprise that loggerhead turtles have good friends at the Gulf State Park and, if they are smart, this is where they will lay their eggs. Every year in June, naturalist Annette Salvatore and park staff member Nancy Yarbrough keep a sharp eye out for nesting spots along the Park Beach and, when they are found, set up wooden stakes around the area. Residents along the beach have followed suit, so if you are beach walking and come upon these small fences, give them a detour.

Loggerheads, due to encroaching civilization, are a protected species. This is due in part to the fact that when the baby turtles hatch, often at night in August or September, they instinctively head for the bright, sparkling surf and stars. Unfortunately, they frequently become confused by car headlights and fatally head for the highway.

If you should be strolling along the beach at night and come across 200 or so baby turtles moving toward the highway, turn them toward the Gulf where they belong. Mother turtles everywhere will bless you!

The **Original Romar House,** 23500 Perdido Beach Boulevard, was the first bed and breakfast in the Gulf Shores area. It was built in 1924 by Spurgen Roche of Mobile before highways or even roads were available to the almost undiscovered Gulf beaches.

Construction materials for the Romar House were hauled in by mules, loaded on barges in Perdido Bay, and floated into the Gulf to the building site. It was an arduous task, but Mr. Roche had built himself the getaway of getaways. He was joined by his friend, Carl Martin, and the two combined a portion of each name to form the now familiar name, Romar. Together they homesteaded many acres by planting corn on the white sandy beach. Although the corn did not thrive, it did provide enough proof of cultivation to meet the homestead requirements.

In 1980, Romar House was purchased by Jerry Gilbreath, a Mississippi attorney, and, in 1991, he opened it as Alabama's first seaside bed and breakfast. The six bedrooms, each named for a local festival, are furnished in Art Deco and have private baths.

The Blue Parrot Bar, where complimentary wine and cheese is served in the afternoon, is of an unusual carved tiger oak. Smoking is permitted here but not in the rooms. A deck overlooks the beach and green Gulf waters and underneath the house is a cool, sandy area with a hot tub spa and cypress swings.

A full breakfast is served. Children over 12 years of age are allowed; no pets. A two-night stay is required during the weekends. Rates are moderate. The telephone number is (334) 974-1625 or (800) 48-ROMAR.

"There is a hurricane watch from Port Arthur, Texas, to Apalachicola, Florida." Hopefully, you won't hear these words while visiting the beautiful Gulf Coast, but if you do, be assured that the area has very efficient weather monitoring. If there is any "good news" about a hurricane, it is that you will have ample warning.

Two terms you should be familiar with are *hurricane watch* and *hurricane warning*. A *watch* means that a hurricane is possible within 36 hours. A *warning* means a hurricane is expected within 24 hours.

If you do have to leave, pack up quickly and return quickly. In many cases, hurricanes make landfall east or west of the prediction and the day after can be clear, sunny, and often a little cooler.

Golf Courses

Good golf courses flourish on the Gulf Coast and the following is a list of some of them, courtesy of The Fairways Golf Company, Don Faggard, President.

Mobile Area Golf Courses

Azalea City. Lovely, long, wide fairways. Has been included in the "Top 36" public golf courses by *Golf Digest*. One of the best layouts on the Gulf Coast. Mobile—(334) 342-4221.

Isle Dauphine. One of the area's most beautiful courses. Located alongside the shimmering Gulf of Mexico. Long, narrow fairways. Dauphin Island—(334) 861-2433.

The Linksman. Adjacent to Dog River, with scenic canals and ponds winding throughout. Mobile—(334) 661-0018.

Magnolia Grove. Part of the prestigious Robert Trent Jones Golf Trail. Three beautiful 18-hole courses cascade over gently rolling hills. One of the very best. Mobile—(334) 645-0075.

Spring Hill. Located on the campus of historic Spring Hill College. Features small, elevated greens. Lots of tradition and fun to play. Mobile (334) 343-2356.

Bay Oaks. Located in southwest Mobile County, featuring an incredible double-dogleg signature hole. Enjoyable to play. Bayou La Batre—(334) 824-2429.

Gulf Pines. Located on scenic Mobile Bay. Water comes into play on seven holes. Pin-point accuracy to small greens a must. Mobile—(334) 431-6413.

Gulf Shores/Baldwin County Area Golf Courses

Craft Farms Cotton Creek Club. Legendary Arnold Palmer designed this one. Rated as one of the best in Alabama. Always in immaculate condition. Gulf Shores—(334) 968-7766.

Glenlakes Golf Club. Scottish links-style golf in a picturesque setting. Shotmaker's course, demanding proper placement off the tees. Foley—(334) 943-8000.

Gulf State Park Golf Course. Located inside the beautiful state park. Very popular with locals and tourists alike. Gulf Shores—(334) 948-4653.

Kiva Dunes. Rated best public golf course in Alabama by *Golf Digest.* Designed by former U.S. Open champion Jerry Pate. A premier facility located on the Gulf of Mexico. Gulf Shores—(334) 540-7000.

Lakewood Golf Course. Marriott's Grand Hotel. Picturesque layout with an island green. Featuring 36 holes. Outstanding facility. Point Clear—(334) 928-9201.

Peninsula. Popular golf community built along Mobile Bay. This Earl Stone layout incorporates existing wetlands and sparkling lakes. A real gem. Fort Morgan—(334) 968-8009.

Quail Creek. Scenic setting along the Eastern Shore. Very challenging greens, featuring great undulations. Extremely popular course. Fairhope—(334) 990-0240.

Rock Creek. A first-class golf course designed with every level of golfer in mind. The elevation changes and natural wetlands make for an incredibly scenic setting. Fairhope—(334) 928-4223.

TimberCreek. Popular, fairly new, with 27 holes. Meanders through rolling hills and hardwoods near Mobile Bay. Daphne—(334) 621-9900.

The Woodlands. Accuracy, not distance, is of the utmost importance in this Larry Nelson-designed course. Features thickly wooded areas and natural marshlands. A very scenic and challenging round of golf. Gulf Shores—(334) 968-7500.

Orange Beach

The city of Orange Beach is bordered by the Alabama Gulf State Park and the Florida state line. The city is bullish about its community and does not want to be mistaken for Gulf Shores.

Orange Beach is so named because the first settlers after the Indians planted orange groves, but they did not survive the few Gulf Coast freezes. Of course, fishing was as important then as it is today, although it is now done more for sport than as a livelihood. Today, the charter fleet at Orange Beach is one of the largest along the entire Gulf Coast. Most of the boats are Coast Guard-approved and up-to-date with the latest safety equipment, but it is always wise to double-check.

Private charter boats usually have their own personal artificial reefs whose location is often a closely guarded secret. Most boats are equipped with Loran, a long-range navigation aid that helps a captain locate his reef. A large public reef was created from chunks of concrete and pilings from the old Perdido Pass Bridge when the new bridge was erected over Perdido Pass.

"If you go deep-sea fishing, you are likely to catch bottom fish such as red snapper, amberjack, grouper, and trigger fish, or you might be trolling for Spanish mackerel, wahoo, tuna, dauphin, and billfish,"

according to Amiel Brinkley, Jr., part-time Orange Beach resident and fishing enthusiast.

"Shark fishing is also popular along the Gulf Coast—some anglers bringing in sharks weighing up to 300 pounds," he said. However, you may be asked to fish for sharks on the "catch and release" program since they are said to be decreasing in great numbers. (Do use caution in releasing a shark!)

You should know that if you catch a scamp, you really have something! Scamp from local Gulf waters is sort of a "phantom fish." It is delicious white meat and is a great favorite in restaurants along the Gulf Coast.

Do you love the look and feel of fine old furniture? Are beautifully handcrafted antiques more your style than wicker and rattan? Then **Currier Antiques and Fine Art** might just be your cup of tea. It is located at 2264 Canal Road (Alabama 180), Orange Beach. Owners Dr. Charles Currier (Tony) and his wife, Nita, originally from Baton Rouge, retired to this area.

Approximately 80 percent of the shop is American antiques. Tony and Nita travel mostly through the South looking for furniture and accessories. You will find lovely Victorian and primitive chests, tables, chairs, and mirrors. In addition, there are Chippendale, Sheraton, and Hepplewhite items. Just one of the lovely estate pieces could be a focal point in any room. The beautiful accessories range from period lamps to unusual wood carvings. The showroom hours are from 10:00 A.M. until 5:00 P.M., Monday through Saturday. The telephone number is (334) 981-2388.

Celly's, 4575 Orange Beach Boulevard (Alabama 180), is a restaurant that has a wonderful split personality. During the week it offers tasty favorites—brick-oven po' boys, pizza, pasta, and hamburgers. But come the weekend evenings, Celly's dresses up in white linen tablecloths and napkins with an elegant gourmet menu such as Veal Scaloppini with fontina cheese and a demi-glace sauce or possibly grilled kangaroo! Why not? Chef Michael Minge, a New Orleans native, attended several cooking schools in Australia. He is also a graduate of a French cooking school in England as well as the Delgado Chef's Program in New Orleans. His wife, Wanda Minge, is a well-known pastry chef with a repertoire of more than 300 desserts. If it is included in the menu, try her Baked Alaska or Neapolitan.

In every sense of the word, this is a full-service restaurant with take-outs and even free delivery for orders over a certain price. Prices are moderate to expensive. Reservations are suggested for summer weekends. Celly's is open Monday through Saturday from 11:00 A.M. to 9:00 P.M. It is closed on Sunday. The telephone number is (334) 981-7500.

The Bayside Grill is off the beaten path but has been discovered by many. There are no reservations, so it is best to come early, sign in, and settle down on the porch where there is a wine and beer bar. This popular restaurant adjoins the Sportsman Marina and the huge fishing crafts add a pleasant touch of local color.

In the main dining room of the Caribbean-style interior, the decibel level is apt to be a bit high on a busy night but the wide variety of Creole-American cuisine is excellent and the desserts are worth the calories. Try the key lime pie. The Bayside Grill is located on Canal Road, Alabama 180, east of Alabama 161 on the south side of the road. It is open from 11:30 A.M. to 10:00 P.M. The telephone number is (334) 981-4899.

Located on Cotton Bayou, with a beautiful view of Perdido Pass and the Gulf, sits **Tacky Jack's Tavern and Grill.**

Breakfast is a must at Tacky's. On the menu are delectable malted waffles, pancakes, homemade biscuits, and grits. A farmer's omelet will probably get your picture on the wall if you finish it—two or three people can make a meal of it. Tacky's also has cholesterol-free eggs.

Upstairs the tavern has a deck outside with a bar and pool tables inside. You will not find anything French on this menu, except the Prime Rib au Jus, which is the specialty of the house. The rest of the menu is good local fare, moderately priced. Tacky Jack's is a fun, come-as-you-are place, but be an early riser to get a seat for breakfast. It is open for breakfast, Tuesday through Friday, from 6:00 A.M. to 10:30 A.M., and Saturday and Sunday, from 6:00 A.M. to 12:00 noon. Tavern hours are from 11:30 A.M. until, Tuesday through Friday, and 12:00 noon until, Saturday and Sunday. Tacky Jack's is accessible by car or boat. The telephone number is (334) 981-4144.

For a serious taste of the tropics, try **Mangos,** where you will find upscale dining at its best. Located in the Orange Beach Marina on Marina Road, this handsomely appointed restaurant overlooks a varied collection of large pleasure boats on Perdido Bay.

The interior walls are a soft shade of mango. In addition, this tasty fruit is teamed with many of the menu items. Grilled Fish Mango is prepared in a lime-butter sauce and garnished with Mango and Pepper Salsa. The house salad, with fresh greens, fruit, and pecans, is tossed with a dressing of mango, lemon grass, ginger, and cilantro. Following the theme, try the bread pudding with, you guessed it, mangos and a rum sauce. Flavored sorbet is served between courses to relax your taste buds. The menu is large and diverse and wines are suggested for each entrée.

Chef Michael Cooper, from Hammond, Louisiana, spent several years in Maui training under European chefs. He says that one of his favorite signature dishes is duck marinated in ginger, sherry, and soy sauce, grilled medium rare, and glazed with a hot pepper jelly. It sounds celestial to say the least. Prices are moderate to expensive. Mangos is open for dinner from 5:00 P.M. every day except Monday. For reservations, call (334) 981-1415.

Classic Charters at Bay Point Marina in Orange Beach has a 65-foot wooden schooner waiting to carry you on a cruise on the placid waters of the back bays. *The Cyrus E. King,* launched in 1962, is named for the original owner's great-grandfather, who was a ship's carpenter on a whaling ship in the 19th century. "The King" is a replica of a Chesapeake Bay "Bugeye," an oyster dredger, yet it is a traditional sailing vessel.

The route, a three-hour trip, twice daily, winds through the bays and around the islands with dolphins in its wake. Classic Charters is located at 5749 Bay La Launch in the Bear Point Marina. Rates are reasonable. The telephone number is (334) 981-5609.

In **Cotton Bayou,** you will mainly catch trout, but at night along the coast of nearby Ono Island, there are specs and reds. Don't forget to use freshwater tackle in the back bays when fishing for spotted sea bass.

If you do any kind of beach fishing, don't be surprised if you have a companion swooping down from the skies in the form of a great blue

heron. He will stand nearby and silently beg to share your catch. Keep a close eye on your bait bucket, for herons are not above petty theft.

In Orange Beach, you will find **Zeke's Landing Restaurant,** a bright, spacious restaurant overlooking Cotton Bayou and Marina. Many of the charter boats dock here, so take some time to eat lunch while watching the comings and goings of the boats. On holiday nights during the summer, you can count on large crowds, so it is best to plan on eating early or late. The telephone number is (334) 981-4001.

Below Zeke's Landing Restaurant is a gift shop, **Seacrets,** where you can browse while waiting to be called for dinner on crowded nights. The shop has everything from Crabtree and Evelyn toiletries to Christmas ornaments. "A Christmas ornament makes a wonderful memento of the Gulf Coast," says Owner Linda St. Charles, who also has another upbeat shop in the Gulf Beach Shopping Center called **St. Charles Place.** Seacrets is open 11:00 A.M. until 9:00 P.M. daily.

There is a small but interesting strip in front of Zeke's along the beach highway. There is the noteworthy **Page and Palette,** a cheerful yet serious bookstore. This is one-stop shopping at its best. Do you want cards? Art supplies? Stationery? (The shop has Crane's.) Do you want napkins for a party? Books? Page and Palette has it all.

Owners Donna and Jerry Anderson have assembled up-to-date stock in every department. Manager Kathy Flynn notes that part of their success as an independent book seller is the fact that they are not limited to the top best sellers. "Because we are independent," she says, "we don't get the same books as everybody else. We have a really diverse store." She's right. Page and Palette is open from 10:00 A.M.

page and palette inc.

until 5:00 P.M., Monday through Saturday, and from 12:00 noon until 5:00 P.M. on Sunday.

Right next door is **The Gallery.** "When people walk through the door, they will see that this is completely different from the novelty-type shops on the beach," says Steve de Shazo, business manager and co-owner. Jack Sanders, partner, adds, "We wanted to provide a place for serious artists to show their work." The two say that there is a wealth of fine art being produced in the area and "it's time to show it off." The Gallery summer hours are from 10:00 A.M. until 5:00 P.M., Monday through Saturday, and from 1:00 P.M. until 5:00 P.M. on Sunday. For off-season hours, call (334) 981-2787.

At the very end of the strip is **Franco's,** the only Italian restaurant in the area. It is truly "delizioso"! No reservations are necessary. It is open for dinner only, from 4:00 P.M. until 10:00 P.M., Monday through Thursday, and until 11:00 P.M. on Friday and Saturday. The telephone number is (334) 981-9800. If you are not in the mood for seafood, the veal is very good, although the seafood fettuccine is the most popular. Franco's even has a children's menu and the staff are admirably patient with children.

The "executive chef," Nancy Hartley, spent two years in Italy studying Italian cuisine. Her assistant, Matthew Stacy, says, "We like to think of Franco's as a quaint, traditional Italian restaurant with authentic Italian food—which speaks for itself."

On the beach side of Alabama 182 (Beach Boulevard) is the popular **Perdido Beach Resort.** One of the main attractions of this beautiful hotel is the only five-star chef in Baldwin County, Gerhard Brill. Originally from Stuttgart, Germany, Chef Brill has cooked for German embassies in Moscow, Beijing, and Bangkok. Just before coming to the Gulf Coast, he was chef for the highly rated Commander's Palace Restaurant in New Orleans.

Chef Brill says, "My favorite dish is Blackened Tuna with Creole Mustard Sauce and fresh crawfish (when I can get it). Everything must be fresh!"

Under Chef Brill's talented touch is **Voyager's Restaurant** in the Perdido Beach Resort, which has won national recognition with the only Golden Fork Award (from the Gourmet Diners' Society of North

America) in the state of Alabama. Chef Brill's Turtle Soup and the famous Caesar Salad are superb and the setting of Voyager's, which overlooks the Gulf, is delightful. The restaurant takes reservations—and it is a good idea to make them, especially on weekends. The telephone number is (334) 981-9811.

One of the most beautiful, scenic spots on the entire Gulf Coast is the **Alabama Point Bridge.** This is a high, handsome bridge spanning the blue-green waters of the Gulf of Mexico as it joins Perdido Bay. The bridge crosses from Alabama Point on East Beach Highway over to Perdido Key.

Here there is a picture-postcard view and even if you have to drive for miles it is worth it. You would probably like to stop on the bridge and gaze, but since that would present a traffic hazard, go to the **Perdido Pass Restaurant and Lounge** on the top floor of the **Perdido Pass Building** on the north side of the East Beach Highway. Here you can sit and soak up the view while munching on the popular Tortilla Basket Salad or the Shrimp and Pasta Dinner. There is a children's menu and no reservations are required, but it is crowded during the summer months. The telephone number is (334) 981-6312. It is open seven days a week from 11:00 A.M. until 3:45 P.M. for lunch and from 4:00 P.M. until 9:30 P.M. for dinner, "depending on the business."

The Perdido Pass Building is an interesting shopping stop also. All the stores are open seven days a week from about 10:00 A.M. until 10:00 P.M.:

> **Island Interiors** has whimsical accessories. **H. I. Hood** has great resortwear. **Seacrecy** smells wonderful and is full of collectibles, including a wide selection of Swarovski silver crystal figurines and Maruri fine porcelain.
>
> Directly behind the Perdido Pass Building on the bay side are marina docking and a variety of water recreational facilities. Take your choice—sight-seeing cruises, before- and after-dinner cruises with complimentary champagne, sailing and fishing charters, snorkeling, para-sailing, and wave runners.
>
> Cross the bridge onto Perdido Key and you will see a road on the south side leading down to the pass. It is a pleasant walk along the water's edge and interesting to watch the boats coming and going under the bridge. Chil-

dren love this stretch of beach because at the mouth of the pass on the beach are enormous sand dunes, just right for children to climb and slide down. There is no lifeguard, so be careful and take note of the nearby sign: "If caught in a riptide, swim parallel to the beach. You will soon be free."

If you really want to "make the scene," as they say, don't miss the **Flora Bama,** which is located near the Florida-Alabama state line on the beach side. This is the only five-star honky tonk on the Gulf Coast. Here you will see all ages, all types, all times. It is open from 9:00 A.M. until 3:00 A.M. and children are welcome until dark. Beach cuisine—hot dogs, hamburgers, pizza, oysters, and crawfish—is served. You can also purchase Florida Lottery tickets and booze.

Perhaps Flora-Bama is best known for its famous "Mullet Toss," usually held the last full weekend of April. This is billed as the largest beach party in the world and it probably is! Each day of the weekend, seven hundred to a thousand people pay to see who can toss a mullet farthest over the state line. Proceeds go to charities.

On Sunday afternoons, weather permitting, a dozen or so parachutists float down to the beach in front of the Flora-Bama. Each one is cheered and toasted as he lands. It seems that to the parachutists, this is simply a means of transportation to their favorite "watering hole." (No one has mentioned how they get home.)

"Alabama? Yes, Y'all, We Drawl"

Who among y'all has South in your mouth?

A whole bunch in Alabama, but fewer than you might expect.

Interviewers in an *Atlanta Journal-Constitution* Southern Life poll were asked to indicate whether the respondents had Southern accents, ranking their accents as strong, detectable or none at all. (We admit that accents are in the ear of the beholder.)

Alabama had the highest percentage of honey-tongued drawlers (57 percent). Florida had hardly any—only 12 percent—further enhancing its reputation as the northernmost Southern state.

The Southern accent was an influence of the slower-

paced Southern climate, says Chriss Doss, an adjunct pro-
fessor of law at Samford University and former president
of the Alabama Historical Association.

"Take the word 'y'all,'" Doss said, "Why say two full
words when you can chop them up and put together a
word that is not so long?"

The difference in accents between states such as
Alabama and Florida may be a question of who settled in
those states and whether they were exposed to people of
other cultures, Doss said.

The Cajun influence in Louisiana came from French
settlers in the 1700s, while German, Irish and English settlers settled in states that included Alabama, Mississippi
and Georgia, he said.

Doss said the difference in the drawl is because of the
migration to the state. (Information provided by the
Atlanta Journal-Constitution [27 June 1993] and the University of North Carolina. Permission to reprint from Cox
News Services.)

If you're exploring accommodations in the Gulf Shores area, you
might do well to contact the **Alabama Gulf Coast Convention and Visitors Center.** The telephone number is (800) 745-7263 and the fax
number is (334) 968-6095. They will fax or mail a complete list of
rental agents for houses, condos, hotels, and bed and breakfasts. Rates
fluctuate and, of course, are less expensive in the winter months.

For information on special events and accommodations along the
Alabama Gulf Coast, call (800) 745-SAND. The telephone number
for Gulf State Park's golf course, campgrounds, and cabins on the
Lagoon is (800) 544-4853.

Although the following places are all in Florida, they are included
in the following short section, since Perdido Key is an extension of
Alabama 182.

Perdido Key, Florida

Perdido Key, Florida

Tucked away in **Colours On The Key** shopping and dining village on Perdido Key is a colorful restaurant named **Characters.** "This," according to proprietor Mack Johnson, "is named for all the out-of-space characters on Perdido Key—of which I am one." In the winter, if the restaurant is closed, you might see a sign on the door saying "Closed due to lack of characters." The Black Bean Soup is one of their specialties and it is the best. In addition, they have an interesting soup "dish," the Bermuda Triangle, which is a cup each of gumbo, Black Bean Soup, and red beans and rice. The Popeye Pie (of course, it is spinach) is satisfying, delicious, and light. Mack has good chargrilled steaks and seafood, too. It is open seven days a week. For reservations or carryout, call (850) 492-2936.

One of the more colorful spots in the Colours On The Key shopping village is the **Hang Ups Art and Frame Shop,** where you'll chuckle, laugh, or smile at almost everything you see. The wonderful, whimsical "Beach Mamas" painted by Perdido resident Paula Payne are a joy. The bird feeders by Ricky Heard are designed of a combination of copper and old, silver-plated bowls, plates, and pitchers and are truly creative. Upstairs is a gallery containing some excellent paintings and sculpture.

Hang Ups, at 14110 Perdido Key Drive, was opened in 1995 by Helen Baggett and Blitz Polston. Helen is a museum and art consultant and Blitz specializes in framing. Several times a year they travel to Europe on a veritable treasure hunt for art for Hang Ups and special patrons. It is open from 10:00 A.M. to 5:00 P.M., Monday through Saturday. The telephone number is (850) 492-1050.

Merrill Miller's Interior and Gifts is a bright and snappy shop that reveals the personality of its owner, Merrill Miller. She has filled her shop with wonderful works of Southern artists—paintings, pottery, and ceramics. The light and comfortable furniture is just right for beach life. To help make your place look like home she has some wonderful freeze-dried plants that will still look alive when you return after being away for weeks. Don't miss the tray of spectacular hand-blown Italian glass ornaments by Vietri, along with other interesting gift items such

as bags, books, and folders, all made from recycled paper. If there was ever a complete interior decorator shop, this is it. It has something for almost any budget. It is located in the Colours On The Key shopping village. The telephone number is (850) 492-9033.

One of *Webster's* definitions of *jambalaya* is "a mixture of diverse elements"; the shop **Jambalaya** certainly lives up to its name. Diane Daigle has gathered many "diverse elements" and opened a cheeky new shop at Perdido Key.

The Cajun music alone will draw you to Jambalaya and once inside you will find all kinds of goodies from candles to crystal. Most of her gifts are originals from local artists and craftsmen in the area; her assortment of books are excellent, especially the Dover series of coloring books for children. Diane's sister Chérie Schadler has published a book entitled *Welcome to Bayou Town!* and comes to the shop to read it aloud on occasion. Hours for Jambalaya are 10 A.M. to 5 P.M. Monday to Saturday and noon to 3 P.M. on Sundays. The address is 14110 Perdido Drive, Suite N-1A, in the Colours On The Key shopping village. The telephone number is (850) 492-2776.

Gulf Coast Coffee Merchants of Perdido is also located in Colours On The Key shopping and dining village and serves up tasty pannini sandwiches built on Italian foccacia bread and fresh salad (this is the same as Gulf Coast Coffee Merchants of Gulf Shores). In the coffeehouse tradition, there are games to play while sipping a cappuccino and a pleasant deck along a canal for fresh-air dining.

It is open from 8:00 A.M. to 9:00 P.M., Monday through Saturday, and seasonally on Sundays. Breakfast is served at 8:00 A.M. and lunch is served from 10:30 A.M. to 4:00 P.M. Evening hours bring special songwriters' concerts with beer and wine available. Prices are very moderate. For takeout orders, call (850) 492-2704.

If you want a day away at the beach, **Lillian's** is a place that has everything you need. How about a couple of lounge chairs and a giant beach umbrella for rent? When you have had enough sun and surf, you can have an outside shower and a shady cabana. Here you can linger a little longer on the beach while you sip a cool drink and eat a gourmet pizza.

Dave and Lillian Walsh started out renting beach umbrellas, chairs, and wave runners. Lillian's personal recipe for pizza dough led her to begin making pizza on the side. Then one day, according to Lillian, "We had orders for what seemed like 80 pizzas." With the help of her family, Lillian has managed to handle the growing business. Dave claims, "If it doesn't look right, we start over. Quality control is very important to us." They take pride in their product.

The menu offers a variety of homemade Italian dishes. The stromboli is a popular item and the pizzas are truly delicious. The crust is thin and crispy and is topped with the freshest of vegetables and herbs. Besides the traditional Italian-style pizzas, they serve a stuffed pizza (with a crust on top and bottom), pizza scampi, pizza Florentine, and pesto pizza (a perfect combination of a light pesto sauce with fresh shrimp, sliced tomatoes, and mushrooms and topped with ricotta cheese—this is heavenly!).

Bathing attire is acceptable inside, but no wet suits, please! There is a large cooler on one side of the dining area filled with cold soft drinks, beer, and wine. What a way to spend a day! Lillian's at 13821 Perdido Key Drive is open from 11:00 A.M. until 10:00 P.M., Sunday through Thursday, and from 11:00 A.M. until 12:00 midnight on Friday and Saturday. For deliveries, call (850) 492-0131.

The Gulf Islands National Park and Seashore on Perdido Key, Florida, is one of the loveliest places around. If you are in Gulf Shores, drive east on Alabama 182. Right after you begin to turn north toward Pensacola on Florida 292, watch for the Gulf Islands Park sign. Follow this road and you will see the entrance gates (there is a nominal admission fee). Just inside the gates and on the right is **Johnson Beach.** Here you will find a pavilion, restrooms, picnic facilities, and ample parking. There is a lifeguard on duty during the summer and the swimming is really fine along this gorgeous stretch of the Gulf of Mexico.

The park itself runs for approximately seven miles, all the way to the end of Perdido Key. The paved road, however, extends only four miles, running between the Gulf and Big Lagoon. There is off-the-road parking so that you can stop to swim, fish, or explore the wide, beautiful beach. Fishing is especially good in Big Lagoon. There are also nature

trails and park rangers are on duty. Plan ahead; remember to bring
water, suntan lotion, or a hat; and walk this splendid stretch of
unspoiled land. There will be nothing here but you and the beach
and the birds. The park is open every day from 8:00 A.M. until sunset.

Just next door to the bridge over the Intracoastal Canal on Florida
292 is **Perdido Key Cafe**—a casual, fun place to eat and watch boats
go by. Many boats dock here, where there are a marina, gas, shelter,
and consistently good food. What more can a boatman ask? The café
is open from 11:00 A.M. to 3:00 P.M. for lunch and from 5:00 P.M. to
10:00 P.M. for dinner, seven days a week. The telephone number is
(850) 492-5600.

Just downstairs from Perdido Key Cafe is **Banana Cabana,** which is
actually a screened porch with picnic tables. Only the bar is open
Monday through Wednesday; seafood, po' boys, and hamburgers are
served from 11:00 A.M. to 10:00 P.M., Thursday through Sunday; and
live bands play on Fridays and Saturdays.

Just off of the old Gulf Beach Highway, you will find three great
places: Fisherman's Corner Bait Shop, the Original Point Restaurant,
and Rusty's Restaurant and Lounge.

On the north side of the Intracoastal Waterway Bridge, under the
bridge at the end of the west side of the road, is **Fisherman's Corner,**
a great bait shop. Here you will find every type of bait imaginable,
including live sand fleas! If you would rather eat than fish, the shop
also has live blue crabs ready to take home. Oh yes! A resident great
blue heron keeps watch over the shop.

Turn west onto Innerarity Point Road for about a mile, where there
is a great but unassuming place—the **Original Point Restaurant.**
Begun in the 1940s, Original Point Restaurant was originally Ivy's Grocery Store and Gas Station, which also sold bait and ice. Ivy's first venture into the food business began with fish fries on Friday nights—"All
You Can Eat for 50 cents!"

Since that time, under the guidance of owner David Lively, the
restaurant has grown and grown and has now spread to a backyard
called the "Pointyard," where you will find bluegrass music on Thursday, Friday, and Saturday nights (with the band beginning as "strolling
musicians" through the restaurant).

You can get wahoo, Cajun popcorn shrimp, spicy hush puppies,
and a mouth-watering mullet sandwich with coleslaw and tartar sauce
on French bread.

Innerarity Point is named for John Innerarity, an Irish immigrant
who bought the point land many years ago. "Aren't we glad?" says
Manager-Hostess Bonnie Powell. "It's a family place, too." She adds,

"Bring the children, bring the grandmother . . . we have fun!" It is open from 11:00 A.M. until 9:00 P.M., Monday through Saturday, and from 12:00 noon until 8:30 P.M. on Sunday. The telephone number is (850) 492-3577.

Take Florida 292A east for about four miles and follow the signs to **Rusty's Restaurant and Lounge,** located on the waterway. This is casual dining and spirits at their best. A tradition since 1957, Rusty's was established in 1950 by the Feran family of Chicago, originating as a boat launch and fishing camp and called Rusty's Rendezvous. As time went by, the fishermen would come in with their catch of mullet and Leo Feran's wife, Dannie, would fry up a batch. That's all it took!

Opened as a restaurant in 1957, all went well until September of 1979 when Hurricane Frederick blew Rusty's away. In 1986, it was rebuilt and is a casual, comfortable, and happy place. There are four dining rooms now—two are screened, one is open but roofed, and the latest addition is a deck.

In the oldest part of the restaurant are wonderful signed photographs of navy planes, ships, and the famous Blue Angels (Rusty's is only one-half mile from the back gate of the Pensacola Naval Air Station).

Rusty's specialty is mullet, and for a crispy fried appetizer the special is mullet backbones ("the part that's left over after they filet 'em"). Why mullet? Right out in front is Big Lagoon with desirable conditions for mullet—clean, sandy bottom and sawgrass feeding grounds. Rusty's also has steamed veggies as a delicious alternative to french fries, the coleslaw is "famous," and children's plates are available. Prices are moderate. It is open from 11:00 A.M. until 10:00 P.M., Monday through Saturday, and from 12:00 noon until 10:00 P.M. on Sunday. For more information, call (850) 492-1657.

Ryan's Catch, 11021 Sinton Drive, is known for fresh, flawlessly prepared fish and the panéed fish rates a double star. The blue cheese salad dressing is one of the best on the beach.

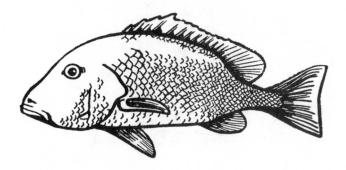

Do save room for Fried Cheesecake, a significant dessert deserving of all superlatives. In other words, it is yummy with a caramelized pecan sauce. The popular restaurant is located in the Southwind Marina on the Big Lagoon just off the Intracoastal Waterway and is accessible by boat.

Below Ryan's Catch is the dockside Tiki Bar with live entertainment on weekends from spring through fall. This is one of the few local restaurants accepting reservations, which is a good idea on weekends. Prices are moderate. It is open seven days a week, generally from 11:00 A.M. to 10:00 P.M. The telephone number is (850) 492-0333.

The **Southwind Marina,** adjoining the restaurant, has four charter boats that are appropriately outfitted for the type of fishing desired. A party boat is also available. For information, call (850) 492-9977.

For information on Perdido Key accommodations, call (850) 492-5422, or send e-mail to chamber@perdido-key.com.

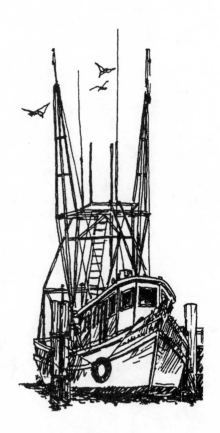

FLORIDA PANHANDLE

Florida Panhandle

Burial mounds found along Florida's west coast show that Indians may have lived in the area as long as 10,000 years ago. Legends of a fountain of youth brought the Spanish explorer Juan Ponce de Leon here in 1513. He claimed the region for Spain and named it for the many flowers he saw there; *Florida* is a Spanish word that means "full of flowers."

For years, the area along the Panhandle has been called the Emerald Coast because of its beautiful blue-green, crystal-clear water. Unlike those of other resort areas, the beaches here contain very little coarse coral and shell, which gives the sand the consistency of powdered sugar.

Pensacola

Pensacola is the Old South blended with a bit of modern Florida and a generous dash of Colonial Spain. Pensacola Bay, discovered by Hernando DeSoto in 1540, is the largest natural, land-locked, deep-water harbor in Florida and has been the key to the city's history and development.

The Spanish established the first settlement here in 1559 and, for the next 150 years, Pensacola lived under the flags of Spain, Britain, and France before becoming a U.S. Territory in 1821.

Three historic districts evoke Pensacola's colorful past: Seville District, Palafox District, and North Hill District. These areas have been beautifully restored and are listed on the National Register of Historic Places. Folk, Victorian, and Creole homes line the avenues—many have been converted into restaurants and shops.

When you enter the **National Museum of Naval Aviation,** be prepared to gasp. It is the second largest museum of its type in the world, containing 250,000 feet of internal exhibit area. For starters, the breathtaking, seven-story, glass-and-steel Blue Angel Atrium features

Map provided courtesy Pensacola Convention and Visitors Center.

four A-4 Skyhawks suspended 30 to 50 feet above you in diamond formation.

The museum has just completed a $12.5 million addition, which includes a huge multimedia theater. Featuring a seven-story IMAX screen, the theater shows a premier movie about naval aviation and features an in-flight view of a Blue Angels' air show.

More than one hundred navy, marine, and Coast Guard aircraft from the early 1900s to the present day share floor and air space; among them, the NC-4 *Flying Boat*, the first plane to cross the Atlantic; an F-2 H-4 Banshee from World War II, an HD-1 Hanrist from World War I, the Command Module from the 1973 Skylab, and the only F-14 Tomcat on public display in the world. There is a replicated flight deck of the World War II U.S.S. *Cabot* aircraft carrier, a flight simulator, cockpits that you can actually climb into, and a flight adventure deck geared toward children. Although all of the aircraft have reached the end of their service life, they are all in pristine condition.

You will probably want to spend the entire day here! Guided tours are held several times during the day or you can wander happily on your own. In addition, several of the aircraft have informational videos showing along side of them. The excellent 40-minute movie is shown hourly.

The museum is located off of Navy Boulevard on the base of the Naval Air Station (signs will direct you). Admission is free, although you need to buy a ticket to the movie. The museum is open from 9:00 A.M. to 5:00 P.M., seven days a week, except for Thanksgiving, Christmas, and New Year's Day.

Don't expect just the men and boys to be excited with this place. Everyone is impressed. There is a sense of history and dedication in this spacious building and the aircraft displays are spectacular. For more information, call (850) 452-3604 or (800) 327-5002. The Flight Deck Museum Shop's telephone number is (800) AIR-NAVY.

Fort Barrancas sits on a high bluff overlooking the entrance to Pensacola Bay (directly across the bay is Fort Pickens). The natural advantages of this location inspired three nations to build forts here. The first one on this site was the British Royal Naval Redoubt built in 1763. The Spanish completed a fort in 1797 and named it San Carlos de Barrancas (*barranca* is Spanish for "bluff"). After the War of 1812, the United States decided to build forts in all major harbors and in 1821 Pensacola was selected for a navy yard. Using the old Spanish water battery as a base, the Americans replaced the old wooden fort with a stronger brick one.

As you leave the Visitor's Center of the fort, you will see how the natural embankment protected the fort from behind. At the top of the path, suddenly before you is a panoramic vista of the fort, white sand, and tree-lined Pensacola Bay, and the wonderful old lighthouse just beyond. The fort is neatly contained, surrounded by a dry moat, and accessible only by a drawbridge. This historic place became part of the Gulf Islands National Park and Seashore in 1971 and, following 18 months of restoration, it was reopened in 1980. It is open from 9:00 A.M. to 5:00 P.M., seven days a week, except Thanksgiving, Christmas, and New Year's Day.

Nearby you can visit the **Advanced Redoubt** of Fort Barrancas. This was built between 1845 and 1859 and is unique among early American forts. Barrancas not only protected the harbor, but it was also needed to defend the peninsula where the navy yard was situated. The Advanced Redoubt was to assist Fort Barrancas in this role by defending against land-based assaults.

The Blue Angels have been synonymous with Pensacola since 1952 when they moved their home base to Pensacola Air Station. Although they train elsewhere, the Blue Angels are in Pensacola several times a year. If you should catch them practicing in the sky, pull your car over and watch them do the "Dirty Roll" and "Half Cuban Eight"— and the most noteworthy "Fleur-de-lis," which will take your breath away.

Many changes have taken place with aircraft and pilots through the years, and we are grateful that in peacetime they are enjoyed as much as ever. The Blue Angels' beautiful, synchronized flying is art in motion above your head. For information call (850) 452-4784.

Yamato's restaurant has made a home in Pensacola since 1974 and, even though the tourists are welcome, the locals call it "family" and keep it busy. This authentic Japanese restaurant has a sushi bar, tatami room (where you must take off your shoes), a hibachi section (you know, where the staff are wizards with knives), and a big dining room for folks who just want delicious Japanese cuisine.

If you are visiting for the first time, you might stick with the teriyaki dishes or Yamato's Genghis Khan, which is a sampling of some of the specialties of the house. Yamato's is located at 131 New Warrington Road and is open seven days a week, from 11:00 A.M. to 2:00 P.M. for lunch and from 5:00 P.M. to 10:00 P.M. for dinner. Check for weekend hours. The telephone number is (850) 453-3461.

It is the Taj Mahal of seafood markets! If you go to **Joe Patti's Seafood,** nothing else will quite measure up. Joe Patti, born in Sicily, came to the Gulf Coast in the 1920s and worked the snapper boats; later his sons founded Patti Shipyard and this huge seafood store that sells wholesale to restaurants and the public.

Situated at the foot of A Street on Pensacola Bay, Joe Patti's is a squeaky clean delight. Walk around and marvel before you get a number. Once you do, an efficient staff member will wait on only you from the beginning of your order until you take it out of the door—signed and sealed in a cooler (yours or theirs) or a thick paper bag (for live crabs).

The freshest-ever seafood is displayed on ice with lemons, limes, and fresh ginger scattered around: shrimp, oysters, mahimahi, yellowfin tuna, scallops, snapper throats, live crawfish, squid, flounder, roe, frog legs, and more. A freezer contains cooked entrées: crab cakes, stuffed crabs, "jambalaya, crawfish pie, and filé gumbo!"

In addition, mixes are available for hush puppies, fritters, and oysters as well as crab boil, smoked tuna dip, and salmon spread. If you want to serve sushi, Joe Patti's has roasted seaweed. It is open from 7:00 A.M. to 6:00 P.M., Sunday through Thursday, and from 7:00 A.M. to 6:30 P.M., Friday and Saturday. This is a pleasant, busy place that has everything.

Baked Crabs

Fresh crabs, cleaned
Butter
Garlic salt
Worcestershire sauce

Preheat oven to 350 degrees. Clean crabs by removing outer shell and insides but leaving legs. Palce crabs, cavity-side up, on a baking sheet with a dab of butter in each one. Sprinkle each with garlic salt and a dash of Worcestershire. Bake for 20-30 minutes. Yield: 3-4 crabs per person.

(Recipe courtesy of *Some Like It South!* cookbook of the Junior League of Pensacola.)

Coffeehouses are springing up everywhere, but few are as authentic as **Good Neighbor Coffee House,** where coffee making is the passion of owners Tracy and Steve Sprackler.

Good Neighbor has no gimmicks. The setting is simple and uncluttered, except for the few antiques lining the walls left by the previous owners. The tables in the coffeehouse are small and located in special sunny spots where you can read your journal or borrow a book from the pocket-book library in the corner. The piano is played by Steve Sprackler when he has time. This is a civilized place where one can enjoy a delicious cup of coffee or cappuccino and have freshly made muffins or sandwiches.

Good Neighbor Coffee House is located at 700 West Garden Street and, if you time it right, you will find good shopping along the block after you finish your coffee. It is open from 7:00 A.M. to 5:00 P.M., Monday through Friday, and from 9:00 A.M. to 5:00 P.M. on Saturday (closed on Sunday). The telephone number is (850) 434-1846.

Since 1972, the **Linen Corner** (698 West Garden Street) has graced the corner of West Garden and Donnellson with lots of style. To say this neat shop is diverse is an understatement. Literally, you can buy for every person on your list in this one spot.

Robin Ellinar and daughter, Cheryl Hart, have gathered linens and lingerie, ties and towels, clothing for ladies and infants, hemstitched place mats, shower curtains, seasonal gourmet foods, and welcome rocks—to name just a few. Robin says, "We never really know from season to season what will be selling. We just decide while we're at market."

Do stop by. It is a pretty safe bet that you won't leave empty-handed. It is open from 10:00 A.M. to 5:00 P.M., Monday through Friday, and from 10:00 A.M. to 4:00 P.M. on Saturday. The telephone number is (850) 438-9887.

The "gang of four" are the owners of **The Market** and **Mainly Shoes** (248 West Garden Street). Anne Frechette, Tish Childs, and Tina Bond have the Market part and Peggy Wollverton has the Mainly Shoes part. They stuff the place with good sports lines and shoes; then they let the customer have at it. You are on your own to select what you want and they leave you alone. However, if you need them, they will come running.

The Market and Mainly Shoes is a spot with panache, and the laid-back attitude of the personnel is refreshing and fun. Both stores are open from 10:00 A.M. until 5:30 P.M., Monday through Friday, and from 10:00 A.M. until 4:00 P.M. on Saturday. The telephone number for The Market is (850) 434-3012 and the telephone number for Mainly Shoes is (850) 438-7114.

A gift shop is a gift shop is a gift shop, but not so with **Artesana** (242 West Garden Street). The layout of the store is so appealing that you will want to stay for a good while. The second floor is stuffed with baskets that pour over the balcony and down the stairs. Artesana carries planters big enough for trees and small enough for bonsai. The paper products are taken from beautiful china designs and the shop has whitewashed birdhouses in primitive shapes of churches, log cabins, country stores, etc. All are very reasonably priced.

Artesana is a full-scale, full-service gift store, and if you cannot find "just the right thing"—well, there's no hope for you. It is open from 10:00 A.M. until 5:30 P.M., Monday through Saturday. The telephone number is (850) 433-4001.

Page and Palette's third store (the others are in Fairhope and Orange Beach) must mean that someone's doing something right! Owner Donna Anderson runs this bright, happy place located at 106 South Palafox.

Donna stocks a great selection of stationery, cards, and art supplies. But it is her floor-to-ceiling books (and the ceilings are tall) that you will want to see. As in all Page and Palette stores, the inventory here is as diverse as it is interesting. It is open from 9:30 A.M. until 5:30 P.M., Monday through Saturday. The telephone number is (850) 432-6656.

New to downtown, but not to Pensacola, is stationer extraordinaire **Ginger Bender.** Coming from San Francisco years ago, Ginger set up shop in a home studio. Happily, she is now down on South Palafox at number 120. In a snappy shop, you can find literally everything you need or want in the paper/desk line, beginning with exquisite custom-designed stationery and invitations.

The choices here are vast: business cards, silver key chains, leather planning diaries, CD holders, photo albums, luggage tabs, recipe cards, mousepads, children's stationery sets (including a "camp kit"), wedding planners, and picture frames—all ready to be personalized if you wish.

A new line of masslinn and rice paper cocktail napkins and guest towels are simply beautiful. Ginger also stocks fine fountain pens, handsome heavy paperweights, birth announcements, and even tiny leather "little black books." Do not miss this ultracomplete shop. It is open from 10:00 A.M. to 5:00 P.M., Monday through Friday; other hours are by appointment. The telephone number is (850) 435-7797.

There is a bar in downtown Pensacola called **Trader Jon's** that has been the haunt of pilots and lovers of flight for more than 50 years. It is a warm, personal place and you will be astonished at the thousands upon thousands of photographs and memorabilia lining the walls. There are more than a hundred handmade model planes hanging from the ceiling, all beautifully crafted with shiny bright colors.

This bar is the personal scrapbook of Martin Weisman, better known as Trader, who is usually present to tell his tales of the history of the place—so grab the specialty of the house, a "wing walker," and take a sentimental journey through this museum of flight. It will stir you. The bar is open from 11:00 A.M. until 3:00 A.M., seven days a week.

Wing Walker

1 jigger rum
1/4 jigger gin
1/4 jigger Triple Sec liqueur
Dash grenadine

Mix well in glass. Add ice and fill with Tom Collins mix. Find a designated driver.

If you are a woman who loves beautiful clothes, **Sarah's** will bring tears to your eyes. At the age of 10, Sarah Brown began working in her mother's shop, Mary's Corner, which was located on the corner of Garden and Coyle for 40 years. She now owns her own swish store at 517 Palafox and shows her sense of style in interior design as well as fashion.

Sarah carries investment-type clothing (which means expensive), but the sports lines appeal to every purse. Her accessories are the whipped cream of the ensembles and could be hung on the wall as objets d'art.

When Sarah says that personal service is the key, she means it. Her competent personnel will help dress you from head to toe with the look that is best for you; the hard sell is not the way she does business. Sarah wants her customers to be her best advertisement.

Once you become a Sarah's customer, you are a "lifer," because she never gives up on you. You may take an item purchased earlier and she will update it—using a scarf, a flower, a shorter hem, a longer hem—whatever it takes to put it back in vogue.

Sarah's is no secret—the store is known far and wide by every clotheshorse along the Gulf Coast. Sarah's is open from 10:00 A.M. until 6:00 P.M., Monday through Friday, and from 10:00 A.M. until 4:30 P.M. on Saturday.

> Style is the dress of thought.
> —Samuel Wesley, 1700

Smack dab in downtown Pensacola, on South Palafox, is **Mr. Manatee's,** a rollicking, open-spaced restaurant where you feel you are in a place to shake the sand out of your shoes instead of being in the center of the business district.

Mr. Manatee's offers a varied menu of chowders, appetizers, and entrées that you can count on to be very tasty. The grill's best choices are their Caribbean specialties such as fried Coconut Shrimp, Cracked Conch Sandwich, and Gator Tail Bites (it is gator). You must be forewarned of the "hot box" that is brought to every table—these six sauces are lethal. The restaurant has a nice deck outside that overlooks a small marina where two slips are available for customers who come by boat.

Mr. Manatee's is located at 619 Palafox and open from 11:00 A.M. to 10:00 P.M., Monday through Saturday, and from 11:00 A.M. to 9:00 P.M. on Sunday. The telephone number is (850) 434-0001.

One block south of Mr. Manatee's are two of the most exceptional shops in Pensacola.

Bayfront Gallery at 713 South Palafox is aptly named, for it is a gallery with collections of art and fine crafts to view as well as to purchase. Bayfront Gallery enables the modest collector to own original pieces of art by foremost artists of the day. Owners Kathy and Leighton Breazeak draw from more than 400 artists in the country whose work in clay, glass, fiber, metal, and wood is pleasing to touch and use in your daily life. Sculptor Don Drum uses heavy cast-aluminum and designs beautiful skillets, covered dishes, and bowls for practical as well as aesthetic uses. A husband-and-wife team from Oregon, who call their business Tin Workmen, produce ingenious shapes from hammered pewter; their delightful measuring cups and fish-shaped spoons would never be hidden in a kitchen drawer.

Hanging on a column in the back of the store are beautiful bells with tones soft and mellow. These bells were created by Tom Torre from Washington, whose medium is recycled industrial material.

American crafts have become a serious art form of today and Bayfront Gallery will stand up anywhere as a place for the collector or investor of important American crafts. It is open from 10:00 A.M. until 5:30 P.M., six days a week.

Across the street from Bayfront Gallery is another rare shop, **Quayside Market.** You enter to a sea of white, starched linen: counterpanes, napkins with Venetian lace, hand-embroidered pillowcases and place mats—all kinds of treasures new and old that are unusual and hard to find. As you go from room to room, you will find other things, such as depression glass, china and silver, old jewelry, and kitchen collectibles. Well, it will take a team of oxen to get you out of Quayside Market. It is open from 10:00 A.M. until 5:00 P.M., Wednesday through Sunday. The telephone number is (850) 432-2577.

The Pensacola Culture Center (400 South Jefferson Street) is not only a work of art outside, but a mecca for all the arts inside. This white-scrubbed structure is the old Records Building and has been transformed, with a theater wing on one side (seating about 500) and business offices for the arts on the other side. The Pensacola Culture Center has a ballet school and a historical society.

At the core of this building is **Stella's,** an Italian-American bistro. It is an open, airy place for people to eat lunch or early dinner. It is really hard to make up your mind when you begin to look at the menu. The salads all sound exciting—yes, exciting—for example, the Moma is made with crisp, smoked bacon, roasted pecan oil and cane syrup vinaigrette, Gorgonzola, caramelized pears, mixed greens, and Roma tomatoes. Napoleon Bakery's French bread is served with all salads. Also available are great sandwiches served on sun-dried tomato bread with roasted garlic mashed potatoes, pasta salad, or the "vegetable of the day" on the side. The "mains" are a whole other ball game—how do you choose between the Portabello Forechelli (a giant portabello mushroom with caramelized onions, melted fontina, Gouda, and Romano cheeses) or Ears and Tails (orechiette pasta tossed with crawfish tails in a creamy, vegetable-laden étouffée sauce)? The hours of this great, upbeat bistro are from 11:00 A.M. to 6:00 P.M., Monday through Friday, and the prices are moderate. Special dinners are often offered before Pensacola Little Theatre productions. For information, call (850) 434-5002.

The Pensacola Culture Center is a hive of activity. You will usually find a good artist exhibited there. Much information is available on current amusements in the city and it would be a good starting point for visitors. The Pensacola Culture Center is open Monday through Friday, from 9:00 A.M. until 8:30 P.M.

Don't you love Americans? In the advent of a nonsmoking world, the trend in cigar bars has begun to take hold everywhere in the United States. Not to be out done by all the big cities like New York and Los Angeles, Pensacola has its own **Cigar Brewery,** owned and operated by Bill Hauser and Chuck Dix.

The Brewery has a comfortable lounge and restaurant geared toward the cigar aficionados of the city. A walk-in humidor houses all the select cigars around the world and, for those not familiar with the quality of cigars, Dix and Hauser are there to assist. All manner of cigar accessories can also be purchased—and yes, lots of women have picked up the habit. For those sensitive to cigar smoke, a couple of tables outside can help you dine more comfortably; however, a ventilation system has been installed in the lounge to eliminate some of the smoke.

The Cigar Brewery is located behind Weaver's Cottage and Tivoli High House in the Historical District on Zaragosa. It is open at 5:00 P.M., Monday through Friday, and at 6:30 P.M. on Sunday. The telephone number is (850) 432-3995.

For serious antiquers, a quality shop is **Cleland Antiques** in an interesting 1840 house in the picturesque Seville Historic District. The Clelands specialize in 18th- and 19th-century American furniture and you will find folk art, Windsor chairs, pine chests, and copper and pewter accessories in primitive to formal styles. Cleland Antiques is located at 410E Zaragosa Street, just off Seville Square. It is open Monday through Saturday, from 10:30 A.M. until 4:00 P.M. The telephone number is (850) 432-9933.

Dharma Blue, rated "a double yum-yum" by a local patron, is a bright, happy café located across from Seville Square in one of the historic homes. On a fine day, porch dining is nice, but don't miss the colorful Caribbean-style interior with the gay, whimsical paintings of Pensacola artist Ann Frantic. A vivid mural of flora and fauna covers the entire wall of the back banquet.

There is a small sushi bar and a tempting menu. For dessert, try the Blueberry Cream Pie. By the way, "dharma blue" is a Caribbean phrase. *Dharma* means "essence of all good things and service to all people" and *blue* refers to a "cloudless sky or sea." Prices are moderate. Lunch is served from 11:30 A.M. to 2:00 P.M. and dinner is served from 5:00 P.M. to 10:00 P.M., Monday through Thursday, and from 5:00 P.M. to 11:00 P.M. on Friday and Saturday. The café is located at 300 South Alcaniz. The telephone number is (850) 433-1275.

Next door, Jeff and Donna Harris have opened **Breezes Coastal Cafe** at 304 South Alcaniz Street in an old wood-frame house. This was a dream-come-true for the couple because they had always wanted to live in a beach town. After owning and managing a café in Birmingham, Alabama, Jeff and Donna made the move to Pensacola in 1996. The café has a small, but adequate dining area inside and a few tables on the porch for outside dining. The menu consists of specialty salads and sandwiches. The daily special is posted on a blackboard on the porch. The food is tasty and fresh. Breezes also specializes in catering. For large orders it is best to call ahead. The menu is moderately

priced. It is open Monday through Friday from 10:30 A.M. until 3:00
P.M. The telephone number is (850) 438-3663.

When asked to name one of the best restaurants in Pensacola,
many natives will say **Jamie's.** This unpretentious French restaurant
is located in an old house on East Zaragosa, one-half block from
Seville Square. The house is small, with "chummy" rooms that have
just a few tables in each one. The thick, white tablecloths, fresh flowers, and simple lace curtains at the windows suggest a typical French
restaurant in Provence.

The cuisine is a perfect balance of excellent meats and fish dishes
with delicate sauces. The Deux Poisson, a favorite, is two fresh fish of
the day with two different sauces. All the lamb and beef are flown in
from the Buckhead Company in Atlanta, which is known for the highest quality meats. Wild mushrooms, so important to French dishes, are
flown in from the state of Washington.

Owner Gary Serafin is proud of the wine cellar. The restaurant has
just received the award of excellence rating from the *Wine Spectator,*
which is an honor it has worked 10 years to achieve.

Jamie's is an intimate restaurant best enjoyed by two to six people
who want to make eating an event, not somewhere to go before the
event. Reservations are recommended. It is open for lunch from 11:30
A.M. until 2:30 P.M., Tuesday through Saturday, and for dinner from
6:00 P.M. until 10:00 P.M., Monday through Saturday. The telephone
number is (850) 434-2911.

The Heirloom Shop, at 507 South Adams Street, is tucked away at
the end of a shady, little street and may be hard to locate; but if you
are interested in French handsewing or smocking, it is worth finding.
Bolts of beautiful batiste, laces, ribbons, and edging are neatly displayed around the shop. Owner Mary Dickson Quina offers classes
for those who want to learn and she also offers pleating and hem-
stitching services for those who already know. The telephone number
is (850) 433-7728.

"Le pain" at **Napoleon Bakery** (101 South Jefferson Street) is baked
daily as only the French can. The breads will be your favorites; every
morning they pile the loaves of baguettes, ryes, and sourdoughs in high
wooden racks to cool. Although high in caloric count, French bread has
no fat and should be eaten the day you buy it—which is no problem
since you will begin pinching it off before you reach your car.

The French pastries in the glass cases are so beautiful they look like paintings; they are all irresistible. You must try a little cake shaped like a mouse, with white icing and chocolate eyes and tail; his ears are slivers of almonds and the inside is a vanilla cake with a rich cream filling. When asked what the French name for this cake was, the tolerant lady behind the counter said, "Mouse."

Pensacola is lucky to have Messieurs Brugiere and Vallrand, who are not only the bakers at Napoleon but the owners as well. Monsieur Vallrand boasts of 18 years of schooling in the art of French baking and Monsieur Brugiere comes from a family of French bakers.

Napoleon is open from 7:00 A.M. to 5:00 P.M., Monday through Friday, and from 7:00 A.M. to 2:00 P.M. on Saturday. The telephone number is (850) 434-9701.

> *Note:* Please use your beginning French with the staff only when the bakery is not crowded!

Pensacola's own Norma Murray has four locations, each one as good as the other. Geared to the busy, corporate crowd, **Norma's on the Run** offers a specialized menu of breads, salads, pastas, and sandwiches. Norma's has a great takeout menu and a good bag lunch. It is located at 28 North Palafox; the hours are from 10:30 A.M. to 3:00 P.M., Monday through Friday. The telephone number is (850) 434-8646. Other locations are Cordova Mall, (850) 476-3702; West Garden, (850) 470-9785; and Bay Front Parkway, (850) 438-9565.

At the corner of Palafox and Garden, take a few minutes to really look around. The wide, grassy median is the shaded Martin Luther King Memorial Park and, in this area of just a couple of blocks, are five beautiful churches.

Near the top of Palafox is the lovely, sand-colored brick First Baptist Church. Below it is the brown, sandstone First Methodist Church (1908) with twin steeples. The Christ Episcopal Church, on the west side of the street, is built of pale stucco in the Spanish style and has a distinctive red-tiled roof. It also has a pretty courtyard overlooking Palafox. Next door is Immanuel Lutheran Church—be sure to notice the exquisite stained-glass windows. Last, but not least, is the quiet, old St. Michael's Catholic Church (1885), where, next door, the rectory has a breathtaking rose garden.

If you are spending time in Pensacola, the **Pensacola Grand Hotel** (200 Gregory Street) has the best location and accommodations. The lobby is the restored L & N Railroad Depot, which was built in 1912. In restoring this beautiful building, extensive care was taken to revitalize as much of the building's original materials as possible.

Pensacola is noted for its live productions offered all through the year. The Grand is just across the way from the Civic Center, making it very convenient to attend whatever function is taking place during your stay. If you are a walker, this is a perfect place to start a stroll through old historic downtown Pensacola.

The hotel is easily accessible from Interstate 10, which runs east and west just north of town. Call (850) 433-3336 or (800) 348-3336 for prices and reservations.

A favorite restaurant of tourists in Pensacola is **McGuire's Irish Pub,** which has been around since 1977. No stone is left unturned for you to have a brawling good time with good food to boot.

St. Pat's is the big day at McGuire's, where the green beer flows and the Irish songs abound; in fact they celebrate for the whole month of March.

For the first time, McGuire's has a new cookbook by Jessie Tirsch, the coauthor of *Emeril's New New Orleans Cooking* and the author of chef Paul Prudhomme's *Seasoned America*. *McGuire's Irish Pub Cookbook* includes recipes of the favorite dishes served throughout the years.

McGuire's romps from 11 A.M. until 2 A.M. seven days a week. You cannot miss it at 600 E. Gregory Street—just look for the big, green bus with a shamrock painted on it. McGuire's accepts no reservations, so call (850) 433-6789 to find out about the crowd. While you're there, don't miss the gift shop.

Pick up a "Historical Guide to Pensacola" at the **Visitors Information Center** at 1041 Gregory Street and take a pleasant walking tour of what was once the heart of the city in the 1700s and 1800s.

Travel north on 12th Street and you will find a study of contrasts—crumbling old houses stand next to beautifully restored homes with manicured lawns. Beginning at Cervantes and 12th Street, you can work your way up to the **Sacred Heart Hospital Building,** which was built in 1915. Aside from being listed on the National Register of Historic Places, the Sacred Heart Hospital Building has kept the architectural integrity that many buildings have been unable to maintain. Housed within this historic building you will find a Montessori school, along with several specialty shops.

If you remember "Grandma's cooking," you need to see what **Madison's Diner** has done to the recipes. Madison's meat loaf is made from certified Angus beef according to Grandma's recipe. "We just add merlot gravy." The bread is homemade and the vegetables are just as Grandma would have them—the garlic mashed potatoes may be just a little bit better. The menu includes beef, chicken, and fish dishes, along with several pastas and a lot of other good stuff. It is open for lunch and dinner from 11:00 A.M. to 9:30 P.M., Monday through Thursday; from 11:00 A.M. to 11:30 P.M. on Friday; from 12:00 noon to 11:30 P.M. on Saturday; and from 12:00 noon to 9:30 P.M. on Sunday. Madison's is located at 1010 North 12th Avenue. The telephone number is (850) 433-7074.

In the same building and just around the corner from Madison's is **C & M Central Market,** a neighborhood grocery. Freshly made sandwiches, salads, and soups are available for takeout or eating in. The grocery stocks oils, vinegars, pastas, cheeses, spices, wines, and other necessities. Owners Catherine and Mandy also cater. It is open from 9:30 A.M. to 6:30 P.M., Monday through Friday, and from 10:00 A.M. to 4:00 P.M. on Saturday. For information, call (850) 434-9888.

J's Pastry Shop got its name from the two brothers who started the business, Jay and Jack Steel—thus the name *J's.* They opened in 1945 and, even though it has changed hats a couple of times, it remains a busy neighborhood bakery, having much the same in baked goods as it did years ago.

How long has it been since you've seen petit fours with pastel icings and wedding cakes with a miniature bride and groom on top? Jay and Jack have those along with Cinnamon Bread, which is made like a jelly roll, and dozens of old-fashioned cookies that you have not seen in a while.

One of the bakers, Alex Cutts (who has been with J's since it opened), remembers baking a birthday cake so big that they had to get a dolly to hoist it out of the bakery. J's is located on 2014 North 12th Street and is presently owned by David Rowland. It is open from

6:00 A.M. to 7:00 P.M., seven days a week. The telephone number is (850) 432-4180.

When you drive up to **Stonehaus Gallery** (2617 North 12th Street), you will smile, for the outside wall has a mock entrance that is unmistakably Peter King's design. Walk around to the right and you will feel the heat from the huge kiln on one side and see a small gallery and workshop on the other side.

Upon entering the large studio in the back, you may see a huge fountain or fireplace being painstakingly constructed for a client piece by piece. Starting with Peter King's and his partner Marni Jaime's beginning design, the finished work requires a team of four, including Peter's brother John King and Rob Hayes, all of whom are integral parts of the project.

Once a year the Gallery has a Christmas bazaar, when they sell many smaller items. Since there are often structural problems that come with larger works, the team relishes this relaxing opportunity to work on smaller designs.

Architectural ceramics are the main interest at Stonehaus now and Peter King's designs have become a national product. His motto is "We want to go where no other architect ceramists have gone before." Indeed, when you walk into someone's home and see a beautiful ceramic doorway, fireplace, or archway that makes you stop, it is probably one of Peter King's designs.

We suggest that when visiting the gallery you call first since it is a working studio; however, it always has some smaller pieces in the front gallery for sale. The telephone number is (850) 438-3273.

What started as a hobby has become a full-scale florist business for Alice Weller and her two daughters, Debbie Turner and Mary Alice Price. They acquired a distinctive atrium structure built more than 60 years ago from the original owner, florist Carolyn Thornton, who worked there almost until she died. Now the ladies "keep the faith" with this old tradition by having the best all-occasion florist shop in these parts—**Celebrations,** 717 North 12th Street.

The shop has a huge stock of materials for the self-designer with all qualities of silk flowers and ready-made arrangements. In back of the store, where at one time were resting and potting rooms, there is now a big warehouse for indoor plants and flowers. You can get long-stemmed fresh flowers every day and—besides the traditional varieties, calla and casablanca lilies and agapanthus are always available. It is open from 8:30 A.M. until 5:30 P.M., Monday through Saturday. The telephone number is (850) 433-2022.

If you have not experienced **Hopkins House Restaurant** (900 Spring Street), you must take in this Pensacola tradition. Set in a quiet old neighborhood in north Pensacola, this boardinghouse has fed people for more than 40 years with the best Southern cooking ever eaten.

Arkie Dell, better known as "Big Mama Hopkins," owned and operated the boardinghouse and served family-style meals until her death in 1987. Her son is determined to keep it exactly as it has always been and thus the tradition continues.

All of your favorites are here—fresh vegetables every day, with cornbread and biscuits to "sop up the pot likker." On Sunday, Tuesday, and Friday the famous fried chicken is served, which even your mama couldn't duplicate. Don't pass up the Sweet Potato Soufflé, which is a melt-in-your-mouth dish, and the Squash Soufflé—another favorite. The menu changes daily and all of it is cooked Southern style.

The restaurant is always bulging with a real mix of people and, since Hopkins House Restaurant shows no favorites, you might need to wait on the porch or foyer for a few minutes. There is nothing contrived about this restaurant—it is strictly the basics—good food, good service, and good prices.

All you need is a good boardinghouse reach and if you don't have one, then ask for the food to be passed and say, "Thank you." Leave a generous tip in the big jar next to Margaret, who is the cashier and assistant manager. Margaret was 13 years old when she began snapping beans and shucking corn for the restaurant. She will tell you all about the history of the boardinghouse and will also share a few recipes.

Hopkins House Restaurant is open Tuesday through Sunday from 7:00 A.M. until 9:30 A.M. for breakfast and from 11:15 A.M. until 2:00 P.M. for lunch. Dinner is served Tuesday through Friday only, from 5:15 P.M. until 7:30 P.M. The telephone number is (850) 438-3979.

The Coffee Cup (520 East Cervantes) is remembered by most people as a stopping place for breakfast on the way to the beach in summer, long before Ronald McDonald was born.

The restaurant still has the best breakfast in town with farm-fresh eggs fixed any way you want them, homemade biscuits, and delicious Nassau grits (forget about getting the recipe). For delicious takeout, you can order baked turkey and dressing and homemade pies, cakes, and cobblers.

Since Larry Thomas took over, The Coffee Cup is the same neat, sunny place it has always been. Breakfast is served until 12:00 noon, Monday through Friday, and the restaurant stays open until 1:00 A.M. on Saturday. The telephone number is (850) 432-7060.

People enjoy going to a restaurant they can count on. Consistency is the byword at **Skopelos** (670 Cervantes). You know it is going to be there; you know the food is good; and you know the prices are right. The restaurant does not rely upon a tourist trade but a clientele that has grown with it. It was the mecca for young couples having dinner during the 1950s and 1960s. These couples have since married and still come to Skopelos with their families.

Because of its loyalty to the neighborhood of Pensacola Heights, its best dish is named Scampi Cervantes after the street on which the restaurant is located. Skopelos is appropriately named for an island in Greece, meaning "rock." It is open from 5:00 P.M. until 10:00 P.M., Tuesday through Saturday, and from 11:30 A.M. until 2:30 P.M. on Friday. The telephone number is (850) 432-4322.

The Marina Oyster Barn has much the same decor as many seafood restaurants along the Gulf Coast. Gulls and Buoys (Girls and Boys) are the labels on the restroom doors and fish netting with starfish attached covers the walls. However, that is where the similarities with other restaurants end, for The Marina Oyster Barn is truly an original.

In the first place, you come from bumper-to-bumper traffic and feel a thousand miles away from it. The restaurant is protected by a park on one side and a beautiful old residential area on the other. Because the Bayou Texar (pronounced "tahar") also borders this lovely area, the residents often hop into their skiffs and paddle to the restaurant.

It is small and comfy with a view from every booth and table. It is also squeaky clean and has friendly, competent personnel: Jane Rooks, the owner for more than 25 years, her son Dale, and Frank Cagle, the manager, who makes this great spot spin like a top.

The menu features seafood "every which way." Jane says they use their special batter on all the fried fish, from shrimp to soft-shell crabs. Because of the brackish water in this area, fresh mullet is always available and Jane feels mullet fanatics love the way it is prepared. Also noteworthy are the Fish Chowder and the homemade chicken and dumplings.

To get to The Marina Oyster Barn, go east on Cervantes until you cross the bridge, then turn north and wind around to 505 Bayou Boulevard. It is open from 11:00 A.M. until 9:00 P.M., Tuesday through Saturday. The telephone number is (850) 433-0511.

Kid's Market, at 2809 East Cervantes, is a welcome sight for anyone looking for a good selection of cotton clothing, casual knits, and special-occasion outfits for children, from infant to preteen. The shop has a great selection of European-style leather shoes in a wonderful array of colors and styles and special-occasion costumes, unique baby and birthday gifts, and a good supply of those downy, soft Nathan J infant sleepers and receiving blankets. The shop hours are from 10:00 A.M. to 5:30 P.M., Monday through Friday, and until 5:00 P.M. on Saturday. The telephone number is (850) 438-1866.

East Pensacola Heights is a neighborhood—remember neighborhoods? This community is Americana revisited. It all begins at **Jerry's Drive Inn** (2815 East Cervantes), a 1950s hamburger joint that will warm your heart. When you go in for the first time, you are surrounded by the "familiar." There is a long bar extending the length and width of the restaurant with tables lining the outside. It is not unusual to see three generations of families at a table with the baby sitting in a "punkin' seat" on top, all eating burgers and fries and chattering away.

Televisions are in every corner, switched to whatever sport is on at the time, from football to "monster mudder races"—races between vehicles mounted on gigantic tires. There is a solid mass of pennants hanging from the ceiling and corny quips are pasted everywhere. There's even one of those spigots that looks as if it is suspended in midair pouring eternal beer into a mug (in neon).

The personnel are easy in their shoes and serve you with gusto while exchanging barbs with the locals. By yourself or with a crowd, you will feel like Jerry's is family. Sha-boom sha-boom! It is open from 7:00 A.M. until 11:00 P.M., Monday through Saturday. The telephone number is (850) 433-9910.

If you want a taste of the Big Apple down South, try the **New Yorker Deli** at 3001 East Cervantes. Although takeout service is available, don't miss the fun of going inside and seeing the tables with cartoons from the *New Yorker* magazine under the glass tabletops. After you have gone from table to table reading cartoons, pick a table and have a seat so you can enjoy looking at all the magazine covers bordering the walls.

Obviously you will want to eat, not just look, so check out the extensive menu. If you are in the mood for something light, try one of the appetizers like Pomifeta—seasoned tomato and feta cheese baked on thick-sliced French bread—or maybe a cup of homemade soup. The sandwiches are true New York style, piled high with meat and cheese on your choice of bread. The entrées are well seasoned and tasty and all of the sauces are made on the premises. The pizzas, calzones, and cheesecakes are authentic New York style and delicious. Prices are moderate. New Yorker Deli is open from 11:00 A.M. to 9:30 P.M., Monday through Saturday. The telephone number is (850) 469-0029.

In winter when you drive up to **Weatherford's Four Season Apparel** (3009 East Cervantes), you will see a huge sign on the side of the building that gives you skiing conditions all over the country for that day. To add a little humor, it even has snow conditions in Pensacola.

Weatherford's is a store for the serious outdoorsman. It can outfit infants to adults with the latest in ski wear as well as clothing for all other activities throughout the year.

Weatherford's also has state-of-the-art climbing equipment and a 33-foot climbing wall. The wall has a 54-foot overhang, a chimney, and a bolted arrette. Owner David Dodson explained that "while the wall is designed and intended for the serious climber, it also provides an opportunity for everyone to familiarize himself with the adventures of rock climbing while remaining safe in a controlled environment." (So there is hope for all acrophobics.)

David has a strict set of rules for everyone using the wall. The last two: "No fast Rambo repelling down the climb. Keep swearing to yourself—watch your mouth and absolutely no spitting." (Evidently a few people have been experiencing a Rocky Mountain high.) Weatherford's Four Seasons Apparel is open from 9:00 A.M. until 6:00 P.M., Tuesday through Saturday. Climbing hours are from 12:00 noon to 6:00 P.M., Sunday and Monday, and from 3:00 P.M. to 9:00 P.M., Tuesday through Saturday. The telephone number is (850) 433-2822.

Tucked away in a sprawling metropolitan area of Pensacola is **The Four Winds International Food Market.** Nancy and James Taraby are the pulse of this operation and the reason for its excellent quality and service. From the moment you walk in the door, it is a "moveable feast," and you are able to indulge in samples of food that have just arrived from all over the world. You may be given a plump dried apricot from Turkey, a fresh date split with triple cream cheese from England, or a chocolate torte from France, to be washed down with a sample of wines.

Mr. Taraby has a history rich in food and beverage. Besides having a degree, he is proud of having apprenticed at the Intercontinental Hotel of Beirut, Lebanon, which is one of the finest hotel chains in the world. Mr. Taraby stands behind a glass counter, working hard while at the same time reciting litanies of recipes to his customers.

One of the things that you must buy is a marinade made at the store. It has an imported olive oil base, with herbs, olives, sun-dried tomatoes, and other ingredients. Mr. Taraby uses this marinade for everything. He bastes lamb and chicken with it, puts it on salads and pastas, and tosses it in a skillet with rice and pine nuts.

The market's cheeses are without equal. It has wonderful meats and sausages, a huge stock of fresh, imported coffees, and barrels of imported olives, not to mention an English snack called "Twiglets," which we defy you to find anywhere else. Mrs. Taraby says her husband is fond of saying, "If we don't have it, it probably isn't any good anyway."

Drag someone to the market who supposedly hates to shop and see what happens. The Four Winds International Food Market is open Monday through Saturday from 9:30 A.M. until 8:30 P.M. It serves food all day and is located at the corner of 9th Street and Creighton. The telephone number is (850) 477-2808.

Fiddlestix is a children's specialty store that is teeming with toys, books, and gifts. One of the owners says, "Fiddlestix has uniqued itself to death," trying hard to find fascinating and educational items for children. The Fiddlestix concept is to have fun while learning; so rather than competing with the large toystore chains, Fiddlestix focuses upon stimulation of the child's imagination.

Fiddlestix has a complete children's bookstore and is always happy to special order any children's book that is in print but not in stock. Adults look for excuses to go to Fiddlestix and it is not unusual to see children dragging their parents whining out the door.

Fiddlestix is located at Cordova Square, 3 Bayou Boulevard, and is open from 10:00 A.M. until 6:00 P.M., Monday through Friday, and from 10:00 A.M. until 5:00 P.M. on Saturday. The telephone number is (850) 478-8304.

Michele's
By The Bay

If you're in the mood for something a little different, you will have a pleasant surprise at **Michele's.** Located at 47 Gulf Breeze Parkway, just east of the Bay Bridge, this unobtrusive little restaurant sits quietly with a wonderful view (from deck or inside) of Pensacola Bay.

It is peaceful and uncluttered; on the tables small sea-green glass vases hold dried grasses and ceiling fans are almost the only other adornment. The menu is diverse and different, prices are in line, and portions are ample.

For a delightful appetizer, try the baked Seafood Mousse served with garlic bread. For a light dish, try the Antipasto or the Grilled Veggie Sandwich served with pesto mayonnaise. A typical seafood entrée is the shrimp, scallops, and crawfish tails in a seasoned sauce served over fresh tomato linguini. You can also get beef or veal and there is a good children's menu. Michele's is open six days a week at

11:00 A.M. for lunch and 5:00 P.M. for dinner. It is closed on Monday. The telephone number is (850) 916-0500.

Needle Delights, a full-line needlework shop, is family-owned and - operated. As a cross-stitch designer, Jeanette Rees "had trouble finding supplies," so she and husband John (retired from the navy) opened the shop in 1992. John does custom framing. This complete shop has anything and everything a "stitcher" could want. You can find any type of thread, cross-stitch patterns, books, beads, buttons, and buckles. The selection of needlepoint canvasses is vast—ranging from tree ornaments to rugs. Classes in all forms of needlework are offered.

Watch for the Christmas Open House in August. Jeanette will have returned from market with all manner of holiday gift ideas and items and there will be refreshments and door prizes. Call to get on their mailing list. Needle Delights is located in Harbortown Village at 913 Gulf Breeze Highway, just before the bridge to Pensacola Beach. Needle Delights is open from 9:30 A.M. to 5:00 P.M., Monday through Friday, and from 9:00 A.M. to 4:00 P.M. on Saturday. The telephone number is (850) 934-1017.

For information on the special annual events and accommodations in the Pensacola area, call (800) 874-1234. Web site: www.chamber.pensacola.fl.us.

To get to **Pensacola Beach,** take U.S. 98 where signs will direct you to the Pensacola Bay Bridge (small toll). The drive across the bridge onto Santa Rosa Island is lovely, with the bay on one side and Quietwater Sound on the other. On both sides are nice public parks with picnic areas. There are a couple of places to rent boats here also.

On Pensacola Beach you'll find lots to do and see. Houses, condos, and motels line the beach, along with snack bars, large restaurants, shops, and small vintage houses. For information about activities and

rentals, call the Pensacola Beach Visitor's Center at (800) 635-4803. Here on the beach, during the "season," you can participate in festivals of all kinds and you will most certainly want to catch a Blue Angels show.

"Best of all Worlds, Food, Fun, Friends, Music, Drinks, Dancing, and Dessert—all in one complex!" That's what the owners say about **Jubilee,** a restaurant and entertainment complex on Pensacola Beach's Quietwater Sound.

In 1986, June and Mike Guerra invested in the boardwalk that June's brother, Dan Baird, had built. They all had faith in the idea of year-round stores and restaurants on Pensacola Beach for area residents as well as tourists. June brought many talents (cooking, entertaining, decorating) along with a lot of enthusiasm to the project. Energetic manager Tom Carmichael joined them a few years later.

At **Beachside Cafe,** you can eat inside or out, all the while watching the kids cavorting on the beach or splashing in the shallow waters of the sound. An extensive menu includes fish, steaks, quesadillas, sandwiches, and burgers. Next door is the newly opened "dessert room," **J-Sweets.**

Topside is **Topside Dining Room,** a recently expanded, fine dining room with a fabulous view of the sound. While you're browsing the menu, look for dishes marked with a *j,* indicating the chef's most requested menu items. In addition to the regular choice of Florida-style cuisine (with a touch of Cajun), the chef dreams up taste-tempting entrées for a new, fresh sheet each week. Since 1987, Cecil Clark, director of music in the Pensacola School System, and his "home band" have played nightly. This place gets five stars all around!

Out on the deck is the **Capt'n Fun Beach Bar** (home of the island's best Bushwacker), with inside and outside deck seating. A recent addition is a great reception room that is available for parties, meetings, etc. Almost everything in the Jubilee complex opens around 11:00 A.M., but hours vary, so call ahead. The telephone number is (850) 934-3108. After seeing all that Jubilee has to offer, stroll out on the large, squeaky-clean boardwalk. There's a small amphitheater and shops galore.

> What is Bushwacker anyway? It's the Pensacola Beach Original Famous Frozen Adult Milk Shake Concoction . . . lethal.

The west end of **Santa Rosa Island** has an entirely different feeling. Just past a couple of motels, development on the Gulf side stops. Instead of high-rise condos, there are a few magnificent high-rise dunes. A historical cross marker on one informs that the first religious service in the Pensacola area took place here: "A mass celebrated on August 15, 1559, the Feast of the Assumption, by Dominican Friars."

After this stretch, the land becomes the property of the Gulf Islands National Park and Seashore and is barely tamed for the next eight miles (a nominal fee will allow you to visit the Seashore for up to a week). Here you'll find extensive camping grounds, bike paths, picnic spots, and nature trails; but for the most part, they are concealed so the effect is of a totally undisturbed beach.

At the end of the road is **Fort Pickens,** the largest of four forts built to defend Pensacola Bay and its navy yards. The fort was com-

INSIGNIA,
13th COAST ARTILLERY

(Sketch courtesy Gulf Islands National Seashore)

pleted in 1834 and was used until the 1940s when missile warfare made the gun batteries obsolete. Building of the fort was a massive project. More than 21.5 million bricks were required for this third-largest fort in the United States. Most of the bricks were handmade locally by skilled slave labor and barged to the island. From Maine came lime for mortar; granite came from New York; and copper for drains was shipped from Switzerland.

Stop in at the Visitor's Center and browse in the excellent bookstore and get a brochure for a self-guided tour. Guided tours are also available as are full moon walks and star watches. Call the Ranger Station at (850) 934-2631, 934-2632, or 934-2634 for information. You will also want to pick up a flyer about the 280 species of birds that have been identified in the area. Restrooms are available, but there are no other amenities. There is a good fishing pier, however.

Hours are from 9:30 A.M. to 5:00 P.M. in the summer and 8:30 A.M. to 4:00 P.M. in the winter (hours change when Daylight Savings Time changes). For condo rental information, call the Pensacola Beach Visitor's Center at (800) 635-4803. For campground reservations on the Gulf Islands National Park and Seashore, call (800) 365-2267. The telephone number for the Visitor's Center at the fort is (850) 934-2635.

Driving east on Santa Rosa Island, you will come to Navarre Beach.

Since Navarre Beach is part of the Gulf Islands National Park and Seashore, there are miles of undeveloped beaches here. Navarre has been rated one of the best beaches in the country. It is small and relaxed, without the traffic and congestion you find in many resort areas. A few pockets for parking along this stretch are available but, for the most part, this gorgeous length of beach is "au naturel."

On the east end there is a public park just over the toll bridge that joins Santa Rosa Island to the mainland (U.S. 98). For information, call 800-480-SAND or locally (850) 939-3267.

Gulf Breeze

Gulf Islands National Park and Seashore

Gulf Islands National Park and Seashore is an enormous park with enormous riches. Sugar-fine white beaches, coastal marshes, forts, trails, and campgrounds are but a few. This diverse park is not a block of land; instead, it is comprised of 11 separate parcels stretching 150 miles from West Ship Island, Mississippi, to the tip of Santa Rosa Island, Florida.

Established in 1971 by Congress, the purposes of the park are to protect wildlife, barrier islands, salt marshes, historic structures, and archaeological sites along the shores of the Gulf of Mexico. The Seashore is under the auspices of the National Park Service. Please see the Index (under *Gulf Islands National Park and Seashore*) for a listing of the separate parks. The web site is http://www.nps.gov./guis.

At the east end of Gulf Breeze on U.S. 98 (about two miles past the Pensacola Bay Bridge) is another beautiful part of the Gulf Islands National Park and Seashore. The Visitor Center here showcases exhibits on the area's history and the **Naval Live Oaks Area** and a short film about the Seashore.

The United States purchased the 1,378 acres, which comprise the Naval Live Oaks Area, in 1828 to ensure a future supply of the invalu-

(Sketch courtesy Gulf Islands National Seashore)

205

able live oak (used extensively then in shipbuilding). Pres. John
Quincy Adams authorized the establishment of a federal tree farm in
the Naval Live Oaks Area on January 18, 1829. It marked our nation's
first efforts at conservation of a natural resource. Live oaks are the
heaviest of all oaks and their resistance to disease and decay made
them even more ideal. One early famous live oak vessel is the U.S.S.
Constitution. During the War of 1812, the *Constitution* received the nick-
name "Old Ironsides" due to the strength of its live oak construction.

The live oak story is told here at the Naval Live Oaks Area with fascinating exhibits and displays. Inside is a wooden replica of a portion
of a ship's hull, complete with cannon. There is also a beautifully
stocked bookstore. Outside is a deck with benches overlooking the
sparkling Santa Rosa Sound. Near the deck is the beginning of a short
(two-thirds mile) nature trail leading to an overlook. What makes the
trail interesting, as well as inviting, are the informational markers
along the way. The markers are placed in front of live oak trees and
show how the various limbs of the trees were incorporated into the
structures of the ships.

In addition, the Naval Live Oaks Area contains a picnic area with
comfort stations and a youth group camping facility. A National
Seashore brochure advises, "Take care visiting Naval Live Oaks, please
take only pictures and leave only footprints." The Naval Live Oaks
Area is open from 8:30 A.M. to 5:00 P.M., seven days a week. The park
is open until sunset. It is closed Christmas Day. The telephone
number is (850) 934-2600.

Creole: A person descended from or culturally related to the
original French settlers of the Southern United States, especially Louisiana.

Cajun: A native of Louisiana, believed to be descended from
the French exiles from Acadia.

If you want some delicious and authentic food, just drive a few miles
east of Pensacola Bay Bridge to **Whistler's Walk Cajun Cafe.** In an unassuming, small building at 2737 Gulf Breeze Parkway, you'll find what
you're looking for—jambalaya, crawfish pie, pirogues, muffalettas, red
beans and rice, and Dixie Blackened Voodoo Beer to name a few.

The place is small, with 10 or so tables, and pleasingly congested.
There are fresh flowers on the tables and two long, high shelves over

the windows house a collection of Coca-Cola bottles and Louisiana State University Tigers memorabilia. A shelf near the door offers jars of hot sauces and jalapeno peppers to buy. On the restroom door is an LSU football schedule and above is a sign that says, "Geaux Tigers." Walls have been decorated with seemingly whatever the owners could find, including an ancient guitar with no strings and a cow poster, but that is okay.

You'll need to get a table and a menu and get in line (yes, there will probably be a line—but it moves fast) and you need to be ready. For starters, get a cup of gumbo, étouffée, or both.

You can create your own sandwich, but why would you want to when the house sandwiches are so marvelous? Among them are a (giant) muffaletta (the likes of which heretofore has not been available this side of New Orleans), a Cajun Veggie, a Baton Rouge (hot sausage with barbecue sauce), and the divine pirogues (shrimp or crawfish with buttered onions and peppers in hollowed-out French bread). Mmm, good!

If you prefer, you can get salads or Shrimp Remoulade and, for 12 years and under, there is a small menu. Whatever you get, be sure to order a side of French bread. All of the bread comes from New Orleans and you'll be talking about it for weeks. For dessert, there's key lime pie and pralines.

Before you leave, please take note of a small sign hanging near the order window. It reads, "Business is great, People are terrific and Life is wonderful." No wonder the food is so good. The café is open Monday through Saturday from 11:00 A.M. to 9:00 P.M. The telephone number is (850) 934-1887. *P.S.:* You can get takeout, too.

Whistler's Walk

The old plantation homes of the Deep South seldom had the kitchens under the same roof as the living quarters. The kitchen was connected by a covered walk to the dining area of the home. At meal times, the hot dishes were carried down this walk from the kitchen to the dining room by the servants of the plantation but with one very strict rule; the carrier had to whistle continuously, thus assuring the diners that he was not eating out of the plates during his trek down the Whistler's Walk.

As you cruise down the highway, the **Beach Bar-B-Que and Seafood,** 5248 Gulf Breeze Parkway, might slip by, but this is a good place to stop and sample the tasty local seafood and barbecue.

The Shrimp and Oyster Po' Boys with side orders of fresh, home-cooked veggies and Jo-Jo Potatoes would be a good choice for lunch. Jo-Jo Potatoes are thinly sliced potatoes fried up almost like potato chips. Or try the fried mullet—all you can eat with hush puppies and coleslaw—said to be the most popular item on the menu.

Owners Della and Diane Johnson have been serving home cooking at the Beach Bar-B-Que since 1991 and the service is friendly and fast. Prices are very inexpensive. It is open Tuesday through Sunday from 11:00 A.M. to 9:00 P.M. Takeouts are available. The telephone number is (850) 932-0210.

If you're cruising along with children and find yourself in Gulf Breeze, Florida (and you've heard for the ump-teenth time, "Are we there yet?"), give yourself a happy break and stop in at the **Zoo,** 5701 Gulf Breeze Parkway. This privately-owned zoo is accredited by the American Zoo and Aquarium Association. Throughout the United States, there are more than 2,000 licensed zoos and aquariums, but only 164 are accredited.

The 50 or so acres are lush Florida landscape and include a beautiful Japanese garden. The monkeys are adorable and the elephant, Ellie, is a talented artist who gives a demonstration twice daily when she paints and uses her footprint as her signature. Other demonstrations include the reptiles, birds of prey, and an eagle flight. Thirty acres are developed for a safari miniature railway and there is a full-service restaurant and gift shop where Ellie's paintings are sold.

This much-loved zoo has a tremendous outreach program in the community and is host to all manner of charity benefits. Since education is one of the zoo's primary goals, a zoo camp is offered during the summer and overnights (called "zoosnoozes") can be scheduled for groups. This includes a nighttime train ride through the wildlife preserve and a behind-the-scenes tour of the zoo. For information, call (850) 932-2229. The zoo is open daily from 9:00 A.M. to 5:00 P.M. during the summer and from 9:00 A.M. to 4:00 P.M. during the winter.

Fort Walton Beach

Fort Walton Beach covers a six-square-mile stretch of U.S. 98 along Santa Rosa Sound and the Gulf of Mexico. Archeological excavations of nearby Indian mounds, yielding artifacts from prehistoric times, have added historical significance to the town.

Walton County was created in 1842 and named for George Walton, one of Andrew Jackson's aides and son of one of the signers of the Declaration of Independence. During the Civil War, local citizens formed a military unit to guard Santa Rosa Sound. This company was stationed at the Temple Mound (in downtown) and the soldiers became known as the Walton Guards. After the war, the town was renamed in honor of the men who served.

Smith's Department Store in downtown Fort Walton has been operating for more than 30 years. H. Gene Smith is owner of the family business, which was started by his father in Panama City. This store is one-stop shopping at its best. Smith's has literally everything a lady could possibly need for any occasion—casual wear, evening wear, hats, jewelry, lingerie, hair accessories, shoes, purses, birthday cards, dolls, stuffed animals, swimwear, and even ostrich eggs. If you should have a weary shopping companion, there are places to sit and rest with magazines and cookbooks for entertainment. A determined shopper might easily spend more than an hour just browsing. The sales ladies are all exceptionally pleasant and helpful. According to one nice lady, Laverna, Smith's is called the "earring capital of the world." Smith's is open from 9:00 A.M. until 6:00 P.M., Monday through Saturday.

You must climb the steps to the top of this, the largest temple mound on salt water, close your eyes, and imagine that there is no busy U.S. 98 below, no roaring traffic, no shops or other signs of civilization as we know it today. Then you can visualize it in A.D. 1400, when the mound was built by the native American Indians of the flourishing Mississippi culture.

Standing on the mound today is the **Indian Temple Mound Museum,** a replica of an Indian Temple where the Indians met for

ceremonies and to elect tribal chieftains. This high piece of ground was also a natural lookout spot used by the Confederates to spy on Union warships during the Civil War.

Inside the small museum are 7,000 artifacts depicting native American Culture and a burial urn, one of only two existing. Burial urns were usually destroyed in the burial rites so it is rare indeed to find one unbroken.

The museum is open from 9:00 A.M. to 4:30 P.M., Monday through Saturday, and from 12:30 P.M. to 4:30 P.M. on Sunday. Admission is $2.01 for adults, $1.01 for children, ages five to 17, and free for children under age five. The telephone number is (850) 833-9595.

What a joy to find a truly fine antique shop. **Darby-Mitchell Antiques,** owned by Gerald Darby, carries English and French pieces with emphasis on country French. Mr. Darby feels his country French collection is the largest and best on the Northern Gulf Coast.

The antique shop has unusual antique accessories, such as the giant Moroccan olive jars, at better prices than in New Orleans. All of the old antique chandeliers are restored and rewired. This shop is open from 10:00 A.M. until 5:00 P.M., Monday through Saturday.

If you're up for a meal with European flair, try **Cafe Italia** with a grassy green vista sloping to the Santa Rosa Sound. Located at 189 Brooks Street, Cafe Italia is quaintly attractive and has indoor/outdoor dining.

You'll find a menu of many of the widely appreciated Italian dishes. Among them, risotto—rice cooked with asparagus, mushrooms, or smoked salmon; of course, veal—ossobuco; and a variety of choices for serious pizza.

Cafe Italia, a traditional, family-owned and -operated ristorante, was opened in 1993 by Nada Echart and her husband, a retired air force officer. Since then, they have been written up several times in *Southern Living* magazine. Possibly, this is the only restaurant in the country that sells shoes. Nada, originally from Croatia, found that her shoes of Borosand, Inc., which are made in her native country, were so admired that she became the sole distributor of the line in the United States.

Cafe Italia is available for wedding receptions and special events to which Nada Echart wears her colorful native Croatian costume. The dishes are moderately priced. It is open daily, except Monday, from 11:00 A.M. The telephone number is (850) 664-0035.

Under the Brooks Bridge in Fort Walton is **Bay Cafe,** a pleasant spot overlooking Santa Rosa Sound. Uncomplicated French cuisine is the bill of fare with daily specials of fresh fish, pasta, and chicken. Bay Cafe has a good wine list and dining on the deck outside is a pleasant respite from the eternal traffic buzzing on the bridge above you.

Bay Cafe is on 233 Aloncia Avenue. Take a right before the bridge onto Brooks Street; the restaurant is at the point at Aloncia Avenue and Brooks Street. Prices are moderate. It is open for lunch from 11:00 A.M. until 3:00 P.M. and dinner from 5:00 P.M. until 11:00 P.M. The telephone number is (850) 244-3550. You may also reach the restaurant by boat.

Seafood Primavera
Bay Cafe

1 lb. fresh crabmeat
1 lb. small shrimp, cooked
½ cup salad oil

(continued)

½ cup red wine vinegar
½ cup mayonnaise
2 tsp. Dijon mustard
2 tsp. garlic, chopped
Salt, pepper, oregano, paprika, and parsley to taste
3 pkg. pasta (fettucine-capellini or combination)
1 cup julienne-sliced zucchini
1 cup julienne-sliced carrots
1 cup chopped broccoli
1 cup chopped cauliflower
3 tbsp. butter
Parmesan cheese

Combine and mix well for about two minutes: crabmeat, shrimp, salad oil, red wine vinegar, mayonnaise, mustard, garlic, salt, pepper, paprika, and parsley. Transfer to cooler.

Cook the pasta in a large amount of boiling, salted water (al dente). Drain well and transfer to cooler.

Cook the 4 cups of fresh vegetables for about 3 minutes in boiling water and drain. Then sauté in the butter. Season to taste, let cool, then mix into pasta and dressing. Sprinkle with Parmesan cheese. Serve on cold plates. Serves 16-18.

The **Boathouse Restaurant** is well worth the trip. Located at 126 John Simms Parkway (aka Florida 20) in Valparaiso, the restaurant is just a few miles north and across the bridge from Fort Walton Beach.

Once a private residence and the East Bay Guard Station, the restaurant has been owned and operated since 1987 by Mary Ann and Bryce Averitte. Bryce has been in the food business since he was 16 years old, first as a butcher and then as the youngest-ever assistant manager at Morrison's Cafeteria. Mary Ann was a banker and in public relations. They make a great team.

Together they've got a charming spot where you can eat inside or out on a great shady deck overlooking the water. For lunch you can get fabulous hamburgers, pulled pork barbecue, and shrimp hoagies (order the superb steak fries, too). At dinner there are gumbo, chicken, scallops, steaks, etc. Now and then they cook up some 'gator and their red beans and rice are famous. Besides simply good food, they also have simply excellent service. Prices are moderate.

It is hard to see the restaurant from the road. There is a sign on the highway where you will turn in and follow a narrow road under the trees. If you're eating on the deck, you'll see and hear planes from nearby Eglin Air Force Base, but rather than an annoyance, they're quite beautiful to watch. The restaurant is open Monday through Friday for lunch, Monday through Saturday for dinner, and Sunday from 10:00 A.M. until 2:00 P.M. for brunch. The telephone number is (850) 678-8839.

Thirteen miles northeast of Fort Walton is **Eglin Air Force Base,** the largest air force base in the country (728 square miles). It was built in 1937 and the nation's newest and most modern aircraft are still tested here. Three-hour tours are conducted January through March and June through August on Monday, Wednesday, and Friday. Call (850) 882-3933 for information about a pass.

"The **Air Force Armament Museum** is a museum for all ages," said director Russ Sneddon. "We have exhibits from World War II to modern times as well as 26 airplanes."

The planes on display include the SR-71 Blackhawk spy plane, a B-17 Flying Fortress and a B-25 Mitchell (both World War II veterans), and a P-47 Thunderbolt, known for the famous aerial dogfights. Also on display are contemporary planes: the F-15 Eagle, F-16 Falcon, F-111 Aardvark, and RF4-C Phantom.

Open since 1985, the Air Force Armament Museum is in a new, modern building on nicely landscaped grounds and is supported by government and private sponsors. Admission is free and the museum is open from 9:30 A.M. until 4:30 P.M. everyday, except Thanksgiving, Christmas, and New Year's Day. It is located just outside of Eglin Air Force Base, West Gate on Florida 85.

The **Gulfarium,** 1010 Miracle Strip Parkway, U.S. 98 in Fort Walton Beach, is a natural if you're on a family seaside vacation. It is the second oldest in the country, well organized, and has the usual marine shows four or five times daily: dolphins, sea lions, and the living sea. Dolphins and sea lions perform together and, although not ordinarily compatible, are working well with each other in the shows.

The Gulfarium is run by Brandy Siebenaler, a marine biologist, and is a member of a National Marine Mammal Stranding Network.

It was in this capacity that they were asked to care for a three-week-old bottled-nose dolphin that was one of a pod of dolphins stranded at Pensacola Beach in 1995. With dedicated care and special formulas, the infant dolphin, name Kiwi, survived and is now a very special feature at the Gulfarium.

For a substantial fee, two or more people, under a trainer's supervision, can spend 40 minutes in the pool with Kiwi. Since Kiwi was raised by humans, she thinks she is one and is a sociable little animal.

There is a snack bar, an extensive gift shop, and a weekly summer day camp for children entering grades three through eight. Show times are from 10:00 A.M. to 7:00 P.M. during the summer and 10:00 A.M. to 4:00 P.M. during the winter. The telephone number is (850) 243-9046.

Destin

Fishing is to Destin as politics is to Washington, D.C. Destin was founded by a snapper fisherman, Capt. Leonard Destin, and commercial fishing was the lifeblood of the area until sport fishing became popular in the 1940s. Today Destin is called "the world's luckiest fishing village."

According to charter-boat captain Larry Rush, "This is because Destin is close to the continental shelf and very deep water. Twenty miles out is a ledge that drops gradually to 300 feet, beyond which is DeSoto Canyon—3,000 feet deep!" This canyon, where huge dinosaurs once must have roamed, is today populated by huge fish—marlin, tuna, sailfish, and sharks.

Another charter-boat captain, Tommy Norred, adds, "Destin is one of the first places to build artificial reefs so the captains know where the fish are." Needless to say, the location of these reefs is a closely guarded secret.

Destin has one of the largest charter boat fleets in the world—more than a hundred boats that ply the incredibly clear, green waters, where you can often see the fish before it strikes. Also improving the odds for fishing is a long eight-month season for the large migratory fish.

Besides the fishing, Destin is the dining destination of the Emerald Coast. Fine restaurants abound and it might be wise to lose a few pounds before you visit so you can afford to indulge.

At the foot of Destin Bridge at 51 U.S. 98 East is an ocean of art at **Wylands' Paradise Gallery.** This is no ordinary gallery as the art pertains solely to the environment. Everyone has seen dolphin sculptures, but none equal Wylands'; and as pricey as they are you will want to adopt one.

Wyland, described by *USA Today* as "a marine Michelangelo," is internationally known for his huge mural covering three surface acres of the Long Beach Convention Center. Another of his famous murals was painted for the Mexico City Seaquarium in exchange for the release of the whale, Keiko, star of *Free Willy*, who for many years had been held in an undersized tank.

215

Other fine nature artists are represented in the gallery. Among them are James Coleman, former Walt Disney animator, and Michael Maiden, whose bronze eagle sculptures appear ready to take flight.

An added attraction to this lovely, tranquil gallery are two 500-gallon saltwater aquariums. This is one art gallery that children will enjoy. Gallery hours are from 10:00 A.M. to 10:00 P.M., daily. The telephone number is (850) 650-1800.

Just as you cross over the Destin Bridge and right on the water is the **Lucky Snapper.** The view of the Gulf, the harbor, and the bridge is spectacular. The open-air dining gives the feeling of actually being in the water. Only the freshest of Gulf seafood is served and, according to owner Tom Rice, he can only serve what the boat brings in. It is tempting to fill up on the tasty Cheese Muffins served before the meal; but the fish dishes are so good, and you will want to save room for the best-ever key lime pie. This is a great place to bring the family for eating and watching the harbor traffic. It is open from 11:00 A.M. to 10:00 P.M., seven days a week. The telephone number is (850) 654-0900.

Just next door is the **Harborwalk Marina.** This marina has everything for your fishing trip—except a boat—but there is gas to run a boat. Inside the store are tackle, maps, books, bait, food, drinks, ice, and coolers. It is a one-stop fishing shop.

One step farther down the boardwalk is **Harborwalk Fishing Charters.** To make that trip even less of a hassle, everything can be furnished, including food and beverages, upon request. Boats are available to accommodate small or large groups, from six up to 49 passengers. For reservations, call (850) 837-2343 or (800) 24-CATCH.

If cruising seems more enjoyable than fishing, there are several options. Motor vessels such as the *Southern Star,* (850) 837-7741, or for a different, more historic style of cruising, schooners like the *Nathaniel Bowditch,* (850) 650-8787, give relaxed, three-hour cruises.

The Reef Runner is a suggestion for a lower-priced snorkeling trip with equipment included. It is located at the Harborwalk Marina, (850) 654-4655, along with pontoon boats to rent if you want to go out on your own.

Diving and Snorkeling

Both diving and snorkeling are superb in Destin. There are several dive shops that can provide you with equipment, instruction, and transportation on boats that will take you to any of nine reefs (five are natural). A "diver's down" flag is a state requirement. Look in the yellow pages for numbers.

There is also some fine snorkeling off the beach—no boats needed. At the Destin jetties at the west end of Holiday Isle, you can see grouper, amberjack, angelfish, and more. Depth here is from very shallow to 25 feet. There is also good snorkeling under the Destin Bridge (you'll need to snorkel at high tide for the slowest current). Beginners should try the Crystal Beach pier pilings, east of Destin on U.S. 98. There is a large sandbar here and it is no deeper than 12 feet.

If the wind is right, go to **Get In The Wind Kite Shop** and pick up a new state-of-the-art kite to fly on the beach. The shop has beautiful stunt kites and kites to be steered with two hands. They also have the single-line kites that fly higher than the high-tech kind.

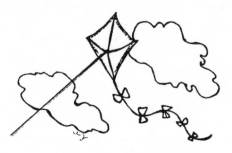

Colorful windsocks make great gifts for people with wharfs and balconies and Get In The Wind Kite Shop has all kinds flying cheerfully from the porch.

This fun shop is located at Barefoot Plaza, 109-B U.S. 98 East, and is open from 10:00 A.M. until 6:00 P.M., Monday through Saturday, and from 12:00 noon until 6:00 P.M. on Sunday. The telephone number is (850) 654-WIND.

Located in the Palmetto Plaza, 127 U.S. 98, **Killough's Interior Design Studio** is a fun visit. It is overflowing with unusual and whimsical objets d'art, china, art glass, pillows, and paintings.

Gary Killough, an Alabama native who has decorated houses all over the Southeast as well as the annual Birmingham decorator's show house, said, "We like to think that unique designs and innovative concepts are our trademark." That seems to be the case. The studio is open from 9:00 A.M. until 5:00 P.M., Monday through Friday, and from 10:00 A.M. until 4:00 P.M. on Saturday. The telephone number is (850) 654-5006 or (850) 243-3899.

Everyone leaving the Panhandle wants to take fresh fish home and **Destin Ice House Seafood Market** (210 U.S. 98) is a good place to stop on your way north. The market will pack fish to travel or air freight it to you, which is its specialty. The Seafood Market is known for having the highest quality of fish, which is why the best restaurants along the Gulf Coast do business here—like the Marina Cafe, Flamingo, Criolla's, Bud & Alley's, and Louisiana Lagniappe, to name a few.

Owner Jim Bass is usually around from 6:00 A.M. on. He has great hints for easy ways to prepare gourmet dishes with all the excellent new seasonings on the market today. For example, Old Bay Classic Crab Cake mix turns out delicious crab cakes, better than those in most restaurants. River Road is a company out of New Orleans that makes a barbecue shrimp mix; when added to shrimp, Worcestershire sauce, and butter, it is as good as Manale's in New Orleans. The idea is to let people in condos enjoy specialty dishes without much time or effort.

The Seafood Market has prize-winning gumbo for sale; there is also frozen stuffed crabs and other prepared food to take out. It has also found a way to have redfish, which is pretty scarce. All is kept cold with eight tons of ice each day. The market is open seven days a week from 6:00 A.M. until 8:00 P.M. during the summer, from 7:00 A.M. until 7:00 P.M. after Labor Day through the end of October, and from 8:00 A.M. until 6:00 P.M. from November through Memorial Day. The telephone number is (850) 837-8333.

Captain Dave's has been around for a long time and still has a huge clientele even though many new family restaurants have opened in Destin. The owners have the know-how to handle big family groups; Captain Dave's takes them all in stride and manages to serve great food at modest prices. The place is always crowded and lively. Visit their second location on Old U.S. 98. Captain Dave's is open from 5:00 P.M. until 10:00 P.M., seven days a week. The telephone number is (850) 837-2627.

Harry T's is a popular, casual hot spot on the U.S. 98 strip with a beautiful harbor view, tasty food from a varied menu, and cheerful service. The Key Lime Pie is some of the best around. What more can you ask?

Harry T's, at 320 U.S. 98, is lively downstairs at night with a band and karaoke, so come prepared to enjoy or bring your earplugs. The telephone number is (850) 654-4800.

The **Boat House Oyster Bar** is a small, popular hangout and a fun place to go in bathing suits, shorts, and flip-flops. Here you will see everything from a Texas billionaire to the local mackerel fisherman. It is the ideal watering hole for the tired and thirsty fisherman since it sits in the middle of the charter fishing docks, right over the water, and, best of all, facing west so you can catch a superb sunset.

The Boat House is also known as the home of Destin's award-winning gumbo, so by all means, try it. Seven nights a week there is live entertainment in the form of a one-man band (there's not much room for more!).

Part of the atmosphere are dollar bills tacked to the ceiling and a sign on the bar saying, "If you are grouchy, irritable or just plain mean, there will be a $10.00 charge just to put up with you." Prices are moderate. It is open from 11:00 A.M. to 10:00 P.M., seven days a week. The bar stays open later. The Boat House is located at East Pass Marina. The telephone number is (850) 837-3645.

Sitting side by side are two of the most revered restaurants in Destin, the Flamingo and the Marina Cafe. These two giants are reminiscent of the 1930s supper clubs, with beautiful decor and renowned chefs who have plaques and medals filling each foyer. Seating capacity is around 200 and, during the season, reservations are needed, for they are always buzzing.

The **Flamingo** is a soft pink stucco building with gingerbread borders (not cutsie). Inside, you are greeted by two tiled flamingos at the reception desk. The dining room is a huge carpeted room with great arched windows, which insure a view wherever you sit. Behind a large panelled screen is a raised bar, where you can enjoy a drink and delicious appetizers. For a starter, the Crab en Croute is made with jumbo lump crabmeat and garlic Béchamel; it is wrapped in phyllo dough, baked, and finished with two butter sauces and honey-roasted nuts—you will not forget this dish.

Entrées at the Flamingo are traditional and, as one patron puts it, "they don't mess with the fish," but grill or broil it with light sauces of white wine or Tequila Lime Sauce. Flamingo's best dish is the Grouper Pontchartrain, which is a pan-fried, soft-shell crab atop a grilled filet of grouper and finished with an array of butter sauces.

Flamingo cannot be given enough superlatives for food, atmosphere, and service; it simply does not take a false step. Prices are moderate to expensive. The telephone number is (850) 837-0961.

Should you be seeking accommodations for body and boat, try **Kokomo,** 500 U.S. 98 on Destin Harbor. There are 10 comfortable units with small kitchenettes and, for a very small fee, a boat slip. An added bonus is the popular Flamingo Restaurant just next door. The rates are very reasonable.

Kokomo also offers a picturesque sunset cruise, deep-sea fishing charters, and guided snorkeling trips aboard a 50-foot custom-built snorkeling boat. For bed, board, and boat, call (850) 837-9029.

Next door neighbor to the Flamingo is the **Marina Cafe,** a terra-cotta building with a shiny copper roof and beautiful mosaic entrance. Five sea creatures are in framed panels and attractively lit from

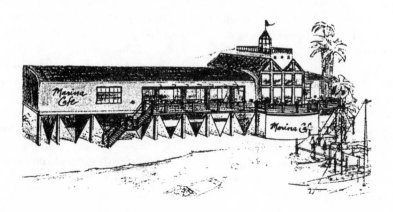

behind, giving the facade a soft glow at night. The interior of the restaurant is the cutting edge of contemporary design.

The split-level dining area overlooks the marina below. One side of the room has intimate booths and a small pizza bar with a wood oven in the corner of the dining room. The cuisine, like the decor, is sharp and innovative and served by two "hop to" waiters for each table. The menu changes daily, but you should hope that the top-grade yellow-fin tuna, with the crust of pepper served rare with ginger and garlic, is available.

Times for each restaurant are from 5:00 P.M. until 10:00 P.M., seven days a week. Prices are moderate to expensive. Both can be reached by boat or water taxi as well as by car. While children are not unwelcome, these restaurants appeal to more adult dining. The telephone number is (850) 837-7960.

A favorite of the "Destinians" (the locals) is **Guglielmo,** a family-owned and -operated restaurant specializing in Northern Italian cuisine. The Guglielmos are originally from Northern Italy and have operated a restaurant in the area since 1991. Currently, it is a father and daughter, chef-manager team, using Grandmother's recipes.

Among the preferred dishes are the traditional Piccato di Vitello and Capellini ala Toseana, a light, angelhair pasta with artichokes, olives, capers, and red peppers. A natural, given the locale, is the Grouper al Forno baked with seasoned bread crumbs, fresh herbs, and spices. It is open nightly from 5:00 P.M. Reservations are recommended. Prices are moderate to expensive. The telephone number is (850) 654-9880. Guglielmo is located one mile east of the Destin Bridge, 529 U.S. 98.

The menu is the surprise at **Harbor Docks** because you're apt to think it is to be the traditional seafood menu when you walk in and see a 14-foot black marlin hanging from the ceiling. However, there is an excellent sushi bar downstairs. The sushi chef is Yoshie, who has catered for such stars as Madonna, Robin Williams, and Shirley MacLaine.

Harbor Docks actually owns a seafood market that provides fine, fresh fish of the day, grilled or blackened to perfection. A bonus attraction is the view of Destin Harbor from about every table and a popular band packs them in nightly. Prices are moderate to expensive. It is open for lunch and dinner from 11:00 A.M. until 11:00 P.M. It is located at 538 U.S. 98 East. The telephone number is (850) 837-2506.

If you are tired of cars and traffic, try the Harbor Queen water
taxi, a bright yellow boat owned by Captains Cathi Jones and
Wayne Anderson. They offer to be your designated driver for
all of Destin Harbor. Open daily. For information, call (904)
585-3321 or (904) 654-5566 or VHF Channel 10. (Reasonable
rates.)

DESIGNATED PICKUP STOPS

1. Boogie's
2. A.J.'s
3. Boathouse
4. Capt. Dave's
5. Harry T's—Marina Cafe
6. Flamingo Cafe
7. Harbor Docks
8. Jewel Melvin's
9. Louisiana Lagniappe

A book that is fast becoming a classic is the *Cruising Guide to the
Northern Gulf Coast: Florida, Alabama, Mississippi, and Louisiana.*
Claiborne S. Young has cruised this course and written about it.
The book parallels by water the route *Coasting* covers by road.

Just east of the Destin Bridge on U.S. 98 at Benning Drive (across
from Sexton's Seafood), located on the harbor are the offices of **Sailing South** (sailing and charters) and **Points of Sail** (school of sailing

and navigation). Just follow the big sand-dollar stepping stones down to the harbor.

If you're interested in learning how to sail, director Anita Page offers both private lessons and classes for basic and advanced sailing between March and November. The school is American Sailing Association-certified. Anita, who has been in this business since 1982, says she tries to keep the classes small so she can give individual attention to her students. You will learn not only the necessary skills to become an "old salt" but also the vocabulary. You'll have fun while you're learning.

In the same building you will find Sailing South. Choose a boat and a destination and they will help you chart your course. Owner Bill Campbell and his staff recommend that you also choose another person to assist you with the sailing. They will spend as much time as you like going over the boat before you take off. If you prefer, a guide can be provided (for a minimal fee) with a few days' notice. The telephone number is (850) 837-7245.

Destin, Florida, is known for its beautiful beaches and seafood restaurants. One of the longtime favorites is **Captain Jewel Melvin's Seafood Restaurant.** Owned by Jewel and Ruby Melvin, this place offers the whole gamut of seafood delicacies. Be sure to check out the mouth-watering specialties, such as the Oyster Boat Sandwich, made with sautéed oysters topped with fried tomatoes, crisp bacon, and green pepper rings and served with Creole mustard on a French roll. The Oyster Stew is exceptional and there is also an awesome Neptune Salad that easily serves four. Most seats in the restaurant have a window view of the water and there is a bar on the porch. Prices are moderate. It is open from 11:00 A.M. to 3:30 P.M. and from 4:00 P.M. to 10:00 P.M., seven days a week. It is closed on Sunday for lunch. The telephone number is (850) 837-2020.

Tom Putnam's great bait and tackle store, the **Half Hitch Tackle Shop** is located at 621 U.S. 98. Like its companion store, the Half Hitch has whatever you need to go fishing—from seine net to a dorky mullet lure. The telephone number is (850) 837-3121.

Since it has been scientifically proven of late that children do not get wired after eating sugar, you can now go with tradition and take them to the **Donut Hole** for breakfast. This bakery/café is family-owned and, since 1977, has been a favorite of locals as well as vacationers. Now, it is not just a place for old-fashioned donuts but also offers a complete breakfast and lunch menu. Try the pancakes or Belgian Waffles with Grandmother's Special Orange Sauce. Omelets are terrific served with the Donut Hole's own baked breads, sliced tomatoes, fries, or grits (plain or cheese).

Swarms of people are always at the Donut Hole, but service is swift and there is not much of a wait. Takeout is available. It is open 24 hours a day, seven days a week. The telephone number is (850) 837-8824.

Donut Hole II is out U.S. 98 and all the good qualities of the old are ditto for the new. It is open seven days a week from 6:30 A.M. until 8:00 P.M. The telephone number is (850) 267-3239.

The **Shores Shopping Center** on U.S. 98 East contains several shops that could contribute happily to a recreational shopping day.

Today's Fashions and Fun, 877 U.S. 98, is a fascinating clothing store because it is ingeniously divided into sections: **Naturally White,** with soft linens, knits, and cottons in shades of white and off-white; and **Somethin' Fishy,** everything with a fish motif. Today's Fashions is brimming with bright, light sportswear, shoes, and accessories. It is open from 10:00 A.M. to 8:00 P.M. daily during the summer months, and from 10:00 A.M. to 6:00 P.M. daily during the winter months. The telephone number is (850) 650-6517.

On the opposite side of the shopping center at 839 U.S. 98 is **The Mill Outlet,** which contains an extensive selection of everything for bed, bath, and table linens. It is open daily from 9:00 A.M. to 9:00 P.M. during the summer and from 9:00 A.M. to 6:00 P.M. during the winter. The telephone number is (850) 837-7244.

Callahan's Island Restaurant and Deli is one of the natives' favorite. There is a mouth-watering selection of meats, cheeses, and pâtés plus imported wines and beer. You can choose your own steak, which will be cooked to suit your taste.

The atmosphere is strictly casual with tile floors and colorful print tablecloths. Tempting, large soup pots simmer on a counter for instant self-service. Everything is fresh and good. For breakfast, try the Santa Fe Omelet; on Thursdays, the Lebanese Salad is one of the popular specials. Takeouts and catering are available. Prices are moderate. It is located at 950 Gulf Shores Drive and is open from 10:00 A.M. until 9:00 P.M., Monday through Friday, and from 8:00 A.M. until 9:00 P.M. on Saturday. The telephone number is (850) 837-6328.

Three very fine restaurants are in different resort areas in Destin. Louisiana Lagniappe Restaurant at Sandpiper Cove, Ocean Club at Tops'l, and Elephant Walk at Sandestin are all consistently good and have a loyal following.

Louisiana Lagniappe Restaurant (*lagniappe* means "a little something extra") really has something extra: a Creole menu that will make you forget the "Big Easy." Kevin and Gwen Ortego, owners, like their Grouper Louisianne topped with fresh lump crabmeat in a seasoned butter sauce and their Pompano En Papillote (pompano baked in parchment paper with shrimp and crabmeat stuffing and a light garlic buerre blanc). Dress is casual and reservations are not taken. Prices are moderate to expensive. It is open from 5:30 P.M., seven days a week. The telephone number is (850) 837-0881.

At the beautiful **Ocean Club,** they know how to lightly sauté fresh fish, which is an art in itself, and then they add the lightest of the sauces, which do not fight the delicate taste. The grilled and blackened fish dishes are also delicious. If you are making a study of Key Lime Pie, the Ocean Club will be one of your top five. Prices are moderate to expensive. It is open from 5:30 P.M., seven days a week. The telephone number is (850) 267-2666.

"Who is he that doesn't like an elephant?" **The Elephant Walk Restaurant and Bar** is the brainchild of a company out of Atlanta called Design Continuum. The interior of this bungalow-shaped building seems to take you to far-off Ceylon, as you sip frothy drinks in the sumptuous bar upstairs overlooking the Gulf. Rattan overstuffed chairs

and couches with kilim cushions and pillows are set in intimate group-ings around a room filled with safari accessories. This is a great place to begin or end an evening. The Elephant Walk Restaurant, below, keeps the dramatic look with floor-to-ceiling faux-ivory tusks and zebra black-and-white chairs. All is coordinated with a beautifully designed jungle-print rug. The Sunday brunch is a special day at the restaurant.

Don't forget to speak to O'Reilly, the beautiful macaw at the reser-vation desk. The Elephant Walk is open from 6:00 P.M. until 10:00 P.M., Sunday through Thursday, and until 11:00 P.M., Friday and Saturday. The bar opens at 5:00 P.M. The telephone number is (850) 267-4800.

Face it—every kid loves **Big Kahuna's.** You cannot avoid it and kids zero in on it when you cross the bridge to Destin.

Do it! If you are young enough, do the big orange tubes and slide down the infinite waterfalls, play in the shipwrecked harbor, and then have lunch. If you are "old," just go to the top of the big plastic moun-tain with your grandchildren, sit, and dream about the pristine beaches and sunsets. It will soon be over and you can get on with your vacation. Big Kahuna's is open from 10:00 A.M. until 6:00 P.M., seven days a week.

As you turn off busy U.S. 98 into the **Silver Beach Motel,** you imme-diately get the feeling that you've gone back to the 1950s. Pink chaise lounges encircle the baby-blue pool. If you want to treat yourself to a special breakfast, consider eating here at the restaurant, which is located in the building facing the Gulf. A smile will probably spread across your face when you step into the pink-and-turquoise dining area. Try to get one of the window tables. Along with a steaming cup of coffee, you will be served a basket of sliced bread so you can enjoy the "hottest toast in town"—made by you with your own toaster. The menu has all the usual breakfast fare, but the house specialty is the French toast and it is sinfully delicious. It is open from 7:00 A.M. until 11:00 P.M. on weekdays and from 7:00 A.M. until 12:00 midnight on weekends. It is closed on Wednesday. The telephone number is (850) 837-6125.

Sockeye's is an in-your-face sporting goods store that heralds in the new century. The powerful murals on the front and sides of the building are painted by Dan ("Spider") Warren of Colorado Springs. They defy you to pass by without stopping at this exciting place.

You enter to the strains of heavy metal and, everywhere the eye rests, action is taking place. Virtual reality is available in every sport. You can surf, fly-fish by a log cabin, or deep-sea fish; and you can actually play five different golf courses (using the new sockeye driver, of course).

Sockeye's is a store where a "stream runs through it" with a trawler resting on the bank of a small town and an old geezer sitting and watching it all. Upstairs, all camping equipment is set up with full-blown tents, canoes, and all manner of camping gear. Outside, a bike shop will put you on a new Jamis or Marin mountain bike as well as rent you roller blades, wake boards, kayaks, canoes, surf boards, and boogie boards.

This place is energizing and so much fun—not to mention the state-of-the-art equipment for every sport, including some that have not been invented yet. Traveling down U.S. 98, you cannot miss Sockeye's, but the address is 2001 Emerald Coast Road. The telephone number is (850) 654-8954.

The Destin Diner is reminiscent of the 1950s and is easy to spot on busy U.S. 98 with its shiny silver, dining-car look. It has a jukebox at every booth, where you can have fun selecting your favorite old tunes to entertain you while you dine. This would be a great place to take the kids—breakfast is served anytime and the burgers and shakes are bound to appeal to any hungry bunch. The diner is open 24 hours and the telephone number is (850) 654-5843.

Gulf of Mexico

To get to the next few places, you will need to make a short detour to pretty, Old U.S. 98.

Having breakfast at **June's Dunes** is like having breakfast at grand-mother's—that is, if your grandmother lives in a rustic, red, two-story house on the beach overlooking emerald Gulf waters. Old-fashioned breakfast fare is served here with a specialty in omelets of all kinds—Italian, Polish, Cajun, Spanish—and for lunch, hamburgers and soups in the winter. It is a fun place to start the day. You can sit upstairs or down, inside or outside on the deck, where you can keep an eye on the kids if they want to play on the beach. June's claims to have the most reasonable prices on the Panhandle. It is located at 1780 Old U.S. 98.

The restaurant is owned and operated by June Decker, who is also a part-time cook. She is open from 5:30 A.M. until 2:00 P.M. The telephone number is (850) 650-0455.

The Back Porch Restaurant on Old U.S. 98 is the only open-air restaurant directly on the Gulf in Destin. The original restaurant was simply an A-frame building with a walk-up window for ordering right from the beach. Today the restaurant has expanded to 10,000 square feet with huge open windows that allow the sea breezes to flow through the dining area. The extensive menu offers fresh seafood steamed, fried, grilled, and broiled. Try the seafood nachos for lunch. Prices are moderate. It is open from 11:00 A.M. to 11:00 P.M., seven days a week. The telephone number is (850) 837-2022.

In the midst of all the high rises and condos is the lovely **Henderson Park Inn,** located along Scenic Old U.S. 98 on a quiet cul-de-sac. The inn's property is next to the newly created Henderson Beach Park and Recreation Area and directly on the Gulf. You will feel miles away from all the hullabaloo. A main building has 20 rooms, most with private whirlpool baths and private balconies and all with a view of the Gulf. In addition, there is a villa of 15 adult-only rooms.

The grounds are beautifully landscaped around the heated pool and spa area and there is an on-site restaurant. The unspoiled mile and a quarter of beach next door at the Henderson Park adds to the quiet feeling of this delightful place. For information or reservations call (800) 336-4853 or (850) 654-0400.

Frangista Seafood and Spirits (1820 Old U.S. 98) has a long history with Destin, starting out in 1948 as the "Beach Cottage" built for the Nitsos family and friends. It is hard to believe, but at that time the old beach road was absolutely isolated and the rooms at the bottom of the Beach Cottage were rented out. Like Destin, business has grown and changed many times on Old U.S. 98, but Frangista stands

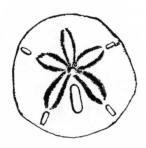

on sacred ground. Traditionally, it has always been a good place to eat and rest and is forever popular with locals and tourists.

The menu is light, treating fish delicately, not drowning it in heavy sauces. Meats are treated much the same with reduction sauces that concentrate on fresh herbs and vegetables. Desserts are another thing—they're rich and gooey—as they should be. This restaurant has a great Old Florida flavor and the service is accommodating without being aggravating.

Frangista is open every day for lunch and dinner, with hours to fit the season. Prices are moderate to expensive and reservations are suggested. The telephone number is (850) 837-2515.

The **Shoe Salon,** located at 9561 U.S. 98, has the best selection of women's sandals on the beach. Plan for plenty of time to browse through the extensive selection of shoes, from fancy evening styles to comfortable beach clogs. It is hard to leave with only one pair and there are also handbags and belts to make the decision even more difficult. The shop is open Monday through Saturday, from 9:00 A.M. to 9:00 P.M. The telephone number is (850) 654-5252.

On a rainy day in Destin do not despair. There is ample to do in the way of "recreational shopping," which may or may not become "serious shopping." Fun, state-of-the-art shops abound.

Smith's Antique Mall is located at 12500 Emerald Coast Parkway, U.S. 98. Here 90 dealers display their goods in a most fetching style. There is a fine selection of almost everything from pottery to porcelain, all ages and types of furniture. It is an attractive combination of an antique and interior market in a spacious, 25,000-square-foot building. It is open from 10:00 A.M. to 6:00 P.M., Monday through Saturday. The telephone number is (850) 654-1484.

The **Silver Sands Factory Stores and Designer Outlet,** located on U.S. 98 East in Destin, has more than a hundred stores. The recent additions of a 75,000-square-foot, $12-million restaurant, brewery, billiard room, and virtual reality game room have revolutionized shopping to a recreational art form. Contrary to the past, families beg mother to take them shopping here.

Located in the rear of the Silver Sands shopping center is the spacious **Morgan's Harbor Docks Restaurant and Brewery,** the largest dining and entertainment center in the Southeast. On the lower level you will find **Creehan's Market,** presided over by renown chef Tim Creehan. In this upscale food market, the bill of fare should appeal to any palate. There is a rotisserie cooking meats over a wood fire, a sushi bar, oyster bar, espresso bar, and, among many other items, brick oven for pizza.

In addition to "eats," upstairs there are elegant mahogany pool tables, comfy chairs, and a splashy game room with a ceiling of vibrant fiber-optic lighting. An out-of-this-world touch is a hot-air balloon floating from the ceiling depicting a Jules Verne motif.

At the entrance of this huge "food hall" are two sand lots for children containing a purple dragon as a slide, giant turtles, and a sunken pirate ship for climbing. It should be no surprise that the designers are alumnae of Walt Disney Studios and have formed an organization called "Totally Fun Company" out of Clearwater, Florida. It is open from 10:00 A.M. to 9:00 P.M., Monday through Saturday, and from 10:00 A.M. to 6:00 P.M. on Sunday. For information, call (800) 510-6255 or (850) 864-9780.

Another recreational shopping experience that is aesthetically pleasing is **Needas,** 13370 West Emerald Coast Parkway, U.S. 98. This is a large shop with an overwhelming selection of clothing for men, women, and children; gifts, china, costume jewelry; and an elegant boudoir room of bridal lingerie. It is very much like a well-stocked mini-mall. It is open Monday through Saturday from 9:30 A.M. to 6:00 P.M. during the summer and until 5:00 P.M. during the winter. For information, call (850) 837-5998.

Clements Antiques, in a spacious yellow brick building, is brimming with European and Oriental antiques as well as intriguing little gift items and beautiful reproductions.

Antique buffs will be interested in knowing that Mr. Clements also owns the well-known Clements auction house in Chattanooga. He spends much of his time in New York working with Christie's & Sotheby's in obtaining his sizeable stock.

In case you're curious, the spectacular bronze giraffe figures in the front yard are priced at $3,000.00 for the large and $2,500.00 for the small. It is located at 9501 West U.S. 98 and is open from 9:00 A.M. to 5:00 P.M., Monday through Saturday. The telephone number is (850) 837-1473.

The Market at Sandestin has to be one of the most appealing on the Emerald Coast. Pastel-painted shops and boutiques are nestled within lush tropical landscapes and covered brick walkways. Benches are placed here and there to rest weary shopping bones.

Just to mention a few of the favorite shops in this exceptional market: **The Blue Marlin,** a men's casual clothing store carrying the popular fish print shirts by Bimini Bay; **J.C.C., Just Comfortable Clothing,** light, cool, coastal ladies' wear; **Tooley Street,** ladies' sportswear; **Black and White,** clothing and accessories, all in black and

white; **The Zoo Gallery,** an appealing art store featuring the whimsical in sculpture, pottery, cards, and T-shirts.

If you shop 'til you drop, you can drop onto the veranda of **Chan's Market Cafe.** Here you can recover with a refreshing cool something while gazing at the soothing waters of the pond that abuts the veranda. Chan's is crowded on weekends, but service and food are good. It is open from 7:00 A.M. to 9:00 P.M., seven days a week. The telephone number is (850) 654-9321.

Riverhill Antiques is a perfect example of a shop where less is more. Inventory is sparse but what is there is choice. Owner Patti Lee has great prices on sisal rugs and good-looking pine pieces. Upstairs the same thing applies to her framed prints and mirrors.

The location of the shop is 10123 U.S. 98. The entrance is a little tricky since it is shared with another shop, Interior Imports. Just look to your right, behind the stairs, and you will spy Riverhill right away. The telephone number is (850) 837-5565 and the hours are from 10:00 A.M. to 5:00 P.M., Monday through Saturday.

Capapie's is one of the best boutiques along the Panhandle. Gayle Warrick's shop carries great cocktail clothes and special orders for all occasions. In addition, her smart-looking sport lines and tasteful accessories prevail. Capapies means "from head to toe" and this fine shop lives up to its name. It is located at 13330 West Emerald Coast Parkway and is open from 10:00 A.M. until 5:00 P.M., Monday through Saturday.

A handy aid in the accommodation search in the Destin-Fort Walton Beach area is the Chamber of Commerce Referral List, which is helpfully divided into classifications: Gulf-access cottages and houses, condos, hotels, and motels with Gulf or harbor view. For this and special events information, call (850) 837-6241. Web site: www.destinfl.com/chambe.htm.

County Road 30-A

If you prefer to travel "in your home," **Emerald Coast RV Resort** is a destination must. This RV resort has achieved the highest rating possible from *Trailer Life Campground/RV Park and Services Directory* and also received the highest rating given by *Woodall's North American Campground Directory*. When you see the facility, it is not hard to understand why these ratings were awarded to Gene and Rosalind Moore and Jim and Rosemary Auld, owners of the resort. This is not a membership park but is open to the public. A driving range, tennis courts, chipping and putting greens, and a swimming pool are all carefully placed among tall pines and beautiful landscaping. The Emerald Coast RV Resort is located at 7525 West Scenic Highway (County Road) 30-A, Santa Rosa Beach, Florida. For reservations, call (800) BEACHRV (232-2478) or e-mail at rvinfo@rvresort.com. You can visit on the World Wide Web: http://www.rvresort.com.

Should you have a yen for antique linens and lace, you will want to check out the **Tea Tyme Antiques** at 17 Tanglewood Drive, Santa Rosa Beach (west end of County Road 30-A).

This is a small frame cottage as quaint as the name. The proprietor, Brenda Fraser, originally from England, scours her native country regularly for antique textiles and items for her shop. Evidently, she finds them as there are scads of linen towels, pillow covers, and bedspreads. It is open from 10:00 A.M. to 5:30 P.M., Monday through Saturday. The telephone number is (850) 267-3827.

In this hustle and bustle area, it is refreshing to find a place that is quiet and the serene **Lake Place** at Santa Rosa Beach is a true oasis. Since it is not too big, you will need reservations. Owners Peter and Susan Mulcahy have created a great restaurant that sits right on Dune Allen Lake. Although they do not accept credit cards and there are no separate checks, no one minds because the food and service are fabulous.

Begin with the delicate Crab Cakes or the Mango Chutney Shrimp (marinated and served in the flakiest-ever pastry shell). Make room for the Crab Bisque or the incredible Ciopinno before ordering such

entrées as Grilled Grouper with roasted garlic, tuna with pink pep-
percorn sauce, or prime loin lamb chops. They have an impressive
wine list (no liquor is served) and limited but sumptuous desserts. It
is a little off the path but do make an effort to find it. The hours are
from 5:30 P.M. until 9:30 P.M., Tuesday through Saturday. It is located
on County Road 30-A, six miles west of Grayton Beach. The telephone
number is (850) 267-2871.

Lunch at the **Santa Rosa Golf and Beach Club,** 4801 West County
Road 30-A, is a feast for the eyes as well as the palate. This handsome,
semiprivate clubhouse was completely renovated in 1997. The interior
is a pale shade of gold; a series of palm tree botanical prints in thin,
gold frames adds an elegant tropical touch. A long glass wall offers
diners a panoramic view of the shimmering green Gulf waters that is
mesmerizing. You almost, but not quite, forget about the food. The
Chicken Salad rates a star and the Grilled Veggie Sandwich is a
healthy winner. Prices are moderate to expensive.

If you're running late for lunch, you can eat on the deck. Deck
dining is available, weather permitting, from 2:30 P.M. to 7:30 P.M.
Lunch is served from 11:30 A.M. to 2:30 P.M. and dinner is served from
4:30 P.M. to 10:00 P.M. For reservations, call (850) 267-2305.

Across the street from the restaurant is the golf club and an 18-hole
golf course, as well as the only tennis courts between Sandestin and
Seaside. Almost half of the membership is composed of local residents and the other half is made up from every state in the United
States, including Canada. The telephone number is (850) 267-2229.

Health is "in" on Santa Rosa Beach with a neat, bright store, **For
The Health Of It,** located at 2217 West Scenic County Road 30-A in
The Rivard Center. If you're visiting this beautiful beach country, it
is not necessary to pack your vitamins, dietary needs, or organic
foods—it is all here, including a massage therapy clinic with three
experienced, Florida-licensed therapists.

Inside the store is the **Organically Yours Cafe,** featuring healthy,
organic culinary creations that are satisfying and tasty even if they are
good for you. Try the "Fast Eddie Bocca Burger" with sprouts, lettuce,
cucumber, avocado, tomatoes, and a "secret dressing." It is soybean

based, but actually tastes like a hamburger. Remember, everything is organic, very fresh, and will please your tummy.

Organically Yours Cafe is open only for lunch, from 11:00 A.M. to 3:00 P.M., and For The Health Of It is open from 10:00 A.M. to 5:30 P.M. The telephone number is (850) 267-0558.

Almost next door and in The Rivard Center on County Road 30-A is the **Indigo Wine Bar.** Sushi is served Monday through Saturday and the Indigo has an extensive, sophisticated wine list—40 of which are served by the glass.

Also available are premium beers, appetizers, and live music. Night owls will rejoice, as they are open from 6:30 P.M. until 2:00 A.M. The telephone number is (850) 267-3733.

Like many proprietors in Santa Rosa Beach, Eric Bloom is an individualist who has lived all over the world but opted to stay in the area. He lives and operates a small café, **Blooms,** out of his frame home— and he does it his way. Eric says he has eaten in many kitchens and finds most of them wanting; so he cooks for his customers in his own pristine kitchen with spotless utensils (each used for a purpose).

When you climb the stairs, you will notice his fresh herb and pepper garden, which he uses for all his cooking. Bloom shops the local market for the freshest seafood, meats, fruits, and vegetables and that is what determines what the menu will be for the day. Prices are moderate, depending on market costs.

Blooms seats 20 people, all at shiny, varnished tables staggered around the room. The kitchen is surrounded by a bar so you can watch the chef cook your meal on the spot. A favorite for locals is the Sunday brunch. The café is open Thursday, Friday, and Saturday evenings, with dinner served after sunset, but please telephone first (850) 267-1834. Blooms is located 50 yards past Ed Walkin Park at County Road 393 on County Road 30-A.

Goatfeathers are the distractions, sidelines and deflections that take a man's attentions from his own business and keep him from getting ahead.

Ellis Parker Butler (1913)
—Quotation on the front of Goatfeathers Restaurant

Indeed, **Goatfeathers** will be a "distraction" from worldly cares, for it is a fun spot for locals and tourists and serves great food. The restaurant has a seafood market next door that ensures about the freshest fish you can get; and the fish are well prepared by chefs, who know what they are doing. For years it has been one of the most popular stops along Scenic County Road 30-A. Goatfeathers is located at 3345 Blue Mountain Beach and open from 11:30 A.M. to 10:00 P.M., six days a week (closed on Wednesday). Reservations are suggested. The telephone number is (850) 267-3342.

If you are traveling by car down County Road 30-A, try to time it so you will arrive at **D & K's Cafe** for dinner. Keep a close eye out for this little, red house set deep in the quiet pines or you may miss it—and that would be a shame.

Doug and Kathy Krumel have renovated this cottage into an intimate, relaxing café serving traditional New Orleans cuisine with a twist of their own. They feel the pan-fried snapper with sautéed shrimp is hard to beat and the soft-shell crab and crawfish dishes in season are local favorites.

D & K's Cafe offers the perfect evening for the serious diner because the atmosphere is easy, prices are moderate, the menu is limited to the freshest foods of the season, and the chef knows how to prepare these foods for the best harmony of tastes. Reservations are suggested. It is open from 6:00 P.M. to 10:00 P.M., Monday through Saturday. The telephone number is (850) 267-0054.

> The name of Basmati's originates from basmati rice grown in India, which has a wonderful taste and aroma.

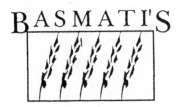

The owners of **Basmati's** had some big shoes to fill after Shueh-Mei Pong sold it. They have not only filled those shoes, but they have made the restaurant a real contender for the best on the coast.

Designer Julia Hanna has certainly contributed to the success of Basmati's with interiors that set a mood of tranquillity and simplicity. The decor is much like the food—creative and appealing—and puts a new face to an old Asian concept. The restaurant is small, but the tables are separated by screens for privacy and the centerpieces are copper-shaded candles that give off a wonderful glow for intimacy (notice the cuts of marble used for accents as well as serving pieces). If the weather is cool, porch dining is available, which overlooks a pretty stretch of water and palmetto fields. Against a background of soft Asian music, sit back and let the competent staff guide you through a meal that is delicious and beautifully presented.

The authentic sushi menu offers nigiri (hand formed) fresh yellow-fin tuna, eel, salmon, mackerel, octopus, squid, shrimp, and cod or salmon roe. Sashimi is available upon request and you can check the chalkboard for specials of the day. The main menu reads like a League of Nations with all kinds of Asian and near-Asian influences. Some favorites are Chinese Barbecue Duck, Cantonese Rack of Lamb, Thai Squid Appetizer, and Teriyaki Beef—all prepared in a variety of ways, keeping the integrity of the cuisine while inventing new dishes.

Basmati's is a restaurant that appeals to the senses and can be enjoyed with another person or a couple of friends. It is located at 3295 West County Road 30-A and is open from 4:00 P.M. to 10:00 P.M., Tuesday through Sunday; sushi starts at 5:30 P.M. Each item on the menu is à la carte, so the bill may be expensive but worth it. Reservations please. The telephone number is (850) 267-3028.

A visit to **Bayou Arts and Antiques** at Cessna Park and County Road 393 is a happy encounter of the best kind. Tucked away in the midst of pines and palmettos on Hogstown Bayou, the shop is entered across a rustic bridge over a marshy stream. A wonderful life-sized heron sculpture stands in the reeds and watches you approach.

Inside, other than antiques, you will find truly one-of-a-kind items, such as striking concrete-and-iron fruit sconces. You may see a hand-crafted hanging planter of bark and branches shaped like a deer head. All are reasonably priced and many have a story to tell. You will also find an interesting selection of local artists' work, including owner Chick Huettel's paintings.

Chick and Cathy Huettel, from Memphis, Tennessee, had vacationed in the area for years before permanently moving to Destin and opening Bayou Arts and Antiques. Much of what they call "recovered" furniture is found by Cathy and renewed and whimsically painted by Chick, who is also a historian and naturalist.

Boat lovers will enjoy a unique attraction—Chick's antique boat collection. This includes an old, worn and weathered crab boat, mullet boat, and pirogue, with all the appropriate fishing traps and tackle.

An added bonus to the shop is the tiny **St. Francis Fisherman's Chapel,** built by Chick, who learned that at one time there was actually a small chapel in that area.

Down a pine-straw path is the blue-framed chapel. Chick painted the interior walls with murals depicting animals and forest on one side, sea life on the other. Outside, a statue of St. Francis of Assisi guards a touching little cemetery of wildlife marked by wooden crosses. Over the doorway is a fisherman's prayer from the 1700s: "Oh Lord, my boat is so small and Thy sea is so great."

The history of the area is haunting. In the early 1900s, Santa Rosa was a small but thriving community harvesting oranges, lumber, and turpentine. Due to a series of natural disasters, the village was abandoned in the 1920s and, except for a few cottages, there is no trace of the stores, churches, hotels, cannery, schools, and mills that once stood here.

"Today's inhabitants," say Chick and Cathy, "are the wildlife of the wetlands." It is open from 10:00 A.M. until 4:30 P.M., Tuesday through Saturday. The telephone number is (850) 267-1404.

(Sketch courtesy of Gulf Islands National Seashore)

Grayton Beach

Grayton Beach State Recreation Area, which is just off County Road 30-A, was chosen as the best beach in the United States in 1994 by Dr. Stephen Leatherman, director of the Laboratory for Coastal Research at the University of Maryland.

Once you see it, you will understand why. The beach appeals to all of your senses. You can feast your eyes upon an unobstructed view of blue water edged with clean, white sand. The smell of the salty air conjures up memories from times spent on other beaches and the feel and sound of the warm sand under your feet are almost sensual . . . this place will relax your soul. Part of the appeal is what you don't see or feel or hear—there is no development, no crowds, nothing to pollute the air or the water—just untouched nature at its best.

The recreation area provides boardwalks over the protected dunes and shower and bathroom facilities along with a large pavilion overlooking the Gulf (for rent to large groups). There are picnic sites, a boat ramp, and a 37-site campground on Western Lake. Water and electricity are available here. For information, call (850) 231-4210.

The recreation area was named for the town of Grayton Beach, which is more than a hundred years old. There are no condos here and, if the residents have anything to say about it, there never will be any. Sandwiched in between Destin and Panama City, the people of Grayton Beach want to keep their unpretentious identity.

In a short time, the Florida sun can render one hot and thirsty and ready for a cool retreat. **Hibiscus Coffee and Guest House** can provide a place to wind down and relax with your favorite book or paper. Coffee is served hot or cold or, for a liquid lunch, try a fresh, fruit smoothie. There is the beginning of a library upstairs and, according to proprietor Kurt Tape, there is a guest room available by the night. For more information, call (850) 231-2733.

Across the street from the Hibiscus Coffee and Guest House and under the shade trees of Grayton Beach on Magnolia Street is **Magnolia House.** On the wide front porch are two huge wreaths encircling the front windows. Owner Nancy Veldman invites you inside to expe-

rience her shop "with music that fills your heart and smells that bring back memories of a time and gifts beyond your imagination." The telephone number is (850) 231-5859.

If you really want to experience Grayton Beach up close, why not rent a bicycle at **Patrone's**? There are also boats for rent and a barnyard zoo where Hamus Alabamus, a 1,000-pound pig, used to reside. We are sorry to report that Hamus died in 1993. The telephone number is (850) 231-1606.

Everything has changed at the **Grayton Corner Cafe** except the location. The new building has a great upstairs deck—perfect for enjoying your favorite beverage while gazing at the beautiful water and famous beaches at Grayton. If you're hungry, try the Smoked Tuna Salad.

Picolo Restaurant and **The Red Bar** in Grayton Beach is becoming the scene-stealer along the Panhandle of Florida. The Petit brothers, Oliver and Phillippe, look more like matinee idols instead of restaurateurs. They have the best concept of how to run a good restaurant than most people in the business. They do not believe in advertising but let the excellent cuisine make the statement.

One of the mainstays is the Italian panéed chicken, which is a recipe given to them by their grandmother. If you are a soft-shell crab lover, you cannot get a better dish than the soft-shell crab over angel hair pasta. The apple dumpling is so good it is beyond description.

The Petits hail from Belgium and have lined the ceiling with posters of international rock concerts. The rest of the decor is thrown together in wild abandonment. Live jazz and bluegrass bands play every night under a mirrored ball and The Red Bar in the back is a good place for beer and hamburgers.

Picolo is laid-back with an easy staff that is young and friendly. The dress code is . . . just be dressed. Everyone with silver hair to pigtails is welcome. Reservations are not taken but regulars may have a slight edge for a table. Cash or checks are accepted but not credit cards. It is open seven days a week from 11:00 A.M. to 4:00 P.M. for lunch and from 5:00 P.M. to 10:00 P.M. for dinner. Prices for a fine gourmet meal at Picolo will pleasantly surprise you. The telephone number is (850) 231-1008.

Affairs is a complete shop that is certainly worth a stop. The owner, Mary Derck, says her shop has "tangible temptations for your home, your loved ones, your children, your wardrobe, your body . . . right down to your feet." Note the exceptional card section in the back.

Hours for Affairs allow shopping from 10:00 A.M. to 9:00 P.M., seven days a week. The telephone number is (850) 231-4282.

Borago

Borago, on County Road 30-A next door to Monet Monet, is a classic Italian restaurant. The interior is peacefully refreshing with cool tile floors; on pale salmon walls there is a trompe l'oeil marble chair rail. The room is reminiscent of an old Italian villa and, other than a huge vase of sunflowers, the decor is minimal. An interesting feature is a tile bar where you can sit and watch the busy kitchen preparations.

If you like Italian, you will most certainly enjoy the Capellini d'Angelo, a pasta with sautéed shrimp, garlic, white wine, capers, and oven-dried tomatoes. A wonderful grouper is prepared with artichokes, sun-dried tomatoes, and pine nuts on wilted spinach. Prices are moderate to expensive.

Borago's location is a plus since a most appealing shop, Affairs, is its next-door neighbor. It is open from 5:00 P.M. to 10:00 P.M., Tuesday through Sunday. For reservations, call (850) 231-9167.

After passing the Grayton Beach turn, about 200 yards on your right, is **Monet, Monet.** You cannot miss it because the beautiful gardens go right out to the highway. Turn into the drive and park in the small parking lot on your right. You may want to walk the garden path before you go into the shop. In the back is a Japanese bridge crossing a beautiful lily pond—you're right; it is a smaller version of Monet's Giverny.

Jonathan Quinn was a financial consultant in Kansas City and decided to follow his passion and build a house and garden much like Giverny in Grayton Beach, Florida. He lives upstairs and has opened a shop for the serious gardener downstairs. He carries books, clothing, tools, terra-

cotta pots, and garden accessories. He has rootings, fresh-cut flowers, and special seeds for sale. The gardens outside are free to the public and exhibitions and lectures take place often. Monet, Monet is located at 100 East County Road 30-A and is open from 10:00 A.M. to 5:00 P.M. everyday except Tuesday. The telephone number is (850) 231-5117.

If you are staying or traveling along the Panhandle, a must-stop is **Criolla's Restaurant** for dinner. Located on County Road 30-A, the restaurant is two miles west of Seaside. It lies in the middle of this beautiful stretch of virgin country—a handsome stucco structure with tile roof and open shutters.

Inside, the decor is cool and serene with soft sea colors of shrimp and clean blues and greens. Good pieces of art hang on the walls with a large painting by Joan Vienot behind the bar. Soft Calypso jazz plays in the background and you know before you sit down you are going to have a wonderful evening.

Even though the place looks like a hideaway, it is touted as one of the best-known restaurants in Florida. *Florida Trends* magazine has awarded the Golden Spoon to Criolla's for three consecutive years. Other prestigious newspapers and magazines, such as the *New York Times, Washington Post,* and *Cook's,* sing its praises.

The chef and owner is John Earles and his "new wave Florida cuisine" is an adventure in dining. The menu consists of food with Caribbean, French-Creole, and Latin-American influence. John takes classic dishes and gives them a new face, using exotic herbs and spices as well as fresh vegetables and tropical fruits. He never stops exploring new tastes and spends every winter cooking in famous kitchens all over the country. Although the menu drastically changes four or five times a year, you will hopefully find the superb Snapper Butter Pecan or his Tuna Mignon in there somewhere.

Criolla's hours are seasonal. Reservations are suggested at any time and dress is casual. The telephone number is (850) 267-1267.

Criolla's Kiss Yo' Mama Soup

½ lb. butter, unsalted
2 cups chopped yellow onion
14 cups fresh corn, cut off the cob (substitute frozen only)
1 cup roasted, peeled, chopped, poblano chilies (substitute canned green chilies)
4 medium-sized chipotle chilies, chopped (substitute canned chipotles)
2 cups rich chicken stock
6 cups milk
1 lb. sour cream
1 lb. Louisiana crawfish tails
Salt to taste
½ cup fresh goat cheese such as chèvre
¼ cup chopped fresh chives

In a nonreactive pot, sauté onion, corn, chipotles, and poblanos in butter over medium heat for 5 minutes. Add chicken stock. Cover and simmer for 15 minutes. Remove from heat and cool for 15 minutes. Purée mixture in a blender or food processor and strain through a medium sieve using a rubber spatula to retrieve as much as possible. Discard pulp. Add milk and return to the nonreactive pot and slowly bring to a boil. Reduce heat to simmer for 5 minutes, stirring frequently. Remove from heat and stir in the sour cream and crawfish tails. Salt to taste and serve. Garnish bowls with dollops of goat cheese and chopped chives. Makes approximately 1 ½ gallons.

Sea Oats

The sea oats that grow so abundantly along our beaches are both attractive and useful. The grassy sea oat is one of the few plants that thrives on the majestic dunes, amid the moving, dry, and salty sand.

Since the dunes are so dry, a six-inch sea oat plant may have roots more than 5 feet long. These long roots help to hold the sand and protect the dunes from wind and erosion. Dunes will grow larger as the oats catch the windblown sand.

Newcomers and visitors are often tempted to take home a handful of these graceful plants, but they may find they have picked the most expensive bouquet of their lives! The sea oats protect the heart of the sand dunes and they, in turn, are well protected by Florida law. (Courtesy *Discovery* magazine, 1988-89. Published by Basham Enterprises, Panama City, Florida. Permission granted by Hank Basham.)

Seaside

Continuing on County Road 30-A between Grayton Beach and Seagrove Beach, the well-planned and much-acclaimed town of Seaside will pop up to delight you.

The dream of founder Robert Davis has become a reality for the world to enjoy. The community was designed with people in mind, for their pleasures as well as their needs. Although each cottage can reflect its owner's personality, there are restrictions to keep them in tune with the overall plan for the town, which is built around a village green. The pastel cottages with porches, railing, or gingerbread trim are nestled closely together to give a most stunning visual effect.

Everything you need is just around the corner: post office, grocery-deli, shops, restaurants, tennis courts, swimming pools, and a world-class croquet lawn and across the highway is the main attraction—the beautiful Gulf of Mexico with its gorgeous beach!

There are special events taking place throughout the year for children and adults alike. Many of the cottages are for rent and there are several bed-and-breakfast inns here. For information, call (850) 231-1320.

One of the best spots at Seaside is the fabulous **Modica Market.** From floor to sky-high ceiling, it is packed with an extravaganza of specialty items. Besides being a fully stocked grocery, the deli is wonderful, featuring creative lunches and takeout food. Try the pizzette

sandwich of grilled marinated eggplant with mozzarella cheese, tomatoes, and roasted peppers swathed in olive oil on a toasted bun—yum!

Breakfast will be the delight of your day at Modica Market. It has a serve-yourself deli with fresh-squeezed orange juice and coffee. There are dozens of breakfast rolls and donuts—all delicious. Outside are 10 newspaper stands with a sprinkling of chairs and tables. The only thing to hurry you is a row of sparrows patiently waiting for your crumbs.

The market is open during the summer from 7:00 A.M. until 7:00 P.M. on weekdays and from 7:00 A.M. until 9:00 P.M. on weekends, and during the winter from 8:00 A.M. until 6:00 P.M.

Ruskin Place is a place for artists to exhibit their work in an open-air environment. It is surrounded by two avenues of three-storied row houses with boutiques and galleries on the ground floor and studios and workshops above. It is open from 10:00 A.M. to 5:00 P.M.

One of the fine galleries is the **Newbill Collection By The Sea,** which offers fascinating collections of contemporary art and American crafts.

Deo Favente is a classy shop at the end of Ruskin Place. Julia Hanna, owner, designs most of her clothes in the natural fabrics of linens, silk, cotton, and rayon (which has a natural base). If her name sounds familiar, she designed the interior of Basmati's, a wonderful restaurant mentioned earlier in this book.

The fact is, Julia Hanna, whether she is designing clothes, interiors, scenic designs, or costumes, is total talent and comes to Seaside with almost 20 years of experience in clothing design under her belt. She first started with an antique clothing shop in Atlanta; she moved to Egypt and worked in theater designing costumes; she then moved to Germany for a four-year program in fashion design. Deo Favente, which means "with God's favor," is the vehicle to display her romantic clothes and accessories, which have an international flavor as well as a Southern influence. She has picked up several other designers of purses and hats not to be found anywhere else. Deo Favente keeps Ruskin Place hours. The telephone number is (850) 231-2017.

Owners of **Studio 210,** Mark and Penny Dragonette built their building themselves. Downstairs is a great coffee shop offering cappuccino, espresso (they use only the fine Lavazza European coffee), tea, and cocoa. In addition, they have traditional Italian desserts—which are shipped frozen to them, directly from Italy. It is a happy task trying to decide which one to order! The cappa profiteroles (a cream puff covered with Chantilly cream, chocolate cream, and whipped cream) is pretty hard to resist. Along with all this delicious stuff, there is art on the walls for sale and some great gift items, including artist Nancy Drew's fun pillows.

Mark and Penny live upstairs and they happily rent the back room on the second floor to travelers. They will furnish you with a couple of bicycles during your stay. Call them. You'll have fun. The telephone number is (850) 231-1790.

A great new addition to the Seaside community is **Fermentations,** a wine bar and shop. There are more than 250 varieties of wine to taste, by the glass or by the bottle, and there is a grand assortment of "tchotchkes" (wine accessories); everything from Riedel and acrylic wine glasses to openers, coolers, napkins, baskets, and corks.

Light lunches and dinners are served and Monday is "blues night" with music from 8:00 P.M. until 11:00 P.M. The shop is located at 25 Central Square and is open Sunday through Thursday from 11:30 A.M. until 9:30 P.M. and Friday and Saturday until 12:00 midnight. For speedy orders, call (850) 231-0167.

Across the street from the post office at Seaside is a patch of shops that are fun to wander through.

Perspicacity is a wonderful open-air market with Gulf breezes blowing while you shop. It has little stalls with all kinds of resortwear, simple cotton dresses, espadrilles, straw hats, bags, and wraparound skirts—easy things to live in while on vacation.

Sun Dog can take care of your reading needs. It is small but well stocked with current and classic literature. Sun Dog has a good variety of children's books as well as books emphasizing nature and environment.

Opened in 1986, **Bud and Alley's** is a happy seaside meeting place. "Named after a dog and a cat, the spirit of the restaurant is to serve creative food of uncompromising freshness in an unpretentious setting."

There are two dining rooms, one facing the Gulf, the other overlooking a courtyard that contains the restaurant's herb garden. The

dining rooms are painted the palest pumpkin and the walls are hung with crisp color photos of the bright houses and buildings in Seaside.

Owners Dave Rauschkolb and Scott Witcoski have created a friendly, busy place where the menu changes seasonally, focusing on ingredients in the peak of the season. They embrace the region by seeking out the finest that Florida farmers, growers, and fishermen have to offer.

When you taste the fabulous dishes—Blue Crab Cakes, Apalachicola Oysters, Carpet Bag Steak, Eggplant Caviar, Seaside Shrimp—you will understand why Bud and Alley's recently received their seventh Top 200 Restaurants in Florida award as well as the *Wine Spectator's* coveted Award of Excellence.

Bud and Alley's is open January through October. They are closed in November, except for Thanksgiving week, and in December, except for Christmas week. Lunch is served from 11:30 A.M. to 3:00 P.M. in the dining room, screen porch, and gazebo; dinner is from 6:00 P.M. to 9:00 P.M. in the summer and 5:30 P.M. to 9:00 P.M. in the winter. It is closed on Tuesday.

Dinner is also served in the herb garden between the garden and the Gulf. Jazz hours are nightly on summer evenings from 7:00 P.M. to 11:00 P.M. The telephone number is (850) 231-5900. This is a good place to go.

Seagrove Beach

For a refreshing change from sand and sea, make a visit to **Pickets** at 10 Nightcap Street. The small shop is set back behind a white, picket fence with a lovely arched gateway. Lush green grass and colorful gardens reach out to welcome and relieve you from the intense glare of the beach. The shop has home and garden accessories and lots of birdhouses. Shop hours are from 10:00 A.M. until 5:00 P.M., Tuesday through Saturday. The telephone number is (850) 231-2036.

"Please don't come here to eat. Come to dine." These words, spoken by Chef-Owner Sandor Zabori, tell the story of this small but impressive restaurant. **Sandor's European Cuisine** is sparkling and spare; there are no booths here and no dim corners; this is simply an uncluttered place that's serious about food.

Sandor, a large, soft-spoken man with a twinkle in his eye, escaped from Hungary in the 1950s and later became a computer engineer, arriving in Pensacola via the U.S. Navy. In the late 1980s, he had a "change of life decision." He says, smiling, "I have always loved to eat, so I decided I would love to cook." That decision made, he enrolled and successfully finished at the Cordon Bleu Cooking School and then apprenticed in some dazzling places, including the La Tour d'Argent in Paris. After a successful time in Pensacola, Sandor's moved to Seagrove in 1996.

The pasta dishes are superb here. The Shrimp and Malaysian Curry and Chicken Paprika dishes are on the menu, along with such savory additions as Indonesian Thai Prawns or melt-in-your-mouth filet served with leeks and Armagnac sauce. Prices are moderate to expensive. Sandor's is located at the intersection of County Road 30-A and County Road 395 and is open for dinner only, Monday through Saturday. For reservations, call (850) 231-2858.

The Smith family obviously knows what they are doing when it comes to feeding folks! There is often a line for breakfast at the **Wheel House Restaurant** (the oldest in Seagrove). You can be sure that the food is good when the locals are seen coming back for more.

Son Greg is the executive chef and when he is not out fishing, you will find him in the kitchen creating new dishes. Fresh seafood is the house specialty. For lunch, the soft-shell crab or fish sandwiches are great, and at night you can choose from steamed, grilled, or fried seafood dishes. The restaurant is open seven days a week from 6:30 A.M. It is a great place for families. The telephone number is (850) 231-5760.

Under the same roof as the Wheel House Restaurant, but down a few doors, you will find a beach supply shop. Owner Elizabeth Flowers has run the shop since it opened in 1972 and remembers when there was nothing more than her shop, the restaurant, and a single four-unit motel across the street.

A serious addition to the list of fine restaurants along this stretch of the Gulf Coast is **Cafe Thirty-A.** The chef is from the well-known Highlands Grill in Birmingham, Alabama, and he is busy preparing savory dishes for visitors and locals alike. The café features a wood-fired rotisserie and ovens, plus a wonderful grill located at the heart of this large wood-frame restaurant—which continues to be packed every night. The secret is "fresh" and that's what you get, whether it is seafood, poultry, beef, pasta, or vegetables—all seasoned to perfection with herbs and spices under the well-trained hand of William McGhee.

Upstairs is the **Fishbone Bar,** where you can sip on your favorite martini chosen from the martini menu or enjoy a cigar on an open deck with a view. Prices are moderate to expensive. Cafe Thirty-A is located on Scenic County Road 30-A in Seagrove Beach, 1 ½ miles east of Seaside, and is open Monday through Saturday at 5:30 P.M. For reservations, call (850) 231-2166.

Roy and Joanne Dollar have marked their shop, **Gunby's** on County Road 30-A, with a small sailboat sporting a red- and white-striped sail. The entrance is covered with branches from the trees surrounding the house, which form an arch over the door. Gunby's, on the curve, has an assortment of antiques, gifts, art, and accessories. Please notice the cat that sleeps on the antique bed covered with a white lace coverlet. If you're in need of interior decorating assistance, Roy and Joanne have lots of talent. The telephone number is (850) 231-5958.

Randy Harelson, artist, author, illustrator, and garden designer, has designed a wonderful, lush garden of nature plants that will grow well in the Florida sun and soil. **The Gourd Garden** has gourds growing on trellises and along the side of a small cottage. Inside the cottage you will find gourds used in every way imaginable and even some unimaginable! Besides the gourds, natural scents and handmade gifts from around the world are displayed in this neat shop and you may purchase plants and seeds to start your own garden. Watch out! The gourd plants grow up to eight inches a day. Randy has an extensive selection of perennials and herbs. It is open Tuesday through Saturday, from 10:00 A.M. until 5:00 P.M. The telephone number is (850) 231-2007.

Granola girls, Carol Garrett and Christie Bowers, are busy baking something special everyday. The **Granola Girls Gourmet Bakery,**

located in the Seagrove Center at 4935 East County Road 30-A, is filled with organic breads, croissants, pastries, and the best granola you can imagine. Once you taste this granola, you will want a lifetime supply. A word of advice: be there early; the secret is out and the entire beach loves what they bake. The bakery is open from 8:00 A.M. to 5:00 P.M., Tuesday through Friday, and from 8:00 A.M. until 6:00 P.M. on Saturday. Call in your order by dialing (850) 231-2023.

Island Hutworks

If you've ever dreamed of having your very own "little grass shack," you'll find one at the **Island Hutworks,** U.S. 98, Santa Rosa Beach. There's a hut for every beach, pool, or children's sandlot. Thatched styles include picturesque tiki huts, umbrellas, grand palapas, small palapas, and even bungalows. The telephone number is (800) 247-1124.

> Who loves a garden, still his Eden keeps.
> —Amos Bronson Alcott

This phrase is engraved on a plaque in front of the large, white-columned house, Eden, and from this the name was derived. Adam and Eve would certainly have enjoyed their namesake homestead with the lush, green grounds and magnificent, moss-draped oak trees. In fact, the trees and setting alone are worth the detour off U.S. 98 onto County Road 395. The direction to **Eden State Park** is well marked with signs.

Built in 1895 by lumberman William Henry Wesley, this typical Southern plantation home is furnished with antique furniture and is open for tours Thursday through Monday from 9:00 A.M. to 4:00 P.M. Guided tours begin on the hour. The style of construction is typical of the Gulf Coast when, before air conditioning, builders took advantage of every opportunity for a breeze. Eden is constructed on piers with a wide central hall and long windows in every room, which allow for maximum air circulation.

Beneath a grove of oaks are picnic tables and barbecue grills overlooking the peaceful Choctawhatchee Bay. A lily pad pond and statuary fountain with a memorial butterfly garden flank the imposing old house.

In 1968, the most recent owner, Miss Lois Maxon, donated Eden to the state of Florida in memory of her parents. The grounds are open daily from 8:00 A.M. until sunset. For more information, call (850) 231-4214. Upon exiting, don't miss an artist's studio gallery called The Other Side of Eden, with an appropriate sign of a serpent and apple.

If you are looking for a good place to take the kids for something other than burgers and fries, try the **Spicy Noodle** on U.S. 98, one mile west of the Phillips Inlet Bridge. The menu includes homemade and imported pastas, salads, and pizzas. While you are waiting for your order, try the Shrimp Spicy Noodle, an appetizer made with jumbo shrimp stuffed with horseradish cheese sauce, then broiled to perfection. A Little Noodle Menu is available for small appetites. The prices are right and the Spicy Noodle is open seven days a week from 11:00 A.M. to 11:00 P.M. The telephone number is (850) 231-0955.

The Terrace Restaurant, located at 13741 East Emerald Coast Parkway on Old U.S. 98 West, offers authentic Mediterranean cuisine along with tablecloth dining in an old European, casual atmosphere. Chefs Thomas and Katherine Kindos prepare seafood, lamb, beef, poultry, and vegetarian dishes with their superb sauces. Thursday, "Greek night," features spanakopeta and roast rack of lamb. The restaurant opens at 6:00 P.M., Tuesday through Sunday. Reservations are suggested. The telephone number is (850) 231-5202.

Panama City Beach

At Inlet Beach, you will want to be sure to get off of U.S. 98 and onto Alternate 98 (98A, also called Beach Front Road). Along here the Gulf-front property has narrowed, high-rise construction is light, and there are stretches of sand dunes where you can gaze across at the unbelievable blue-green water and the sugar-white beach. On the other side of the road, there are older beach rentals that have been operating for nearly 50 years, a few small restaurants and oyster bars, and an occasional shop. At Laguna Beach, **The Seahorse,** a "they've got everything" kind of place, is a piece of déjà vu.

You will notice traffic picking up, but stay on the road because you need to see it to believe it. From here to Panama City Beach (about 18 miles), it is wall-to-wall condos and motels on the beach side (some are brand-spanking new and 15 stories tall, while some are circa 1940 and one story with kitchen). Across the road, also wall to wall, are T-shirt-body piercing-beach gear-souvenirs-shells-daiquiri-beer-swimsuit-suntan lotion-air brush-et cetera shops. Traffic creeps while beachgoers dart and stroll back and forth across the road and motorists gawk.

As you are traveling this crowded stretch of Panama City Beach, you will see one motel after another and most look alike. However, when you spot the **Flamingo Motel,** you will want to take another look. This privately owned motel has a beautiful, tropical garden surrounding the beachside pool. The rooms are clean, bright, and tastefully decorated; the rates are reasonable; and the hospitality unbeatable. The Flamingo Motel is located at 15525 Front Beach Road and for reservations you can call (850) 234-2232.

East-Side Cafe, located at 13500 Front Beach Road, is a delightful treat. As soon as you walk into the restaurant you feel cooler and calmer. The tile floors and neatly spaced tables add to the relaxed atmosphere. Lunch is served from 11:00 A.M. to 2:30 P.M. and dinner is served until 10:00 P.M., daily. For lunch, try the Seafood Club, made with crab cake, lettuce, tomato, bacon, and shrimp salad. Two favorite pasta dishes for dinner are the Shrimp, Prosciutto, and Basil Pasta and the Chicken Penne Pasta. The telephone number is (850) 230-0804.

PANAMA CITY BEACH

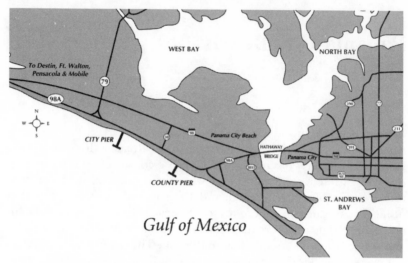

Map provided courtesy Bay County Chamber of Commerce, Panama City, Florida.

To find it you need to be sharp. **Liz and Jane's** is a delightful outlet for ladies' (and some children's) leisure clothing located right in the middle of all the Panama City Beach hoopla. Friends Liz and Jane combined talents in 1989 to develop their own variation of the comfortable, relaxed garment. Beginning in Liz's laundry room to make clothes to sell at craft fairs, the ladies used their innovative energy to expand their business to 2,400 accounts in 50 states and several countries.

The dresses, tops, pants, and shorts are made in four fabrics—cotton, linen, jersey, and fleece—and are designed for maximum comfort. The majority of the manufacturing is done "out back," where giant silkscreen and embroidery machines operate constantly. Made in the U.S.A.? You bet!

The stonewashed collection is versatile and carefree; designed for the woman who wants to feel 100 percent herself. Ever evolving and diverse, the line is the ultimate wear for work, church, weekends, or travel. These coordinated clothes are made for missy sizes six to 14 and plus sizes 11 to 24. The smallish shop is the only outlet and is as welcoming as the clothes are. It is easy to shop here and reasonable. Their shop is located at 15606 Front Beach Road and is open from 10:00 A.M. to 6:00 P.M., Monday through Saturday, and from 12:00 noon to 5:00 P.M. on Sunday. The telephone number is (334) 234-7522.

Near the east end is the **Edgewater Beach Resort,** which covers 100 acres and is surrounded by a privacy wall and gatehouses. You need to be a guest here to see all the resort has to offer, including the 11,500-square-foot swimming pool, one of the largest in the country. For information, call the resort at (800) 874-8686.

Flag Warning System at the Beaches

Red Flags	Danger, Undertow
Yellow Flags	Beware of Undertow
Blue Flags	Calm Seas

A couple of places the locals love are here on the beach. Located at 5121 Gulf Beach Drive and open "from eleven until" is **Schooners.** Perhaps it has something to do with owner Jim Cannon's name, but every afternoon they fire off a cannon at sunset. Order fish and chips or the burger. There is entertainment, too. Great! The telephone number is (850) 235-3555.

At 6627 Thomas Road on the beach is a great family restaurant called **Run Away Island.** This brightly colored spot, with flags of the Caribbean Islands hanging from the ceiling, offers tropical salads, sandwiches, conch fritters, and the like. Besides good food, what sets this place apart is a playground for the children so Mom and Dad can relax while the kids order from an extensive, reasonable child's menu. Run Away Island is a good Sunday afternoon place. It is open from 11:00 A.M. until in season and winter; however, hours may change out of season. The telephone number is (850) 234-9525.

Just outside Panama City Beach, the road splits and Alternate 98 veers toward Panama City. Take the other fork, which is Thomas Road, for about five miles. The traffic is considerably lighter, the shops are considerably fewer, and the condos are considerably spaced out, while the beach and the water are still incredibly beautiful.

You will pass Montego Bay, a fun place where you can go in your shorts and flip-flops. Try the Oysters Montego. If you stay on this road to the end, you'll come to **St. Andrews State Park** (or you can return to U.S. 98 via State Road 392).

St. Andrews State Park covers more than 1,000 acres of coastal

(Sketch courtesy Gulf Islands National Seashore)

dunes, wetlands, and forests and an authentic turpentine distillery is located there. There are two fishing piers, campgrounds, picnic facilities, and a boat ramp; a concession has snacks and limited grocery items. The extensive shoreline and the rock jetties offer exciting places to study marine life as well as swimming.

Shell Island, a pristine barrier island, is situated just across the ship's channel from the park. A shuttle departs every half-hour (in season from 9:00 A.M. until 5:00 P.M.; off-season from 10:00 A.M. until 3:00 P.M.). A three-hour snorkeling trip includes instructions and equipment.

At the end of the island is one of the prettiest beaches anywhere. The beauty, of course, is the gorgeous water and here, at land's end, the water is shallow; it is a great place to take your kids and a picnic and just snorkel around. There are no, repeat no, facilities on the island, which makes it all the more beautiful. For information on the park, call (850) 233-5140 and for the shuttle (850) 233-0504.

Diving

Two popular dive sites exist in the area. The *Tarpon* (circa 1887) was a 159-foot iron-hulled steamer. For 34 years it carried turpentine, naval stores, and passengers between Mobile, Alabama, and Carrabelle, Florida. During a storm in 1937, the ship sank and lies in 93 feet of water. The Loran coordinates are 13979.6/47001.9 (7.8 nautical miles off Panama City Beach).

The *E. E. Simpson* (circa 1877) was a 93-foot tugboat. This boat pushed freight barges and pulled stranded vessels to safety between St. Andrews Bay and Pensacola, Florida. In 1929, while trying to free a stranded ship in rough seas, the *E. E. Simpson* sank and lies in 25 feet of water. The Loran coordinates are 14121.6/46942.6 (1.5 nautical miles off the Pass at the east end of Shell Island).

Panama City

Panama City was settled prior to the Civil War and the first permanent settlers were English Tories. There are several stories about how the city acquired its name; one is that developers came up with it in order to secure shipping contracts for fruit from Panama. St. Andrews Bay, named for the saint by the Spanish explorer, de Narváez, surrounds much of the city, providing great water activities as well as a protected harbor.

World War II kept Panama City bustling as factory workers migrated to the South by the thousands to find work assembling munitions and building ships. Today, Panama City is known for its white beaches, blue, blue water, and hustle and bustle.

Captain Anderson's Restaurant is synonymous with Panama City; you can hardly mention one without the other. You certainly will not miss the glittering fish heralding the approach by road to this famous place. Every year it is listed among the top fifty restaurants in America; *Southern Living* made it number one by magazine readers; and *Florida Trends* has rated it in the top ten for more than a dozen years—so you have it. However, after all the ado, Captain's still remains a fine restaurant you will not want to miss.

For more than 30 years, the Patronis family has owned this restaurant and it still has all the classic dishes. You might as well just sit back and study the extensive menu. One of the excellent choices is the great broiled fish section; fresh pompano, grouper, scamp, amberjack, and yellow-fin tuna are available to be broiled in olive oil with chopped spring onions and parsley. The favorite is the World Famous

Seafood Platter, with stuffed deviled crab, golden fried shrimp, scallops, and fried fresh fish. You can add half a broiled lobster if you like. The grilled bay shrimp and the Angus beef dishes are other favorites. Although the restaurant is family friendly, it is rather pricey to take a big family to dinner there.

Captain Anderson's is quite an operation and it is bracing up for the new millennium with another generation of Patronises at the helm. It is open Monday through Saturday from 4:00 P.M. to 10:30 P.M. You may come by boat or water taxi; it is located at 5551 North Lagoon Drive. The telephone number is (850) 234-2226. No reservations are required.

Prior to 1975, B. J. Putnam was a charter-boat captain in Destin, but when advised by his doctor to stay out of the sun, he began a new career that would still allow him to be involved in fishing. He opened the famed **Half Hitch Tackle Shop,** which is now run by his son Tom.

Located at 2206 Thomas Drive, this place is a fisherman's dream come true. From floor to ceiling are rods, reels, and cane poles, while aisle after aisle of lures are on one side and frozen bait is on the other. There are rod-and-reel rentals, reel repairs, and a huge stock of tackle.

In addition, you can get charts, maps, tide tables, and information about legal lengths for fish and closed seasons. Up front are two blackboards posting salt- and freshwater updates. Whoever "opens up" in the mornings posts all pertinent information, including weather. It is a great place. The business card reads, "Half Hitch Tackle . . . 'Where

the Captain Buys His.'" This shop has all you need and then some. It is at Thomas Drive in Panama City and 621 U.S. 98 in Destin. Hours are 5:00 A.M. to 8:00 P.M., Monday through Saturday, and from 5:00 A.M. to 6:00 P.M. on Sunday. The telephone number is (850) 234-6992. The web site is www.halfhitch.com.

Marriott's Bay Point Resort is a year-round resort with carefree living for permanent residents and guest vacationers. Many of the condo villas and cottages overlook either the bay or the golf course. **Bay Point Yacht and Country Club** fronts on its own private marina, which is only one mile from the Gulf's open waters and the Intracoastal Waterway. Located three miles southwest of Panama City off Thomas Drive, Bay Point is also accessible by boat via the pass at St. Andrews Bay.

This is a get-away-from-it-all place with pleasures of all kinds in the offering: sailing, playground, day care center, two gorgeous golf courses, and 12 clay tennis courts. For information, call (850) 235-6966.

Marriott's Bay Point Resort is one of the largest convention complexes on the Gulf, with seven restaurants and six swimming pools. Another impressive statistic is that Bay Point is headquarters for the annual Billfish Invitational Tournament, which awards the largest prize amount, $350,000.00, in the Continental United States. Prices are seasonal. For information, call (800) 874-7105 or (850) 234-3307.

Corams Steak and Cakes, 2016 Thomas Drive in Panama City Beach, is not a bad way to start the day. This is an old-fashioned diner in the best sense of the word. The service is brisk and cheerful and if the coffee doesn't wake you up, the house specialty, "Heavenly Hash," will—for sure. This is hash browns, jalapeno peppers, onions, chopped ham, tomatoes, and green peppers. Your taste buds will stand up and cheer. Corams is open 24 hours a day, seven days a week. The telephone number is (850) 234-8373.

The world's largest Palapa Hut at **Hathaway Landing** adds a genuine tropical touch to Panama City Beach. This giant hut, constructed of 50,000 palm leaves and cypress poles, is 70 feet high and overlooks West Bay and Hathaway Marina.

A tempting, white strip of beach runs alongside the hut for ideal sitting, sipping, and boat watching. Aside from tropical drinks, there is a light bill of fare and live entertainment on weekends. Built in 1993, the Palapa Hut has been remarkably free from storm damage.

Seaplane rides and sailboat cruises are available and a dive shop offers scuba and snorkeling equipment and trips. Also on the busy premises is the **Marina Grill,** which is open from 11:00 A.M. to 11:00 P.M. The prices are moderate. The telephone number is (850) 233-0008.

The new patio-style **Cantina** serves *tapas,* which in Spanish means "little dishes" similar to American appetizers or English starters. The Cantina is moderately priced. It opens at 4:00 P.M. The telephone number is (850) 233-2007.

Leave the beach one evening and you're in for some very pleasant surprises. Just a mile or so east of the Hathaway Bridge and right on U.S. 98 (at number 4423) is **Canopies.** In this elegant, former home built in 1902, you will find superlative dining. Overlooking ancient oaks and a lawn sloping to St. Andrews Bay, you can dine on the Bay's Blue Crab (the She Crab Soup is super) or grilled fish, especially the seared tuna, accompanied by Made-in-the-House Bread and Straw-berry Butter. There is a cozy bar where you can order, too. You will be writing home about the unbelievable crabmeat dish, served in a pastry for an appetizer or in soup under the pastry, which is then puffed and browned. There is all this plus an extensive wine list in a charming Victorian setting. Canopies is open seven days a week from 5:00 P.M. The telephone number is (850) 872-8444.

Now don't think for a minute that if you've seen Panama City Beach you've seen it all. Panama City is a lovely old town, tree-lined with restored and updated shops, a theater, an art center, and restaurants, with little bays and bayous that wind around town.

Le Shack is on Beck Avenue and just a block away from the bay. Once a service station and therefore once tiny, Le Shack has grown over the years . . . but not too much.

It is a deceptive building—it actually holds about 80 people, but is "quaint, eclectic, and romantic" according to owner Ted Bill. Having been in business for nearly 20 years, Le Shack must be doing something right. Part of what's "right" is the fabulous Shrimp and Crab Lido appetizer, a baked dish of bite-sized shrimp and crab tossed with seven cheeses from seven nationalities and just enough sour cream. Ted says, "It's phenomenal!"

Follow this with either the Spicy Garlic Prawns or Filet Mignon (cooked the exact opposite of blackened to create a zesty dish) or the Layered Snapper (with artichoke hearts, mushrooms, and shrimp)

baked with a cream sauce. Is your mouth watering yet? Then call for a reservation, especially on the weekend. Le Shack is open seven nights a week, from 5:30 P.M. until 10:30 P.M. The telephone number is (850) 763-6748.

Scamp and Crabmeat Francais "Recipe"

Filet of scamp—egg washed
Crabmeat
Lemon or lime juice
Wine
Butter
Saffron
Garlic

Pan fry scamp for a quick crust. Top with crabmeat. Broil using lemon or lime juice, some wine, some butter, some saffron, some garlic.

When questioned about amounts or measurements, owner Ted Bill said, "Any good cook can figure it out!"

While you're in the area, venture on down Beck Avenue to **Hunt's Oyster Bar.** Here you can feast on raw, baked, or steamed oysters; boiled shrimp; and a hot dog for the kids. Besides the best oysters around and beach television, Hunt's has a super slogan you should remember wherever you are: "Never go into an oyster bar that's pretty!" Hunt's is open from 11:00 A.M. until 9:30 P.M., Monday through Saturday. After oysters, you can wander across the street to the attractive **Benton Theatre,** restored from its former duties as a police station and now home of plays and visual arts. The telephone number is (850) 763-9645.

One of the most scenic spots in Panama City is **Oaks By The Bay Park,** located on 10th Street and Beach Drive, behind the Ramada

Inn and overlooking St. Andrews Bay. The tranquil, tropical setting, with a view of shrimp boats plying the waters of the bay, makes it a great place for photographs.

On your way down 10th Street, you will hit the **Panama City Marina,** where you may want to stop a minute and look at all the shrimp boats docked here. This marina is surprising for its size as well as location; it is so quiet and beautiful, especially at sunset, that you may not want to leave.

An interesting aspect of the park is a rare, four-headed palm tree, Butia Capitata-Pindo Palm. Since it is the only one of its kind in the world, it is protected by an iron fence and a metal bracing support.

Another impressive park resident is a Heritage Oak named "The Old Sentry." For 250 years, this sprawling, sturdy old oak has been standing guard by St. Andrews Bay. There is also an archaeological site occupied in A.D. 1200 by Fort Walton Indians.

The handsome **Paul Brent Gallery** at 413 West Fifth Street is located in the heart of the Panama City Downtown Art District. Artist Paul Brent has captured the very essence of Florida on canvas with his stylistic interpretation of exotic wildlife and landscapes in his cool pastel palette. He is one of seven Florida artists elected to the prestigious membership in the National Watercolor Society and his paintings and prints are widely acclaimed.

If you are remotely interested in art, you will enjoy this gallery. It includes handcrafted jewelry, sculpture, pottery, and Paul Brent's paintings and prints as well as a very fine framing department. It is a gallery with wide appeal and something for everyone and everyone's pocketbook. The gallery is open from 8:00 A.M. to 5:00 P.M., Monday through Friday, and from 9:00 A.M. to 5:00 P.M. on Saturday. The telephone number is (850) 785-2684.

One of the tried-and-true restaurants in downtown Panama City is **The Cheese Barn.** For more than 20 years it has been in operation—

appealing to adults and children alike. If you want an intimate dinner, it has little alcoves for two to four people; it also has rooms for larger, more boisterous, group dining.

The menu is varied and consists of favorite international dishes from France, Germany, Cajun country, Mexico, and Italy. The lunch menu, served from 11:00 A.M. to 4:00 P.M., is light pasta, soups, salads, sandwiches, and the quiche of the day. The children's menu is very reasonable and has all the favorite things to tempt even the picky eater. The Cheese Barn is located at 440 Grace Avenue and is open from 11:00 A.M. to 8:30 P.M., Tuesday through Saturday. The telephone number is (850) 769-3892.

If you're rambling around downtown Panama City, you might want to take a coffee or lunch break and pop into the comfy **Panama Java Coffee Bar** at 223 Harrison Avenue. Weather permitting, there is outdoor seating; inside is like a comfortable living room with sofa, chairs, games, and books, as well as small dining tables.

The menu consists of a variety of sandwiches, black beans and rice, and, of course, a tempting array of coffees. You might want to try the Panama Java Royale, an espresso blended with chocolate and milk and topped with shaved chocolate and whipped cream. If your conscience rejects this, go with the fresh carrot juice. This popular hangout is open Monday through Saturday from 8:00 A.M. to 11:00 P.M. and on Sunday from 10:00 A.M. to 6:00 P.M. For takeouts, telephone (850) 763-8220.

One hesitates to use the formidable term "dining experience," but when you dine at **Ferrucci** you will have a most pleasant experience. You enter into a quiet, sophisticated room with walls beautifully sponge-painted (by Ingrid) a mellow gold. The dining room is marked with an almost absence of decorations; there are few nice prints and photos and just enough parlor palms.

A new concept in restaurant architecture here is the kitchen placement. It is at the end of the dining room, only partially hidden behind a plant-topped counter. You can see Chef Michele cooking and he can see you smiling. Due to extremely efficient air ducts, the room is neither smoky nor noisy.

Offered are antipasto (try the homemade mozzarella or the mussels) and simply heavenly pasta (order the Spaghetti al Pomodoro Fresco). When asked the secret of his lightest-ever Tomato Sauce, personable Michele replies, "The finest imported Italian virgin olive oil and imported Italian tomatoes." He says this with the same enthusiasm he obviously uses for cooking. For the "secondi"—second course—you must sample one of the superb veal dishes. Now leave room for dessert, specifically tiramisu—light lady fingers dipped in espresso, layered with mascarpone, and sprinkled with cocoa. Eccellente!

Born in Italy, Michele comes by his talent honestly—his grandfather's restaurant in Naples opened in 1908. Michele's wife, Ingrid, says, "We are committed here. The places that are successful are 'Mom and Pop' operations and that's what we are." Michele and Ingrid aren't old enough to be Mom and Pop, but the cuisine tastes of a long and dedicated heritage of fine cooking. When he's not cooking, "Pop" also sweeps leaves from the courtyard. Ferrucci is located at 301 Harrison Avenue and is open from 11:00 A.M. to 2:00 P.M., Tuesday through Friday, and from 5:00 P.M. to 10:00 P.M., Saturday and Monday. The telephone number is (850) 913-9131.

Eighteen East Fourth Street is old, vintage Panama City and is the home of **Studio 2000,** an exceptional art school for children. If you are lucky enough to be a resident, your child can benefit from the classes all year-round, but even if your stay in Panama City is limited, sign up for the short programs offered in the summer (sort of a buy-it-by-the-class setup).

Mary DeSieno, owner and director, says Studio 2000 "belongs to the students" and they bring life to the program. Well, if the children are the life then Mary is the pulse, and together they are creating some master strokes from children, ages three years, to young adults, ages eighteen years. Mary acts as a guide not a teacher; she is the conduit that leads to all the art forms provided at the studio, including drawing, painting, printmaking, sculpture, collage, jewelry making, architectural drafting, and design.

Something special is at work here that goes beyond virtual reality, computers, and all the other wizardry of our times; it is the development of creativity in the young—what could be more exciting than that! For information, call Mary at (850) 747-9162.

If you are fond of shoes, find your way to **Buddy Harris Shoe Store,** 562 Harrison Avenue, in downtown Panama City. This is an appealing store with shoes beautifully displayed throughout on hanging glass shelves. Scattered about, you will find life-sized china dogs overseeing the human activities.

Buddy Harris, who has been in the shoe business since 1968, said, "There's a trend toward more comfortable shoes and the young women of today are just not accepting uncomfortable shoes." He pointed out that the Euro-look is in now with strong heels and broader toes.

The shoe selection is impressive, and just a few of the shoe lines at Buddy Harris are Cole Haan, Stuart Wiseman, Ferragamo, Mephisto, and Arche. It is open from 10:00 A.M. to 5:00 P.M., Monday through Saturday. The telephone number is (850) 769-5200.

Historically, the center of activity in old Panama City was located in the middle of downtown, where the Dutch Colonial-style **McKenzie House** is now being restored. Across the street a pretty park has been built where you can stroll or walk your dog, day or night. The McKenzie House is located at 17 East Third Street.

Robert Lee McKenzie was the first mayor of Panama City and was instrumental in bringing commerce to the city. He and a group of entrepreneurs had dreams of linking the railroads to the port and shipping lumber to Atlanta. This same group of men changed the name of the town of Millville to Panama City, supposedly because they envisioned that their railroad lines would be comparable to the shipping lanes in the Panama Canal.

"Starting the day off right" takes on a whole new meaning when you start your day with breakfast at **Bayou Joe's Marina Grill.** You'll be so stress-free and satisfied that you will probably want to move near here.

Just off of Luverne Street at 112A 3rd Court and sitting on Massalina Bayou, Bayou Joe's is a small restaurant with a porch and a view of the bridge, boats, and birds. Fortunately for you, there are no adornments to distract you from the peacefulness. Sit yourself down, order the V-8 juice, sigh, and get ready to "lay back."

The menu begins with the following: "Please do not be in a hurry: we have a tiny kitchen and each meal is prepared to order"—and is it ever good. The Bayou Omelet (shrimp, grouper, and Tom's Cheese Sauce) will have you wanting to call your friends. French Toast (thick and fluffy) with powdered sugar and paired with smoked sausage is hard to beat.

Lunch, too? Yes . . . burgers, barbecue, Caesar salad. Dinner? Yes . . . fresh local seafood (grouper and shrimp are always available), salad, and grilled bread. Isn't it great to find a place so uncomplicated? The silverware comes wrapped in a washcloth—"Hope it doesn't match your bathroom!" the waitress will warn you with a smile. She'll also bring you some bread to feed the fish if you would like.

When you *have* to depart, take a good look around. This marina is the oldest one in Panama City, built in 1942. As you go slowly along the boardwalk leaving this languid, loose place, you'll know you'll be back—maybe by boat next time. It is open from 7:00 A.M. to 9:00 P.M., seven days a week. The telephone number is (850) 763-6442.

Ebro Greyhound Park, just 15 miles north of Panama City, offers racing nightly, except Sunday. There are matinees on Wednesday and Saturday. For additional information and directions, call (850) 234-3943 or 1-800-345-4810.

A pleasant, stopping-off place is **Oaks Park,** right outside of Callaway on U.S. 98. The park is about 15 minutes from Panama City. Whether you're going or coming, it affords a great opportunity to stop for a picnic and let children run off some steam.

The park is so dense with oak trees that hot summer sun cannot penetrate; it is located on the water, where adults can relax and watch the children play on the good equipment provided by the park.

Golf Courses

Good golf courses flourish on the Gulf Coast and the following is a list of some of them, courtesy of The Fairways Golf Company, Don Faggard, President.

Pensacola/Milton/Gulf Breeze Area Golf Courses

Lost Key Golf Club. Arnold Palmer designed this beauty, featuring narrow fairways, lots of water, and undulating greens. Built around the natural terrain of an Audubon sanctuary. Perdido Key—(850) 492-1300.

Marcus Pointe. Located on 610 acres of rolling wetlands. Always in top-notch shape. One of the area's favorite courses. Pensacola—(850) 484-9770.

The Moors. This popular Milton course plays host to the Emerald Coast Classic, a favorite stop on the Senior PGA Tour. Links-style course with gorgeous greens. Milton—(850) 995-4653.

Perdido Bay Golf Resort. Long, demanding course with water on almost every hole. Played host for 10 years to a PGA Tour stop. Pensacola—(850) 492-1223.

Scenic Hills. Demanding test, requiring both length and accuracy. Outstanding layout. Played host to the U.S. Open's Women's Championship. Pensacola—(850) 476-0380.

Tiger Point. Features two beautiful and challenging courses (East and West). The Jerry Pate-designed East layout will test the skills of the finest players. Gulf Breeze—(850) 932-1333.

Navarre/Fort Walton/Destin Area Golf Courses

Bluewater Bay. Located north of Fort Walton, featuring 36 championship holes. Enhanced by lakes, marshes, and wooded areas. A beautiful setting. Niceville—(850) 897-3241.

Emerald Bay. Located near the Gulf of Mexico, Robert Culp has designed a truly magnificent golf course. Meticulous attention to detail is always present. Destin—(850) 837-5197.

Hidden Creek. Large greens, immaculate fairways. Not much water, but plenty of bunkers. A first-class facility all the way. Navarre—(850) 939-4604.

Indian Bayou. This 27-hole beauty is one of the area's favorite courses. Large, lush greens, fairly wide fairways, and lots of water. A must. Destin—(850) 837-6191.

Seascape. Winds through woods and around shimmering lakes. Accuracy is a must. The very scenic course requires subtlety and finesse to tame. Destin—(850) 654-7888.

Shalimar Point. Located on the shores of sparkling Choctawatchee Bay, just north of Fort Walton. Lush and gorgeous. A real treat. Shalimar—(850) 651-1416.

Panama City Area Golf Courses

Hombre. Beautiful locale with dogwoods, azaleas, and numerous lakes. Water comes into play on 15 holes. Regular stop on the Nike tour. Panama City—(850) 234-3673.

Marriott Bay Point Resort. Located on a sprawling wildlife reserve, Bay Point features two championship courses. Lagoon Legend is one of the most difficult in the nation with a slope of 152! Club Meadows is friendlier. Panama City—(850) 234-3307.

If you are seeking accommodations on Panama City Beach, keep in mind that the 18-mile beach is heavily congested in the center with condos and rental units on the east and west ends. The Panama City Beach Chamber of Commerce offers a fairly complete referral list. For this and special events information, call Visitor Information at (800) 722-3224; Web site: http://interoz.com/pcbch.chamber; e-mail address at pcbchchamber@interoz.com

The Forgotten Coast

The Forgotten Coast

Beginning at Mexico Beach is a part of the Florida Panhandle known as the "Forgotten Coast." Although there are rental houses, golf, tennis, and fishing, for the most part this gorgeous stretch of beach is very low-key. From Mexico Beach to Wakulla Springs you will not find glitzy restaurants, cocktail lounges, miniature golf, or bungee jumping. Thankfully, what you will find are family beaches, marinas, grassy bays for fishing, forests, islands, and lighthouses—all on two-lane roads.

WILLOWEISE ©'86

Mexico Beach

Located about 20 miles east of Panama City is **Mexico Beach,** where from any place in the city it is only a five-minute walk to the beach. Separated from the rest of Bay County by the sprawling Tyndall Air Force Base, Mexico Beach offers a beautiful and serene haven. There are three gorgeous miles of beach here. Along with the beauty, the swimming is ideal, since the undertow is slight. The seaward pull of receding waves breaking on shore can be especially strong along the Gulf beaches. Because St. Joseph's Peninsula extends into the Gulf like a barrier island, it breaks up this pull and the swimming is safe and pleasant.

A long city-owned pier provides ideal fishing conditions and charter boats abound. You will find motel and beach rental accommodations. Located within the city limits are excellent campgrounds. Call the Chamber of Commerce at (800) 239-9553 for information on this quiet family area.

If you would like to spend quiet, relaxed time here at Mexico Beach, the **Driftwood Inn** might be just the spot for you. Owners Peggy and Tom Wood have created an oasis for the weary to "recharge." Both units and houses are for rent and have been furnished with unique antiques in a "Beach Victorian" style. A covered deck equipped with swings allows out-of-the-sun seating to view the glistening waters of the Gulf of Mexico. The boardwalks connecting the units are banked with colorful flowers, which add to the beauty of the inn. The Driftwood Inn is located at 2105 U.S. 98. The rates are moderate and a continental breakfast is served in the lobby every morning. For reservations, call (850) 648-5126.

For a short and sweet side trip, all you need to do is head north on Florida 386 or Florida 71 for about 20 miles to Wewahitchka, home of world-famous Tupelo honey. Florida is one of the six honey-producing states. The white Tupelo tree, with its distinctive nectar, grows profusely along the rivers in this area and is one of the major nectar sources for honeybees. Real Tupelo honey is light golden with a pale greenish cast, and the flavor is mild and delicious.

The honey is produced in a unique fashion. Hives are placed on elevated platforms along the river's edges and, during April and May, the bees fly out through the Tupelo blossom-laden swamps returning with their precious "cargo." This river valley is the only place in the world where Tupelo honey is produced commercially.

L. L. Lanier and Sons are producers of certified Tupelo honey. If you would like to purchase some honey, turn east at the intersection of Florida 71 and Lake Grove Road, for approximately two blocks. When you see the Lanier sign, turn in the driveway, which is bordered by enormous azalea bushes, and continue to the backyard where a sign will direct you. This honey is mighty fine!

Wewahitchka is also known for nearby **Dead Lakes,** an 80-square-mile area that produces excellent freshwater fishing. The lakes formed many years ago when nearby rivers flooded a cypress swamp, leaving thousands of eerie stumps and a great fishing habitat (the bass are big!). These uniquely shaped bare trees make the place a must for photographers and artists. A pine forest shelters a picnic and camping area. Call the Dead Lakes State Recreation Area at (850) 639-2702.

Port St. Joe

Right "next door" to Mexico Beach, although in a different time zone, is **Port St. Joe.** Originally called Port St. Joseph, the city was established in 1835, partially as a rival for the booming cotton trade controlled by Apalachicola. Later it was the site of the state's first Constitutional Convention in 1838.

The forests surrounding the present Port St. Joe have been its mainstay since the first permanent residents settled in 1904 to harvest turpentine. Later a rail line was extended to utilize the town's fine deepwater harbor for exporting lumber.

Port St. Joe's other claim to fame is its warm, shallow bays, which produce some of the country's most succulent, sweet scallops. You can harvest your own in St. Joseph's Bay and the season usually begins around July 4. However, rules about where and when you can harvest are stringent, so check with local authorities before beginning. Diving enthusiasts will enjoy sunken ships and underwater historic relics. For information, call the Chamber of Commerce at (850) 653-9419.

Julie's on Reid in Port St. Joe has the best buffet at lunch and dinner you will find in the area. The salads are made with fresh vegetables and the homemade dressings are especially tasty. The menu offers a wide variety of other choices and the daily specials are always good. The Grilled Chicken Pasta is hard to beat. The desserts are all made by Julie and are worth the calories. The restaurant is open from 11:00 A.M. to 2:00 P.M., Monday through Friday, and on Saturday for lunch. Dinner is served from 6:00 P.M. to 9:30 P.M., Tuesday through Friday. The telephone number is (850) 229-8900.

Just as you turn down St. Joseph's Peninsular toward the state park is **Cape San Blas.** Site of the Cape San Blas Lighthouse, this area is acclaimed as one of the top five beaches in the country. Rental accommodations vary from luxury condominiums to rustic cottages. Salinas Park has beachfront picnic areas and picturesque boardwalks, and here you can rent a boat (with or without a guide) or you can go scalloping.

Go Fishing
. . . but first get a license . . .

Almost everyone needs a fishing license in Florida. There are exceptions, so check the fine print at bait-and-tackle shops. The fees from the licenses are used to enhance the state's saltwater fisheries through improvement and restoration of fish habitats.

For a real getaway with no telephones, no traffic, no television (unless you choose it), and no hassle, try one of the cabins located on the site of **Old Civil War Saltworks** on Cape San Blas Road. Little is left of the Confederate Civil War Saltworks, but you can read some history on the area at the display located on the site. The cabins accommodate from two to four people and the houses can accommodate larger families. No pets are allowed and there are no parties or large groups—this is quiet, restful vacationing. There are canoes for use on the bay and the scalloping is great here. Don and Ardie Schreck keep this place spotless and, according to Ardie, if you come once you will want to come again. It is sort of like going to camp with the whole family. For more information and reservations, call (850) 229-6097.

For information about rentals on the beach or the bay on Cape San Blas, contact Tom Todd Realty at (850) 227-1501 or (800) 876-2611.

Because of impending development around Port St. Joe, new roads have been built, many of which go through stretches of virgin country. It is very nice to take a long drive down County Road 30-B or County Road 30-E and see undisturbed wetlands with many water

birds lining the edges. Gigantic pines with fields of palmettos underneath create a postcard scene that is fast changing. The drive to Indian Pass on County Road 30 affords a nice 15-mile trek before you reach the end of the road.

About two miles from Indian Pass is a country store called **Indian Pass Raw Bar,** where you can acquire some minor staples. The store has four or five tables with rolls of paper towels on each one. The program is to go to the cooler, crack a cold drink, and sit down to the best raw or baked oyster dishes you can eat anywhere (a little gumbo on the side is also suggested). Owner Jim McNeil tells you his oysters come from the west end of Apalachicola Bay, which assures you that they are the freshest they can be. He also has steamed crab legs, Indian Pass coleslaw, and good Key Lime Pie.

You will absolutely love this place with its vintage Gator football schedules on the wall and Jim's collection of old soft-drink bottles on the shelf. You will be sure that it is your find, your spot, and you will probably sit there for most of the day forgetting where you were going in the first place. Call for hours. The telephone number is (850) 227-1670.

One of the most colorful aspects of the Florida Panhandle are the legends and lore of pirates and lost treasure ships.

A popular route for Spanish galleons was from Vera Cruz, Mexico, along the Gulf Coast, where they were often victims of tropical storms or hurricanes.

The most infamous pirates visiting the northern Florida coast were

PIRATES ANCHORED OFF DESTIN

Stede Bonet, Jean Lafitte, and (probably the most notable locally) Billy Bowlegs, who even has a festival celebrated in his name. He was born in 1763 in Maryland, was a British loyalist, and fought in the Revolutionary War, after which he was assigned to a British regiment in Pensacola. Here he rebelled and went AWOL. Some of the Creek Indians in the area became his allies.

So began his long career of piracy. To judge from his photograph, he was a handsome man who loved the ladies and had several wives, one of them an Indian chief's daughter.

According to legend, Billy Bowlegs left buried treasure and sunken ships in his favorite haunts, Santa Rosa Island and Choctawhatchee Bay. Recently his ship, *The Mysterio,* was indeed discovered at the far end of Choctawhatchee Bay by a determined treasure hunter, Bud Worth. Finally, with all the drama of an Indiana Jones movie, two ancient chests with gold coins and silver bars, as well as four cannons, were dredged from the depths.

Another time, gold doubloons were discovered and it is said there are perhaps more buried under the sand dunes. So, if you're not into diving, get a metal detector and go for the gold. (Chick Huettel, *Adventure in Destin Waters* [Santa Rosa Beach, Fl.: Hogtown Publications], 1986)

The **Cape San Blas Lighthouse** is located approximately 10 miles south/southwest of Port St. Joe and is best seen from the beach of St. Joseph Peninsular State Park.

If you are a lighthouse seeker, the lighthouse at Cape San Blas is barely there, but heroic efforts have saved as much as possible of this old relic that dates back to 1859. The lighthouse still has the chips, caused by musket fire in the Civil War, in the French-made lens. It has been moved many times and storms and erosion have just about finished it off.

St. Joseph Peninsular State Park has a fascinating history. The Spanish discovered and inhabited the land in this region, but there is evidence that nomadic tribes of archaic Indians came to the area, probably for the source of seafood that the Bay of St. Joseph had in abundance. Early maps dating back as far as 1513 show the names of St. Joseph and San Blas (which is also on the peninsula). Bartram, in his travels in 1700, makes reference to the exceptionally fine grapes grown at St. Joseph Mission. It is known that there was an English outpost of sorts on the peninsula around 1800 and in the mid-1830s the lighthouse was built.

St. Joseph Peninsular State Park is on County Road 30-E, south of

Port St. Joe. The park is at the west end of the narrow peninsula and, in addition to having park facilities, it is also the site of a wilderness preserve.

The 2,516-acre park is almost totally surrounded by water. There are facilities for overnight camping, a marina, and a bait shop. The beaches are really beautiful and in some areas there is a lifeguard on duty. Furnished cabins are on the bay side of the park.

The park is also well known for its huge barrier dunes. It is an excellent birding area and hiking is a great way to observe the wildlife (hikers must register with the superintendent before entering the wilderness preserve). Some facilities are accessible for the handicapped. For information, call the park manager at (850) 227-1327. (Chuck Spicer, "State Joseph State Park," *Coast Line* 1, no. 6 (1993): 12)

Apalachicola

At one time, Apalachicola was the third-largest port on the Gulf, rivaling Mobile and New Orleans, and in the late 1800s the docks were booming with the cotton industry. Apalachicola's name is also synonymous with oysters, since nearly 90 percent of Florida's oysters (and 62 percent of the Southeast's oysters) come from Apalachicola Bay and St. George Sound. The uniqueness and delicacy of the oysters' taste are due to the subtle blend of fresh and salt waters in the area.

Historic Apalachicola has many lovely Victorian homes and buildings. About three square miles of the city have been designated a National Historic District and you can take a walking tour (directions at the Chamber of Commerce, 128 Market Street, [850] 653-9419). Besides homes, you can see cotton warehouses, several churches, the Gorrie Museum (which includes a fascinating model of the first ice machine), and the waterfront, where shrimp and oyster boats dock and seafood processing companies crowd the wharves.

Mainland beaches are few here, but the three nearby barrier islands offer everything imaginable—swimming, fishing, bird watching, hiking trails, and campsites.

The **Coombs House Inn,** a historic bed and breakfast in a restored Victorian mansion, is located at number 80 Sixth Street in the historic district of Apalachicola. The home was built in 1905 by James N.

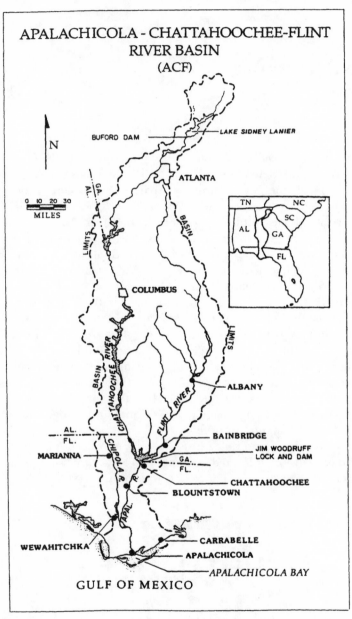

APALACHICOLA - CHATTAHOOCHEE-FLINT RIVER BASIN (ACF)

Map furnished by the Northwest Florida Water Management District

Coombs, a wealthy timber baron. One of the major hurdles faced by the new owner, Lynn Wilson Spohrer, was the fact that the house had only one bathroom. Mrs. Spohrer added 10 new baths in such a manner that it is difficult to tell which one was the original. Marilyn and Charles Subert are the resident innkeepers and serve a continental breakfast in the original dining room, which is decorated with colorful English print draperies and turn-of-the-century furnishings. For more information, the telephone number is (850) 653-9199. No pets, please.

Be sure to stop at **Trinity Episcopal Church.** This beautiful white pine structure was cut into sections in New York and floated to Apalachicola on sailing vessels down the Atlantic Coast and around the Florida Keys before being reassembled with wooden pegs in 1837. The organ, circa 1836, is still in the church. Unfortunately, the bell did not fare as well; it was melted down to make a Confederate cannon.

Wherever Chef Eddie puts down his roots, he will have a following. He has developed an old gingerbread cottage into the **Magnolia Grill,** which recently received 4 ½ hats from the *Tallahassee Democrat,* as well as accolades from *Southern Living* and *Florida Trends.* He rates among the top 200 restaurants in Florida.

People come from far and near to taste Eddie's signature dish, Pontchartrain, consisting of fresh local dauphin en croute, topped with a scampi sauce, artichoke hearts, and sliced toasted almonds. Just reading the menu will pull you to Apalachicola for an epicurean feast.

The Magnolia Grill is small with rich, paneled walls and high ceilings. Eddie and Bettye Cass will make you feel you are visiting old friends and will help you choose the best wine for whatever entrée you choose. Approaching Apalachicola proper, the Magnolia Grill is at 133 Avenue E, U.S. 98. The whitewashed cottage is sandwiched between two buildings. Keep a sharp eye out. For reservations, please call (850) 653-8000.

In the middle of town on Market Street, beside the county's only flashing red traffic signal, is the **Apalachicola Grill, Seafood and Steakhouse.** The grill is a large, family-style restaurant serving fresh fried and chargrilled fish of the region and is a wonderful stopping-off place for lunch.

The owners profess to have the largest fried fish sandwich in the world and you will believe them when you order one. It comes with heaping mounds of golden fried "catch of the day" (usually tilefish— a mild, flaky, white-fleshed Gulf species). Prices are moderate and a child's menu is provided. It is open from 11:00 A.M. to 3:00 P.M. for lunch and from 6:00 P.M. to 10:00 P.M. for dinner, Monday through Saturday. The telephone number is (850) 653-9510.

Adjacent to the Apalachicola Grill, Seafood and Steakhouse is the **Riverview Seafood Market,** offering a variety of fresh fish, condiments, and accompaniments that can be packed for travel. The market also prepares a special crabmeat stuffing with more than 40 percent lump crabmeat (to be used with your own recipes) and steamed shrimp. It is open from 11:30 A.M. to 6:00 or 7:00 P.M., Monday through Saturday. The telephone number is (850) 653-2666.

Walking the streets of Apalachicola is the best way to enjoy the town. One can sense that change is on the way and many new restaurants and shops have opened and are prospering in this new boom. Much of the charm of this old town is still intact and there is much restoration of old buildings that have fallen into disrepair. Get an ice cream at **Old Time Soda** or a dessert at **Delores's Sweet Shop** and make the journey—three miles will cover it. Apalachicola may go the way of many Florida towns and not be the same when you return.

Robinson and Sons Outfitters is truly the place for the well-dressed fisherman to keep up his image. The store is literally packed with great looking, up-to-date, serviceable clothing for the outdoor enthusiast. This Orvis dealer has everything from books to read about your favorite sport to well-trained guides to actually take you to it. Brothers Chris and Tommy Robinson will guide you to the best places in the area to fish. Call (850) 653-9669 to book a trip. It is located at 94 Market Street.

A great treasure in Apalachicola is 82-year-old Ginaro Zingarelli, known as "Jigs" to his friends. Mr. Zingarelli still works at his print

shop on the corner of D and Commerce streets, as he has for 40 years, and still prints on an old linotype machine.

If he is in his shop working, you may want to stick your head in and talk to him. He is a native of Apalachicola and has seen many changes. Actually, change doesn't bother Mr. Zingarelli and he doesn't understand people bellyaching about the inevitable. He likes Benjamin Franklin and quotes him when it is appropriate to the conversation. The *Tallahassee Democrat* wrote a huge article on Mr. Zingarelli and, when asked if he had a copy, he said, "Just one and I am saving it for my brother."

If you drive down the coast and land in Apalachicola, another gift shop is probably the last thing you want to see. The **Sunflower** is aptly named because it is a shop filled with sunshine and fun with, believe it or not, things you have not seen before.

Owner Betsy Doherty hails from Vermont and has the Yankee ingenuity to make the Sunflower a success. She is a smart buyer and draws from good name companies that have imagination and savvy. She never resorts to the cutesy or craftsy merchandise you see so much of along the coast.

Her gourmet section has great accessories for the outdoor cook: wine-soaked wood chips, sacks to smoke foods easily, cookbooks, and barbecue sauces—plus all kinds of long-handled utensils to grab the food you have lost through the grill. Her garden section carries the best herbs from O'Tool Herb Farm, as well as flower seeds packaged

in all kinds of contrivances, gardening gadgets, thingamabobs, dohick-
ies, and widgets to make life easier for fanatic gardeners.

Bringing quality to a place makes change easier to accept and Betsy
has given as much as she takes to the Apalachicola community. Sunflower is located at 14 Avenue D and is open from 10:00 A.M. to 5:00
P.M., Monday through Saturday. Summer hours are from 12:00 noon
to 4:00 P.M. on Sunday. The telephone number is (850) 653-9144.

Locals are fascinated with **Roberto's Eclectic Italian Cuisine** on the
corner at 15 Avenue D. Just when you plan to have dinner here, it is
closed with a set of new hours on the door. The lucky few who do have
dinner here say it is delicious and they want very much to return.

The café is tantalizing from the outside looking in and a menu is
tacked to the door to pique your interest even more; but the illusive
Roberto keeps his secret for a catch-as-catch-can patron. If you have
dinner at Roberto's, contact *Coasting* via the publisher. Send any cor-
respondence to Pelican Publishing Company, P.O. Box 3110, Gretna,
Louisiana 70054-3110.

From what can be surmised, the Veal Roberto is the best dish at the
restaurant. The hours are usually from 6:00 P.M. until, Tuesday
through Saturday; after Labor Day, you should call; it is closed for
the winter months, but maybe not; Roberto's may be open for lunch
someday; the Tuscan wine bar is open from 4:00 P.M. until, Thursday
through Saturday, but, if it is too crowded . . . no bar. Reservations
are a must but walk-ins are welcome. Don't be fainthearted; persist!
The telephone number is (850) 653-2778.

While you are here, you should be aware that the **Apalachicola
National Estuarine Research** reserve is located nearby. The reserve,
which is the largest in the nation, consists of nearly 200,000 acres of
land and water and supports thousands of plants and animals, many
of which are endangered.

Nearby is the **St. Vincent National Wildlife Refuge Center,** one of
more than 500 refuges managed by the U.S. Fish and Wildlife Service.

Prior to becoming a refuge, St. Vincent Island was used primarily
as a private hunting and fishing preserve. The two previous owners

(Sketch courtesy Gulf Islands National Seashore)

introduced a variety of exotic wildlife to the island. A large population of sambar deer from Southeast Asia still roam the island today, along with a healthy population of whitetails.

Once a year, a hunt for the sambar deer is permitted after a random drawing from 50 to 200 applicants. The hunt has strict regulations and the deer must be hunted with primitive weapons or archery. Applications for this hunt may be obtained at the St. Vincent National Wildlife Center at 479 Market Street, or you may write to St. Vincent National Wildlife Center, P.O. Box 447, Apalachicola, Florida 32329.

Other protected species on St. Vincent Island are the bald eagle, loggerhead turtle, indigo snake, wood stork, and peregrine falcon. In 1990, the refuge became one of several Southeastern coastal islands where endangered Red Wolves are being bred. After the wild pups have been weaned, they are taken to reintroduction sites in North Carolina and the Great Smoky Mountains. (Information concerning St. Vincent Island provided by St. Vincent National Wildlife Refuge.)

The **Estuarine Walk** is in Apalachicola (261 7th Street) and is an educational exhibit open to the public between 8:00 A.M. and 5:00 P.M. on weekdays. All ages will find it interesting.

One of the best assets for Apalachicola is the arrival of Jane Doerfer on the scene. Miss Doerfer is the author of *Going Solo in the Kitchen,* a cookbook for one, which has recently been awarded the distinction of being one of the top 13 cookbooks by *Good Housekeeping.*

Going Solo in the Kitchen is the only established cooking school devoted to teaching cooking for one. In this five-day course, the student is immersed in the culinary philosophy and style Doerfer has espoused for more than 20 years. It is a cuisine that uses what is seasonal and geographically available, with lots of fresh herbs and vegetables and very little fat. Apalachicola offers Jane all of this, as well as the freshest oysters, shrimp, and seafood in the country—it has been a good marriage.

The school operates out of a 19th-century plantation cottage overlooking the shrimp boats on the Apalachicola River Basin. The house was moved by Doerfer to its present location in 1992 and renovated by architect Hugh Hewell Jacobsen. Student lodging is provided nearby at the historic 1907 Gibson Inn.

For more information, you can write to Going Solo in the Kitchen at P.O. Box 123, Apalachicola, Florida 32329; or call (850) 653-8848 or (850) 451-5294.

At 125 Water Street is **Boss Oyster,** a must-go-to place. Although there is other fare (ribs, burgers, chicken), the seafood is the specialty here. It is hard to beat the steamed shrimp or the triggerfish, but those oysters . . . oh, yes!

You can have them raw, steamed, roasted, or fried. Or order the baked oysters with different toppings—recipes all submitted by guests (feel free to submit one yourself). The Oysters Max (capers, garlic, Parmesan cheese) and the Oysters St. George (asparagus, shallots, colby cheese) are outstanding. It is a comfy come-as-you-are place, where you can eat inside or out on a wonderful covered deck by the river. You can often see the just-harvested oysters being washed on a platform next to the restaurant. It is open at 12:00 noon on weekdays and 9:00 A.M. on weekends. The telephone number is (850) 653-8139.

There is also an inn and marina combination on the banks of the river in downtown.

The **Rainbow Inn and Marina** is located at 123 Water Street and offers transient dockage as well as motel facilities directly on the Apalachicola River. For reservations or docking information, call (850) 653-8139.

Caroline's Riverfront Restaurant is part of the Rainbow Inn and Marina and is open seven days a week from 6:30 A.M. until 10:30 P.M. For early birds, the restaurant offers a quiet place to watch the sun rise over the Apalachicola River. The breakfast menu includes items such as homemade buttermilk biscuits with tomato gravy, country ham with red-eye gravy, sautéed fresh fish of the day, and fried oysters, and grits.

Red-Eye Gravy

Red Eye Gravy really requires a piece of well-cured country ham with most of the fat left on (but in a pinch, other kinds of ham or bacon could be used). Fry ham in its own fat in an iron skillet until browned on both sides. Transfer to a plate. Add one-third to one-half cup of strong, black coffee to skillet, scraping up any ham bits that have stuck to the pan. Stir all this about but do not allow gravy to boil. Pour over the ham and grits or biscuits.

A good place for a drink at The Rainbow Inn is upstairs over the restaurant on the deck. A quiet restfulness seems to settle over the river and the town as daylight dims into twilight. There is something magical about sitting outside to watch the day come to an end.

People come to **The Gibson Inn** for different reasons. Some come to wait out a storm before taking their boats across open waters. Some spend time before a big hunting or fishing expedition. Some are tourists exploring unspoiled territory. Some come just to crash and take time out of too busy lives. Whatever the reason, people love The Gibson Inn.

Formerly named The Franklin, the hotel was built in 1907 by James Fulton Buck. He was from a lumbering empire in South Carolina and he used handpicked black cypress and heart pine meant to last. In 1923, the Gibson sisters bought the hotel and changed its name. In 1942, the army bought and used it as an officers club for Camp Gordon Johnston.

Presently, it is owned by Michael Neil Koun and Michael Merlo, who purchased and restored the hotel in 1983, staying true to the original architecture. There is never a time you will not see a bucket of paint and a ladder somewhere in the hotel, for the price of this old beauty is eternal maintenance.

The Gibson Inn has 31 rooms, each decorated with period pieces and each totally different from the next. The lobby is wide open with beautiful hardwood floors flowing into a cozy bar with a restaurant behind it. Delicious meals are served three times a day. The dining room takes you back in time with its brass gaslights and old photographs.

Holidays are fun at The Gibson Inn and two weekends a year are mystery weekends, during which a group of friends try to solve a mock murder. The telephone number is (850) 653-2191.

Hooked on Books is a nice bookstore in the annex of The Gibson Inn. The telephone number is (850) 653-2420.

What's in a Name?

Although Apalachicola is a beautiful name with a beautiful meaning ("Land of the Friendly People," from the Indian), it is a mouthful to say. Locals simply refer to their town as "Apalach."

If fishing as well as eating is your thing, be sure to take the time to go to a couple of the fishing camps nearby. Wonderfully rustic, these camps offer some mighty fine eating. Check out the Bay City Lodge or Breakaway Marina and Motel. Both have charters, bait and tackle shops, marine service and supplies, dry boat storage, and cabins, along with restaurants.

Whether you're casting for trout or drifting in the cool waters for bass, you can't beat the fishing on Apalachicola River. These camps are just a "mullet's leap away" from some of the finest fishing in North Florida. Mornings they'll cook you a fisherman's breakfast and/or fix you a bag lunch and when you return they'll cook your catch. If you've had no luck, there will still be dinner for you! There are guides if you need one and a fish cleaning service. Now what else could you possibly want? **Bay City Lodge** can be reached at (850) 653-9294 and is open year-round with reasonably priced cabins and motel rooms with cable television and air conditioning. Manager Tom Gordon says the best time to come and fish is "when the conditions are right." This could be a great father-son trip or just bring a bunch of fishing buddies. You may bring your own boat if you prefer. This facility is wheelchair accessible.

Breakaway Marina and Motel has boat storage, bait, and tackle. According to manager Jerry Cauthen, it is somewhat unique to find a marina located in fresh water. He says you can go fishing any day. If it is too rough to get out to salt water, you can fish the rivers or bays. Jerry also added that this is a good place to ride out a hurricane. The restaurant is open for breakfast, but only for motel guests. Anyone is welcomed for dinner on Wednesday through Saturday and on Sunday for lunch. It would be a good idea to call (850) 653-8898 and make a reservation.

The **Apalachicola National Forest** encompasses one-half million acres. Several roads enable you to drive through a good-sized chunk of it, but to really see the forest, you need to hike or canoe or spend the night in one of the campgrounds.

Main entrances are off Florida 20 and Florida 319. There are minor roads that form cross links—Routes 267, 375, and 65. Accommodations are limited to camping. With the exception of Silver Lakes, all sites are free, with only basic facilities.

One section of the forest, **Trout Pond,** is open April through October and is intended for the public as well as disabled visitors. This portion has a wheelchair-accessible lakeside nature trail and picnic area on Route 373. For more information, call (850) 643-2282 or (850) 926-3561.

Before hiking or camping in the forest, check with the Rangers for maps and weather information.

Gorrie Bridge

This bridge is on U.S. 98 and is built over Apalachicola Bay, connecting Apalachicola and Eastpoint. It is named for Dr. John Gorrie, who arrived in these parts in 1833. While trying to keep his malaria patients' rooms cool, he devised an ice machine. Unfortunately, he died before the idea became the basis for the modern refrigerator and air-conditioner. There is a museum dedicated to him in Apalachicola that contains a model of his device.

Eastpoint

The Apalachicola Bay area is known for producing "world-famed" oysters . . . but it is Eastpoint that ships them to the world. Oyster processing houses line the bayshore, where oysters are shipped by the millions, traveling in 18-wheelers to all parts of the nation.

Eastpoint had its beginnings in the early 1900s, when the community was the site of an experiment in cooperative living. The name is apparently derived from the community's location on the east point of a peninsula where the mighty Apalachicola River empties into Apalachicola Bay.

As you drive in from the west, you will see many oyster and fish markets lining U.S. 98. Most of these markets, located right on the bay, sell retail, so hopefully you will have a cooler.

Osprey Homes

If you see some platforms high atop tall wooden poles with a mess of twigs and branches on top, you're seeing osprey nests (humans put up the poles, the osprey does the rest). Ospreys love tall places and often you'll see some "illegal" housing that they have erected on telephone poles. A favorite neighborhood is the row of power poles adjacent to the Gorrie Bridge in Apalachicola. Ospreys are large birds of prey in the hawk family. They are about 2 feet long with a wingspan of nearly 6 feet and have enough white feathers on their heads to resemble a bald eagle. The American Osprey breeds and winters in this area; they feed on fish that stay close to the surface and are of little value to man.

The Barrier Islands

The three barrier islands that surround the mainland are all important bird areas. Many varieties nest along the sandy shores and all islands are critical rest stops for migrating birds during the spring and fall. The similarities end there.

St. George Island can be reached by a bridge and offers nearly 30 miles of powder-soft sand beaches and great fishing (charter, surf, or bayside). During the early 1900s, the island's pine forests were turpentined and on many of the large slash pines you can still see scars from this activity. The trees have other scars, too, resulting from training exercises during World War II. One resident remarked that "the trees still have so many bullets in them that they are deemed unfit to go to the sawmill to be cut for lumber."

At one end of the island is **St. George State Park,** which charges a nominal fee for either day or camping admission (call ahead for camping) and has nine miles of undisturbed beach. There are hiking trails, an observation deck, and a small boat launch. The telephone number is (850) 927-2111.

St. George Island is the last large Gulf-front area where high-rise development is not present. There are a few good restaurants, a couple of lounges, a convenience store, and the prominent and pretty **St. George Inn.** Barbara Vail, owner of the inn and native of Philadelphia, says she and her late husband, George, traded snow for hurricanes when they moved to the island in 1985. They actually built the inn themselves in less than two years. Barbara spends

her days keeping her guests comfortable and running the restaurant, which is open for evening meals. There is a nice wine list to complement the menu. The St. George Inn is moderately priced and the rooms are available by reservation. The telephone number is (850) 927-2903.

The Buccaneer Motel is located on the Gulf side of the island and there are a few condominiums for rent. There are quite a few private homes on the island and many of them are available for rent.

At the west end of the island is a man-made channel that provides good fishing, and across this channel on Cape St. George stands the historic Cape St. George Lighthouse. Shell collecting is great on this island, which is accessible only by boat.

To find the Forgotten Coast, **Jeanni's Journeys, Inc.,** is one of the best ways to go. Jeanni McMillan has been camping and exploring the Panhandle area for 25 years. She has taught school in Singapore, has been an environmental planner, and has trekked the Himalayas— while meditating there, she realized where she belonged and came back to her beloved coast to set up programs designed to explore the Barrier Islands off of St. George.

The programs are rated from easy to moderate to difficult. They include exploring the island on a 20-foot Key West or 23-foot Aqua Sport, shelling trips, Apalachicola river trips, and special kayak and canoe trips. Jeanni also has kiddie rainy-day excursions and art projects. All kinds of camping equipment is available to rent for overnight camping on a deserted island, where you can be dropped off and picked up the next day.

You can book your own adventure by calling Jeanni's Journeys, Inc., at (850) 927-3259; e-mail her at jj-inc@juno.com; or go by the office located at 139 East Gorrie, St. George Island. Her office is open from 11:00 A.M. to 6:00 P.M., Monday through Saturday. The season is open March 1 through December 30.

Boiled Seafood from the Oyster Cove
St. George Island
(Courtesy of Biff Newsham)

For every gallon of water used and for about 5 pounds of seafood:

¼ cup salt
2 tbsp. cayenne pepper
2 tbsp. lemon pepper seasoning
1 tbsp. garlic powder
3 bay leaves

Let spices boil a minute or two before adding the seafood. The real secret is to drop in whatever seafood (shrimp or crawfish) is to be used when water is at a rolling boil. The water will stop boiling when the seafood is added. Just before it starts to boil again, turn off fire and let sit and soak a few minutes. Serves 8-10.

St. Vincent Island is the largest of the barrier islands, containing 12,000 acres. Accessible only by boat, the island is a National Wildlife Refuge and is open to the public during the daylight hours. It is uninhabited except for turtles, eagles, turkeys, whitetailed deer, and, hanging around the freshwater ponds, plenty of alligators. Be careful landing by boat—the tidal currents are quite strong.

The final link in the barrier chain is **Dog Island,** just off the coast of Carrabelle. Owned by the Nature Conservancy, most of the island is a preserve and the only way to get there is by boat (or ferry) or private plane. Once there, you will see a single sand road, a few permanent residents, and the tiny **Pelican Inn.** The inn was recently bought by Jane Doerfer, who is making it into a livable state for people to completely get away. The seven rooms have complete kitchens and clean bedrooms—and that's all. There are no telephones, no television, no stores, and no food service—you'll need to bring your own.

There is fishing—bay, charter, or cast netting—and you can rent a skiff or a Hobie catamaran or hunt for shells. It is very quiet here. In the fall and spring you can hear the migratory birds and in winter you

can hear the ducks in their ponds in the dunes. The few people who come here find there is no better place for peace. For more information, call (800) 451-5294.

Cypress Knees

The tall, pyramidal bald cypress tree thrives in the Southeastern swamps and bay shores, where conical "knees" grow up from the roots. These knees aid in providing air for the submerged parts of the trees. The leaves are soft and feathery and have a faint evergreen odor and the durable wood, very resistant to rotting, is prized for posts, railroad ties, and construction. You will see quite a few cypress trees with knees along the road between Apalachicola and Carrabelle.

If you're rolling along U.S. 98 on the west side of Carrabelle and see a weathered sign declaring "World Famous," you have reached **Julia Mae's.** This is a rustic café on the canal and, since 1977, has been a local favorite of fishermen and seafood lovers. The homemade pies are by Julia Mae's sister and the coconut is said to be the most popular. The prices are very reasonable. The café is open from 11:00 A.M. to 10:00 P.M., seven days a week. The telephone number is (850) 697-3791.

Carrabelle

Carrabelle, "The Pearl of the Panhandle," is one of the two incorporated cities in Franklin County, Florida, and is known as the "fisherman's paradise."

This small town was established in the late 1800s and was built around several large sawmills. The lumber was shipped out by small sailing vessels. The post office, built in 1878, remains in its original location and is the gathering place where residents exchange fishing tips and keep up with the local gossip.

One of the many treasures in this coastal community is the fact that Carrabelle is home to the world's smallest police station, which is located on U.S. 98 in a telephone booth!

Neighborhood haunts are good places to visit and **Harry's Bar** in Carrabelle is one of those places. Open every day from 7:00 A.M. until, Harry's is a rendezvous for many kinds of people—locals and those just passing through. Carole will talk you into one of her special drinks, such as Absolut Lemonade (no *e* in absolut). The drink is made with Absolut vodka, sweet-and-sour mix, and cranberry juice or Lemon Largo, which is lemonade with tropical schnapps (Carole likes to serve her lemon drinks). Ask about an ageless beauty who drove a big, gold caddy and hung out at Harry's Bar.

There is no address for Harry's, just that it is on Marine Street. It is owned by Jerry and Carole Adams.

After you leave Carrabelle and Eastpoint (heading east), stay on U.S. 98. Right after it crosses Ochlockonee Bay and immediately to the east, you will see **Lighthouse Point Resort.** This is not a large place, but it is lovely. Here are furnished condos, tennis courts, a swimming pool, a fishing dock, and an on-site private marina. In other words, all the good things about the "big" places with none of the hassle. All condos have waterfront views and there are restaurants nearby. For information, call (850) 984-0171.

For those who prefer camping, on the other side of U.S. 98 is **Holiday Campground,** also on the Bay.

At the end of the road is sometimes a rainbow. At the end of this part of the road is the beautiful **Wakulla Springs Lodge** and the **Wakulla Springs State Park.** Located at the eastern edge of the Apalachicola National Forest, about 30 miles from Carrabelle, the Lodge and Conference Center offers spacious accommodations, with every one of its 27 guest rooms overlooking the springs or the park. The Lodge, built in 1937, retains the stately ambience of yesteryear with marble for the floors from Tennessee, Moorish archways and doors from Spain, and wonderful lobby rafters aglow with Aztec designs.

In winter months, guests can relax in front of the great stone fireplace for bridge or checkers and in the summer swim in the magnificent springs. The spring flows from an underground river at a rate of 600,000 gallons per minute. Its basin covers 4 ¼ acres, reaching a depth of 185 feet, yet objects are clearly visible at the deepest point. Even after much research, the origin of the spring is unknown.

This lovely place sits in the heart of the 2,900-acre park, where a wide variety of wildlife lives. The state of Florida acquired the park in 1986 and the Florida Park Service offers glass-bottom boat tours and jungle boat trips, past lush palmetto-filled land straight out of *The Yearling*.

The lodge and park, located on Florida 267 (about 10 miles north of U.S. 98 or 15 miles south of Tallahassee), are open year-round. On major holidays, the lodge chef serves a famous smorgasbord featuring holiday fare. All during the year, events and programs are held in the park—ecology hikes, sunrise and twilight boat cruises, and Bird Sounds, a birding program for the sight impaired. Ranger-led snorkeling programs are offered during the warmer months. For information on the park, call (850) 922-3633 or (850) 224-4590.

Now it is just a few miles to the St. Marks National Wildlife Refuge and the St. Mark's Lighthouse, where part of the state of Florida turns and heads south.

MISSISSIPPI

Mississippi

Three powerful Indian tribes ruled the Mississippi Region: the Chickasaw, the Choctaw, and the Natchez. Between 25,000 and 30,000 Indians lived in the Mississippi region when the first white explorers arrived. In 1682, the entire Mississippi Valley was claimed for France and this region included the present-day Mississippi. For many years, the Gulf Coast of Mississippi has been one of the nation's most popular winter resorts, with its large sunny beaches and fine hotels. Today, with the advent of gambling boats, this portion of the Gulf Coast is a year-round

(Sketch courtesy of Richard Scott, Jr., from *Battles Wharf and Point Clear* by Florence and Richard Scott.)

resort. The towns along the fabulous coast are in a string and you'll
have to watch carefully to see where one ends and the next begins.

We suggest you pick up a Mississippi Gulf Coast map when you
are in Mississippi (from either a chamber of commerce or a visitors center) so that you may better find your way around.

Pascagoula

A huge shipbuilding center and busy port, Pascagoula offers many recreational opportunities. Almost surrounded by pine ridges and mysterious bayous, the city is named for an Indian tribe that once lived there.

The famous **Singing River** is located near U.S. 90 and is known for its mysterious music, which resembles the sound of a swarm of bees in flight. Best heard in late summer and early autumn in the stillness of late evening, the music seems to grow louder as one listens. An old legend connects the sound with the mysterious extinction of the Pascagoula tribe.

While you're in Pascagoula, plan to visit the **Scranton Floating Museum** at River Park, just north of Ingalls Shipbuilding. This floating museum offers an opportunity to explore a shrimp boat firsthand. There is also an Environmental Learning Center with aquariums, "living" touch tanks, and a hands-on seashore exhibit. Scranton Floating Museum is open from 10:00 A.M. to 5:00 P.M., Tuesday through Saturday, and from 1:00 P.M. to 5:00 P.M. on Sunday. For more information or to arrange a group tour, call (228) 762-6017.

Three restaurants in Pascagoula are favorites among the locals. If asked, almost anyone would probably name one of these:

Fillets is located at 1911 Denny Avenue (U.S. 90) and serves a down-home menu with all the Southern favorites. Everyday specials include chicken and dumplings (the cook loves to make dumplings on Tuesday), liver and onions, chicken and fish (broiled or fried); and there are great turnip greens, too. The staff is warm and friendly and welcome families of any size. It is open from 11:00 A.M. to 9:30 or 10:00 P.M., according to the crowd, seven days a week. The telephone number is (228) 769-0280.

About seven or eight traffic lights west of Fillets is Ingalls Avenue. Turn south and drive a fourth of a mile down to **Bozo's,** a 42-year-old fish market and deli. Three generations of Delcambres have owned the market and Keith Delcambre says the crawfish are the best any-where. "We are the first to have 'em and the last to get 'em," he says.

All you need to know is to wear your grubs and sit down to a pile of crawfish spread out on butcher paper and eat 'em until you burst (you might need to be hosed down before you are on your way). The Shrimp Po' boy runs a close second—dressed and served on a foot-long bun—shrimp literally spill over the side of the sandwich. Bozo's also has a lot of fresh fish to buy. It is open from 8:00 A.M. to 8:00 P.M., seven days a week. The telephone number is (228) 762-3322.

Just past Bozo's at 2018 Ingalls and 14th Street is **Marguerite's,** an Italian restaurant that is truly loved by the people of Pascagoula. For 22 years, this place has served delicious food and is now run by Liz O'Cain and her mother, Katherine Hunt, after the death of father and husband, Bill Hunt.

The numero-uno dish is Sautéed Shrimp and Mushrooms in Garlic Butter Sauce served over Spegatini. The second favorite is the Veal Milanese (sliced veal, breaded, sprinkled with Romano cheese, and sautéed in lemon-drawn butter). Stuffed Eggplant Lamberto and a good seafood platter round out the menu.

Marguerite's does not take reservations and will accept Visa and MasterCard only. It is open from 5:00 P.M. to 10:00 P.M., Monday through Saturday, and until dark on Sunday. The telephone number is (228) 762-7464.

Just a few blocks north of U.S. 90, lying alongside the Singing River, is a virtual cornerstone in Mississippi's history. **Old Spanish Fort** is the area's most valued landmark as well as probably the oldest struc-ture in the United States between the Appalachian Mountains and the Rocky Mountains. The name, though, is misleading, because Old Spanish Fort is neither Spanish nor was it a fort.

The modest building was a French carpenter's shop built in 1718 and is all that remains of the approximately 10 buildings on an old estate that was enclosed within a stockade for almost 50 years. The grounds, consisting of approximately three acres, are now lush with giant azaleas and huge expanses of grass that lead down to the river. Three cannons dot the grounds, two captured by Andrew Jackson at New Orleans and one taken near Mobile at Spanish Fort. It is not known whether this is where the name Old Spanish Fort originated. Another possibility is that in 1766, three Spanish boats docked here, presumably to consider the outpost as a fort, but after two weeks, the Spaniards changed their minds and sailed away.

Old Spanish Fort still stands today. Much has been restored, but you can still see the original 18-inch-thick walls made of a durable mixture of clay and Spanish moss and covered with ground oyster shell plaster. There is an adjacent museum building with many displays and artifacts and there are a few picnic tables. Old Spanish Fort is open year-round from 9:30 A.M. until 4:30 P.M., six days a week, and on Sunday from 12:00 noon until 4:30 P.M. It is closed on major holidays. The telephone number is (228) 769-1505. It is a beautiful spot.

OLD SPANISH FORT

Gautier

A few miles west of Pascagoula is Gautier, Mississippi. In Gautier you'll find the **Mississippi Sandhill Crane National Wildlife Refuge,** which was established in 1975. The headquarters and visitors center is located just one-half mile north of Interstate 10, Exit 61, at Gautier-Van Cleave Road. Here you can get information on this 19,000-acre refuge. The center is open Monday through Friday from 7:30 A.M. until 4:00 P.M. You are invited to hike, photograph, or bird-watch on the trails during visitor center hours. For more information, contact the refuge manager by writing 7200 Crane Lane, Gautier, Mississippi 39553; or by calling (228) 497-6322.

While in Gautier, take a very small detour to **Singing River Originals Pottery.** Josie Gautier, granddaughter of Fernando Gautier, founder of the city, started Singing River Originals Pottery in 1950. While traveling in Florida, she saw some shell jewelry that was shoddily made but sold like hot cakes. Miss Josie began her business, she said, "when I was an old woman."

Her first mold was made from a speckled trout she caught off the U.S. 90 Bridge. From that point, all of her crab, shrimp, and fish molds were cast from the real thing. Although Miss Josie died in 1992, each ceramic piece is created from handcrafted molds that she painstakingly made—her inspirations came from her love of nature and wildlife, which still surround her shop, now owned by her niece, Harriet Gautier Portas.

As you tour the shop (located in one of four houses built by Josie's father and uncles in the 1800s), you will find unique serving dishes with blue crabs and Gulf shrimp on them and seafood plates with matching napkin rings.

Gwen Washington, whose family has been with Singing River Originals Pottery for three generations, works quietly on the back porch. From there she can look through enormous live oak trees to the Singing River—the expansive yard looking much as it must have looked a hundred years ago. Singing River Originals Pottery is open Monday through Friday, from 10:00 A.M. until 4:00 P.M., and is located south of the Singing River Bridge on Oak Street. The telephone number is (228) 497-2012. On Mondays and Fridays, it is best to call ahead.

Just north of the Singing River Bridge you'll find **Huck's Cove** tucked under live oaks and nestled along the river. Go down the steps to a deep, shady porch complete with swings and old life rings on the wall. From there, the deck meanders around the water, past little open-air "half cabanas" housing tables framed by banana trees and plants. In fact, lush plants abound—sitting all around the deck on pieces of pilings, crab traps, and wooden buckets—it is Key West in Mississippi.

Inside, under ceiling fans and boat flags, you can get salads, sandwiches, seafood, or a "Paradise Burger." Windows are open to the deck and you've got a breeze and a view no matter where you sit. There is also a nice bar and a most pleasant staff. It is a good place to go. Huck's Cove is located at 3000 Oak Street (on the northeast side of Singing River). The bar and restaurant are open every day at 11:00 A.M. (12:00 noon on Sunday), and dinner is served every night except Tuesday. The telephone number is (228) 497-4309.

Ocean Springs

The quiet, oak-lined streets and serene atmosphere of Ocean Springs, Mississippi, contain a history that goes back almost 300 years. Pierre LeMoyne d'Iberville stepped ashore here in 1699, establishing for France the first permanent settlement in the vast central area of North America.

The area began growing with the advent of the shallow-draft paddle-wheel steamboats that had to make frequent stops to take on wood and fresh water between runs from New Orleans to Mobile. The name Ocean Springs was coined by Dr. George Austin, a New Orleans physician who established a sanitarium to take advantage of the health-giving springs found in the area. Today, Ocean Springs is a thriving community with the charm of coastal homes, winding lanes, and peaceful trees.

There are two restaurants in Ocean Springs that have the best food this side of New Orleans—Germaine's and Jocelyn's. The histories of these two restaurants are so connected that it would be hard to write about one and not about the other.

Germaine's is the new name of the old Trilby's restaurant, which has been a landmark in Ocean Springs for more than 50 years. Jane and Jack Gottsche bought it in 1990, changed the name to Germaine's (after their daughter), and have set about making it a gem of a restaurant.

The Trout Amandine rivals Galatoire's in New Orleans, but the lump crabmeat dishes are the favorites of Germaine's patrons. The delicious Rum Cream Pie is its signature dessert and the Raspberry

Sauce that goes atop a meringue with French ice cream is a dessert for which you would make a special trip. It is open for lunch, Tuesday through Sunday, from 11:30 A.M. until 2:00 P.M., and for dinner, Tuesday through Saturday, from 6:00 P.M. until 10:00 P.M. The telephone number is (228) 875-4426.

Germaine's Rum Cream Pie

Graham cracker crust
5 egg yolks
1/4 cup sugar
1 envelope unflavored gelatin
1/2 cup cold water
1/2 cup dark rum
1/2 pint whipping cream
Shaved chocolate pieces

Fill one 10-inch pie plate with graham cracker crust and freeze. Do not bake. Beat egg yolks, add sugar until creamy. Dissolve gelatin in cold water and bring to a boil. In a steady stream, pour slowly into egg-sugar misture. Add rum. Chill until mixture mounds on spoon. Beat whipping cream, add chilled mixture, and blend well. Pour into frozen pie shell and freeze at least 6 hours or until ready to serve. Top with shaved chocolate pieces.

Jocelyn and Harold Mayfield managed the original Trilby's restaurant. Jocelyn now has her own restaurant, **Jocelyn's,** on U.S. 90 in Ocean Springs. In an old house painted lilac, you can have a wonderful meal, with Jocelyn and her family taking care of things. She says that the best dishes are the crabmeat au gratin and the seafood casserole. Jocelyn's is open Tuesday through Saturday, from 5:00 P.M. until 10:00 P.M. Call for reservation for more than five people. The telephone number is (228) 875-1925.

You can have private luncheons and dinner parties at noon and anytime on Sunday if the group has fewer than 25 people. There is also has a complete catering service for weddings and other occasions.

Officially opened in 1987, **The Doll House** (next door to Germaine's) is a private collection of dolls, displayed in a lovely blue-and-white Victorian-type house with six viewing rooms. Although Mrs. Blossman does have some antique dolls, she admits that here is simply a doll lover's collection. After 30 years of collecting, Mr. and Mrs. Blossman built this home so that children of every age could come and enjoy. To make it all the more delightful, the admission, which is nominal, is by donation to benefit the YMCA Pet Shelter Fund. The Doll House is open from 1:00 P.M. until 5:00 P.M., Tuesday through Sunday. The telephone number is (228) 872-3971.

> Pick up a copy of the *Ocean Springs Record* and read the hilarious police calls published every week. They have been aired on "Saturday Night Live" and other national shows.

For family-style fun, **Aunt Jenny's Catfish Restaurant,** located in a historic house at 1217 Washington Avenue, hits the spot. Famous for outstanding fried catfish, the restaurant also specializes in other country fare such as fried chicken, coleslaw, and the proverbial hush puppies. It is open Tuesday through Saturday from 5:00 P.M. until 9:00 P.M. and on Sunday from 11:30 A.M. until 8:00 P.M. The telephone number is (228) 875-9201.

Anthony's Under the Oaks (right next door) is owned and operated by the folks at Aunt Jenny's and offers fine food and delightful waterfront dining. Every table in the house overlooks the gorgeous view of Fort Bayou. (There are beautiful sunsets over the water here

in the summertime!) And there is even a gracious, oh-so-Southern wraparound porch so you can sit and rock a spell after all the indulgence. For those arriving by water, there is a place to dock a boat and walk right up to the restaurant. (Information on Aunt Jenny's and Anthony's courtesy of Sallye Irvine, *Food and Wine* writer.) This restaurant is open Monday through Saturday from 11:30 A.M. until 1:30 P.M. for lunch and from 5:30 P.M. until 9:00 P.M. for dinner. Sunday brunch is served from 11:30 A.M. until 2:00 P.M. The telephone number is (228) 872-4564.

The **Gayle Clark Gallery** is located in the historic L & N Depot. This neat gallery opened in 1981 and has grown to be one of the finest in the Southeast. Ms. Clark's works include a sophisticated line of sterling jewelry in bold shapes, small bronze sculptural pieces, and some sterling flatware. In pewter, she creates decorative bowls, plates, and giftware as well as her annual Christmas ornament.

Gayle Clark has been a resident of Ocean Springs for 30 years and her work reflects the rich coastal landscape she calls home. The gallery is open from 9:30 A.M. to 5:00 P.M., Monday through Saturday. The telephone number is (228) 875-3900.

If you brought your bike, you're in luck. The **Live Oaks Bicycle Route** extends 15.5 miles along the streets of Ocean Springs. It begins at the Train Depot, where you can get a map, leads to Davis Bayou, and returns to the Depot. You'll see the Historic District, Fort Maurepas, Shearwater Pottery, two beaches, and part of the Gulf Islands National Park and Seashore. There are excellent opportunities for picnicking, bird watching, and fishing, so come prepared!

Next door to the historic L & N Train Depot is **Centennial Square,** with several interesting shops such as the **Local Color Gallery,** which has Walter Anderson Calendar Prints—one for each day of the year. These prints are for sale, framed or unframed, and, according to owner Larry Cosper, can be wrapped and shipped to your desired destination. What a great birthday gift! It is open from 10:00 A.M. until 5:00 P.M., Monday through Saturday. **Local Color Gallery, Too** has works of regional artists.

Miners Toys, at 927 Washington Avenue, is much more than an excellent toystore; it is a place where the owners have grown and been involved with the Ocean Springs community for more than 10 years.

Miners has great collections of things, especially the beautiful dolls: the large and small Madame Alexander, the French Corolle that smells like vanilla, the German Gotz dolls, and the American Designer dolls by Lee Middleton. All come with clothes and doll furniture to collect. Miners also carries the Breyers Horses with the barns and equipment from bales of hay to buckets of apples.

Ron Wall is becoming well known for his hand-painted pewter pieces of miniature Civil War soldiers and all the paraphernalia that goes with them. Although expensive, this collection can be a lifelong hobby for boys aged eight to eighty. Besides the educational toys and games of all kinds, Miners has little, inexpensive treasures to be given to someone who has been extra good.

Everything in the store is quality and up-to-date—and you don't have to be a child to enjoy it. It is open from 9:30 A.M. to 5:30 P.M., Monday through Friday, and from 9:00 A.M. to 3:00 P.M. on Saturday. The telephone number is (228) 875-8697.

An interesting landmark in Ocean Springs is **Lovelace Pharmacy,** built in 1926. The soda fountain and shelves of penny candy have long since gone, but after so many years, it still operates as a pharmacy with some of the original fixtures intact.

Prompt, courteous service is the order of the day and you will have a good feeling knowing this old building is still used for its original purpose. Lovelace Pharmacy is located at 801 Washington Avenue and is open from 8:00 A.M. to 7:00 P.M., except Saturday, when closing time is 6:00 P.M., and Sunday, when closing time is 1:00 P.M. The telephone number is (228) 875-4272.

"I'm just a baby bookseller!" says happy owner Marilyn Lunceford of her second career in a newly opened bookstore. In a charming old pink-and-white house at 1209 Government Street (just two short blocks east of Washington Avenue), you will find **Favorites: Books,**

Art, Etc. "The house was really dilapidated when I saw it," Marilyn recalls. "I took a big, bold, courageous step and fixed it up." She has done a superb restoration job. The first thing you will notice upon entering through the antique door is an anteroom with a comfy wicker settee, white lace curtains, and a fabulous piece of circa-1930s linoleum on the floor.

In one room (with a marvelous stenciled floor) is pottery for sale by Jim Francis of Mississippi Mudworks. In the dining room is a long table for reading or writing and the kitchen is full of cookbooks. Propped on shelves above the books are paintings by local artists, all for sale.

This is a cheery, happy place and it is obvious that a second career is pleasurable to Marilyn, a retired air force nurse. "I knew I was on the right track when, during the week I made my decision to make the purchase, my horoscope read, 'You are going to be the author of a new career!'" Favorites: Books, Art, Etc. is open Monday through Friday from 10:00 A.M. until 6:00 P.M. (5:00 P.M. on Saturday). The telephone number is (228) 875-0082.

The hottest new spot in Ocean Springs is the **Bayview Gourmet,** a cheerful café directly across the street from Favorites.

Breakfast at Bayview is like being in someone's sunny kitchen. Take time to sample the breakfast menu, which consists of fresh eggs, any style, and, if you would like, omelets (try the Bienville Avenue with crabmeat and Bay Shrimp topped with cheese and hollandaise sauce). All of the favorites are here: Belgiun waffles, French toast, buttermilk pancakes, grits, and large muffins. The difference is the way it is done. Bayview's coffees are the specialty, with espresso, cappuccino, café latté and café mocha. French-press coffees are prepared at your table using Arabica beans.

The same excellent quality in food continues into the lunch menu with delicious soups, garden and pasta salads, and gourmet sandwiches using fresh-baked foccacia and bruschetta bread. The Bayview Gourmet is open from 7:00 A.M. to 7:00 P.M., seven days a week. Even though this place is a local favorite, the traveler would do well to make a stop at this very special spot. The telephone number is (228) 875-4252.

Martha Reichard has opened a pleasant place for lunch. Located in the heart of town at 715 Washington Avenue, **Martha's Tea Room** offers lunch six days a week—Monday through Friday, from 10:00 A.M. until 2:00 P.M., and Saturday from 11:00 A.M. until 3:00 P.M. She has carryout or will cater your private party.

There is a good offering of sandwiches, salads, and quiche, as well as a delicious steamed veggie plate served with brown rice. The soup of the day is accompanied by homemade bread, which you can also buy by the loaf. It is nice to eat by the window and watch as the world goes by on the sidewalk. The telephone number is (228) 872-2554.

The **Salvetti Brothers** have come to Ocean Springs and planted themselves in the middle of town in the old Ben Franklin five-and-ten-cent store. Just look for the Italian flag that flies outside the restaurant.

The brothers, Michael and Patrick, have worked in New York and California; now, with Randy Emboulas, a well-known New Orleans chef, they are giving the community of Ocean Springs a fine ristorante Italiano.

Fettucini Alfredo, Fettucini Carbonara, and Cheese Tortellini are but a few of the wide range of Italian dishes offered on the menu. The spaghetti meat sauce is a delectable combination of meat and tomatoes with fresh herbs and other ingredients, all simmered for many hours, which results in a smooth sauce that is light and sweet to taste—bellisimo!

All kinds of Italian background music can be heard, from Pavoratti to Dean Martin. You will also dine on red tablecloths with grape vines strung above your head. Salvetti Brothers Ristorante Italiano is open for lunch and dinner, seven days a week. The telephone number is (228) 875-0120.

The best collection of Glen Miller drawings is at Salvetti Brothers. This New Orleans artist has sketched the historic buildings of Ocean Springs—catching the personality of each one with great flair and imagination. The drawings can be purchased almost anywhere in the city and are reasonably priced.

After lunch at one of the restaurants in Ocean Springs, **Candy Cottage** might be your next stop. Usually pralines are being made in the window and, in addition to the classic Pecan Praline, there is Bourbon, Coconut, Chocolate Mint, and a new Oatmeal Praline that is deliciously different.

The pecan logs sold at the Candy Cottage were originally the recipe of the owner's great-grandparents, Mr. and Mrs. Andrew N. Foote. The pecan logs are solid, with whole pecans and caramel throughout—they have no fillers of nougat or marshmallows. Chocoholics will drool over fudge and chocolates of every kind. The shop will ship anywhere and has great gift baskets. It is located at 702 Washington and is open from 10:00 A.M. until 5:00 P.M., Monday through Saturday. The telephone number is (228) 875-8268.

A dowager at an art exhibit once gushed to Andy Warhol, "Don't you just love art?" Warhol's reply—"Art who?"—so captured the imagination of Sharon and Trailer McQuilkin that they named their art gallery in honor of the remark. **Art Who?** (623 Washington Avenue) is located in a turn-of-the-century building that was once home of the *Ocean Springs News.* Sharon, a former model and interior designer, and Trailer, a sculptor, represent more than 150 Southern artists.

The gallery also showcases a piece or two of Trailer's work—botanically accurate wild flower sculptures done in copper. These exquisite pieces are so delicate that it is hard to believe they have been fashioned from sheet copper and assembled with a butane torch so that "no joints will show." This unbelievable work has been displayed in an Easter window at Tiffany's in New York. Trailer has recently been commissioned to do rare and endangered wild flowers, which will be a six-year project for Calloway Gardens in Georgia.

Sharon has recently taken part of the gallery and added two rooms for a bed and breakfast. She has ingeniously decorated these two bedrooms with great art and furnishings from local businesses. Each room is a showplace and everything is for sale.

The rooms have all the amenities: full baths, wet bar, refrigerator, television, ample closets with ice machine, washer, and dryer down to the walk outside with private parking in the back. A walk across the street to Le Croissant will get you a free continental breakfast of fresh croissants and coffee in the morning. Art Who? is a delightful place to stay if you want privacy and some quiet time at prices that are moderate.

Gallery hours are from 10:00 A.M. to 5:00 P.M., Monday through Saturday. For information concerning reservations, you may call (228) 875-3251.

Once again in the cottage at 612 Washington Avenue, you can smell the wonderful aroma of bakery goods as you walk by. From 1909 to 1950, this little house was a bakery and now the Fraisse family have come from France to open **Le Croissant French Bakery**—lucky Ocean Springs.

The croissants are their specialty, large or small, with chocolate or fruit filled and as a sandwich—they are perfection. The Fraisses also bake brioche, muffins, cinnamon rolls, and loaves of French bread daily. A small lunch is served, consisting of the soup du jour with sandwich or salad.

On Saturday, the bakery becomes a family affair with the four children working in front while M. Fraisse bakes in the back. It is located at 612 Washington Avenue. The bakery is open from 7:30 A.M. to 4:00 P.M., Tuesday through Friday, and from 9:00 A.M. to 4:00 P.M. on Saturday. Also open on Sunday morning. The telephone number is (228) 872-4366.

On the corner of Washington and Porter is **Five Seasons Whole Foods Market,** a bright, airy health food store that means business and is not just a place to pop in for vitamins. Jan Walker, owner, knows her stuff and has been in the business for more than 20 years. She opened Five Seasons in 1991 and, even though she does not advertise, her business is flourishing.

Five Seasons has at least 10 different types of rice (which you may buy in bulk), macrobiotic specialties, homeopathic remedies, body care products, and natural vitamins and minerals. Jan has an exceptional assortment of books on diet, health, and natural life-styles. Most importantly, a naturopathic doctor and a certified nutritional counselor are always at the store to help guide you to better health. Five Seasons is open from 9:30 A.M. to 5:30 P.M., Monday through Saturday. The telephone number is (228) 875-8882.

Nestled under an ancient spreading oak, **Oak Shade Bed and Breakfast** is located near the water and within walking distance of the best of old Ocean Springs. One block off scenic Washington Avenue at 1017 La Fontaine, the residence was once the home of the Ocean Springs harbor master. Bicycles are available and children are welcome. It is open year-round. Phone (228) 872-8109 and ask for Chris or Marian.

The main thoroughfare of Ocean Springs, Washington Avenue, is an interesting street, but the jewel of the avenue is the **Walter Ander-**

son Museum. Completed in 1991, the museum was built to celebrate the works of Walter Anderson, a renowned local artist acclaimed by some to be the South's greatest.

The museum houses many pieces of art, of which the most important are said to be the murals. However, the Walter Anderson paintings of "The Little Room" (which was not discovered until after his death in 1965) and "The Community Center Room" are absolutely fascinating. You can spend hours studying the fantastic, vividly colored wildlife decorating these walls. Changing exhibits complement the permanent work of this interesting, mystical artist who spent the last 18 years of his life painting on isolated Horn Island, 10 miles off the Mississippi coast. On several occasions, Walter strapped himself to an island tree during violent weather in order to experience the fury of the storms, which is evident in some of his works. He revered the flora and the fauna of the area and immortalized them in his unique style.

The Walter Anderson Museum is open seven days a week: from 10:00 A.M. until 5:00 P.M., Monday through Saturday, and from 1:00 P.M. until 5:00 P.M. on Sunday. Admission is $4.00 for adults and $1.50 for children (no charge for children under six years old). The telephone number is (228) 872-3164.

At the end of Washington Avenue, on the beach, is a replica of the 1699 **Fort Maurepas,** which was the first European colony in the Mississippi River Valley region. From this fort, Alabama, Mississippi, and Louisiana were eventually colonized. This replica was built using copies of the original plans found in the French archives. Twice yearly, the fort hosts re-enactments of French Colonial history. Guided tours may also be arranged. Contact the Fort Maurepas Society at P.O. Box 1741, Ocean Springs, Mississippi 39566; or the Ocean Springs Chamber of Commerce.

Shearwater Pottery was established in 1928 by the late Peter Anderson, who was joined in his venture the next year by his two younger brothers, James and Walter (*see* Walter Anderson Museum of Art). The pottery is located on 24 acres of beautifully wooded land facing the Mississippi Sound. The land was purchased in 1918 by Peter's mother, who called the place Fairhaven and, on occasion, used it as a small art colony where people came to pursue their creative inter-ests and to relax in the tranquil atmosphere.

Peter's four children are presently a part of Shearwater Pottery. James, the youngest son and present potter, began working with his father in 1966 and has obviously inherited his father's eye for beauty in shape and glaze. He uses two types of clay for his pieces—Missis-sippi clay from the Lucedale area and white ball clay from Kentucky for his glazed work.

The pottery shop is located at 102 Shearwater Drive. The show-room is open from 9:00 A.M. to 5:30 P.M., Monday through Saturday, and 1:00 P.M. to 5:30 P.M. on Sunday. The workshop is open from 9:00 A.M. to 12:00 noon and from 1:00 P.M. to 4:00 P.M., Monday through Friday. The telephone number is (228) 875-7320 and tour groups can be arranged.

In Ocean Springs is the **Davis Bayou Campground,** a part of the Gulf Islands National Park and Seashore. The campground consists of more than 400 acres of wetlands and marsh leading to an addi-tional 70,000 acres of seashore existing in and around the Barrier Islands, which are accessible only by boat. In the visitors center you will find programs and exhibits on park resources, which include trails, camping, islands, beaches, and marsh tours.

There are several nature trails in the park where you can observe alligators, fish, raccoons, and a wide variety of birds. Excellent camp-sites are available with hook-ups and a bathhouse is centrally located in the campground. A fishing pier and a boat launch overlook Davis Bayou channel and there is a huge, shaded picnic area with five large pavilions, a softball field, playground, and restrooms.

The Visitor Center is the best place to start your visit. Inside is a fascinating display about the importance of the islands and wetlands that the park is dedicated to protecting. The display features water-color reproductions of prolific local artist Walter Anderson; these reproductions represent his "notes" of Horn Island, 10 miles out into the Mississippi Sound. The artist would row out in his open skiff and spend days painting, often using his upturned boat as shelter.

Displayed among Anderson's work are the faithful wood carvings of carpenter-turned-artist, John Seageren. These accurate and beau-tiful carvings are done from basswood and represent the variety of wildlife on the Barrier Islands. A 13-minute video presentation, "Tides, Winds and Waves" is available for your viewing.

The park is open from sunrise to sunset; after sunset the park is open only to registered campers. The Visitor Center is open from 8:00 A.M. to 4:30 P.M. in the fall and winter and from 9:00 A.M. to 5:30 P.M. during the spring and summer. For large groups, permits, or information, call (228) 875-9057 or (228) 875-0821. The Visitor Center is located at 3500 Park Road.

Biloxi

Biloxi, Mississippi, was one of the first permanent white settlements in the Mississippi Valley. Founded in 1717, the name comes from a Sioux Indian word for "first people." Biloxi was the capital of French territory and has been under eight flags. Since the 1870s, Biloxi has been a leading oyster and shrimp fishing headquarters.

On your arrival in Biloxi, at Point Cadet, is the **Maritime and Seafood Industry Museum,** located just west of the bridge. You will find the museum in a circa-1933 Coast Guard station within Point Cadet Plaza. This museum, opened in 1986, contains exhibits and artifacts that relate the story of the seafood industry along the Mississippi Gulf Coast.

The Kiwanis Club of Biloxi has erected a fascinating hurricane exhibit with many photos and a 20-minute film. Museum curator Val Hulsey notes that the museum sponsors a Sea and Sail Adventure Day Camp for children, ages six to 13. It is open from 9:00 A.M. to 5:00 P.M., Monday through Saturday, and from 12:00 noon to 4:00 P.M. on Sunday. For more information, write to P.O. Box 1907, Biloxi, Mississippi 39533; or call (228) 435-6320.

Almost directly across the street is the **J. L. Scott Marine Education Center and Aquarium.** Here are live exhibits, films, and displays for the entire family. Forty-eight aquariums showcase a multitude of native fish and other creatures.

Part of the University of Southern Mississippi Institute of Marine Sciences, the Aquarium's centerpiece is a 42,000-gallon Gulf of Mexico tank—home to sharks, sea turtles, and other large residents. Another exhibit contains a partial skeleton of a whale beached on Ship Island.

Located at 115 Beach Boulevard, the Aquarium is open from 9:00 A.M. to 4:00 P.M., Monday through Saturday, with a nominal admission fee. For information about seminars, field trips, and day camps, call (228) 374-5550.

As you enter the beginning of a 26-mile coastal drive, you will immediately see a melange of businesses, boats, and magnificent old homes (many were built as summer homes for inhabitants of New Orleans). For a thorough look at this road and all it has to offer, you might want to see it from a trolley tour. The **Beachcomber Streetcar Line** operates seven days a week, from 9:30 A.M. until 10:30 P.M.

The trolley travels the entire length of the Mississippi Gulf Coast— from Bay St. Louis to Biloxi. You can buy a one-day pass and ride the trolley all day long. The Beachcomber Trolley runs every 40 minutes between Gulfport and Biloxi and every 80 minutes from Gulfport to Pass Christian and from Pass Christian to Bay St. Louis. Trolley stops are marked with signs. For further information, call (228) 896-8080.

If you would like to know about Mardi Gras on the Mississippi Coast, you can visit the office of the **Gulf Coast Carnival Association.** It is located on the second story of the old Magnolia Hotel on Rue Magnolia Street. The full-time secretary helps to coordinate the events during Mardi Gras as well as provide

(continued)

information to the public. The office is open 12 months of the year and the telephone number is (228) 432-8806. Festivities begin in December and every city along the coast has a parade. For further information about Mardi Gras, you may want to pick up the book *Coasting Through Mardi Gras: A Guide to Carnival Along the Gulf Coast.*

Before you really get started, though, take a minute to become aware of the **Great Seawall.** This 25-mile concrete seawall stretches between U.S. 90 and the sand beach and was completed in 1928. An idea of Hobart Shaw, a Gulfport city engineer, the seawall was constructed for shore protection and considerably increased the value of beachfront property. The construction also set the stage for the 1951 development of the Mississippi Gulf Coast's 26 miles of man-made sand beach.

You might want to tour the **Biloxi Lighthouse,** a 65-foot cast-iron structure built in 1848. For tour appointments, call (228) 435-6293. You might also want to stop by the Chamber of Commerce to pick up a map of the Mississippi Beach Historic Homes Driving Tour.

Although you won't be able to see it in action, a very important component of the 403rd Wing of the Air Force is stationed in Biloxi at Keesler Air Force Base. The 53rd Weather Reconnaissance Squadron is a one-of-a-kind organization; it is the only unit in the world flying weather reconnaissance on a routine basis. The mission of the 53rd Weather Reconnaissance Squadron ("Hurricane Hunters") is to recruit and train personnel to provide surveillance of

tropical storms and hurricanes in the Atlantic, Caribbean, Gulf of Mexico, and the Central Pacific for the National Hurricane Center.

In 1943, Maj. Joe Duckworth twice flew a propeller-driven, single-engine North American AT-6 "Texan" trainer into the eye of a tropical storm, once with a navigator and again with a weather officer. These pioneering efforts paved the way for further flights into tropical cyclones. The 53rd WRS was activated in 1944 and since that time has called many airfields home. The squadron came to its location at Keesler in 1973.

The 53rd WRS is authorized 20 aircrews, each with six positions. To perform their missions, the Hurricane Hunters have 10 WC-130 aircraft; these aircraft penetrate the eye of the storms at different altitudes, depending on the severity of the storms, and are capable of staying aloft nearly 18 hours. An average mission might last 11 hours and cover almost 3,500 miles. During this time the flight meteorologist collects and reports weather data every minute. This vital information is relayed by satellite to the National Hurricane Center in Miami. (Information courtesy of Public Affairs Office of the 403rd Wing, Kessler Air Force Base, Mississippi.)

If you would like more information about the 53rd WRS, check out their web site at www.hurricanehunters.com.

Rev. Abram J. Ryan (Father Ryan), poet laureate of the Confederacy and pastor of St. Mary's Catholic Church in Mobile from 1833 to 1877, rejoiced in this beautiful house where he lived for 14 years. Although not as tranquil as it was when it was built in 1841, the **Father Ryan House** bed and breakfast (located four blocks west of the Biloxi Lighthouse at 1196 Beach Boulevard) is still elegant and romantic.

Nine rooms on three floors all have private baths; several have private porches overlooking the Gulf. Others have views of the garden and brick courtyard in the back and two recently added suites are in an adjacent building. Full breakfasts are served in the Lemon Room, a peaceful place overlooking the courtyard. A small but pretty swimming pool is also in the back, concealed by a screen of fragrant Confederate jasmine. Off-street shaded parking is available.

You can't miss the beautiful 100-plus-year-old palm tree that is growing up out of the front steps. The story is that it sprang up after Father Ryan took final leave of the house. The telephone number is (800) 295-1189 or (228) 435-1189.

> Just a hundred feet away Seaward, flows and ebbs the tide and the wavelets, blue and grey moan, and white sails windward glide o'er the ever restless sea.
>
> —Father Abram Ryan
> From "Sea Rest," 1872

A centerpiece of the Mississippi Gulf Coast's historical sites is **Beauvoir,** the home where Confederacy president Jefferson Davis spent the last 12 years of his life. Davis lived, worked, and entertained notables of his day at this beautiful residence, which was built in 1854. Today, landscaped grounds covering 54 acres contain houses, pavilions, a Confederate cemetery, and a museum that chronicles the Confederate experience and highlights the life-style of the South's "First Family." Beauvoir is open daily from 9:00 A.M. until 5:00 P.M. The telephone number is (228) 388-1313.

After all this touring, you may be ready to get away. At the **Point Cadet Marina,** you can board a re-created two-masted oyster schooner for a full- or half-day trip as well as for charter trips for special occasions. For more information, call (228) 435-6320.

The Barrier Islands

The Barrier Islands constitute much of the Gulf Islands National Park and Seashore's acreage. Composed of white sand carried seaward by rivers draining the Appalachian Mountains, these long, narrow islands serve as blockades to ocean waves and violent storms that would otherwise strike the mainland coast.

The islands are ever changing. Waves wear away the eastern ends and the islands are therefore shifting steadily westward. Further alter-

(Sketch courtesy Gulf Islands National Seashore)

ations are made by violent storms that overwash the islands and by winds that shift and sculpt the dunes. Such changes are constant.

The Barrier Islands in the Gulf Islands National Park and Seashore are West Ship Island, East Ship Island, Horn Island, and Petit Bois Island in Mississippi and Perdido Key and Santa Rosa Island in Florida. These islands provide visitors with wonderful spots to relax and reflect. While visiting, please take care of these vulnerable places.

Why not relax on **Ship Island** (Gulf Islands National Park and Seashore)? Here, 12 miles off of the coast, Congress has set aside some of the last undeveloped barrier islands for public enjoyment. In 1969 Hurricane Camille cut the delicate island in two, creating East Ship Island and West Ship Island. Nearly four miles long, this unspoiled stretch of land is home to a variety of plant and wildlife; and quiet expanses of beach invite you to swim, picnic, explore, or just relax. During the summer months, you can also have guided tours of **Fort Massachusetts,** one of the last masonry coastal fortifications built in the United States.

Reaching the island is an adventure. The boat trip will take you across the Mississippi Sound (used by European explorers who arrived on these shores in the early 1600s) and you might just pass schools of dolphins. Tickets for the ferry are sold on a first-come, first-served basis and are available one hour before departure from Gulfport Yacht Harbor, U.S. 90 at U.S. 49, (228) 864-1014.

Blessing of the Fleet

O, Lord God, graciously hear our prayer and let Your goodness and mercy bless these boats and all who sail on them. Grant them a good and fruitful voyage and a safe return to their families. Grant continued prosperity to our seafood industry on the Gulf of Mexico, in the name of the Father, and the Son, and of the Holy Spirit. Amen.

—From the Blessing of the Fleet Mass
Bishop Joseph Lawson Howze, D.D.
May 4, 1996

"The annual Blessing of the Fleet is a symbolic renewal of the faith required by those who continually entrust their lives to wiles of the sea. 'The first formal Blessing ceremony on the Coast was held in June 1929,' said Bishop Joseph L. Howze, Catholic bishop of Biloxi. To the

Coast residents then involved, it could hardly have come sooner; it was that year that the stock market crashed and sent the nation into the Great Depression. Through often-tested faith and hard work, this area has always seemed to have the spiritual stamina to pick up the pieces and keep going. In this modern age, the Blessing of the Fleet still serves as a reminder that our lives and fortunes are perpetually controlled by forces greater than ourselves." (Frank Blankenship, "Blessing of the Fleet," *Gumbo.* 4 (May 1997): 9. Used by permission)

There are literally dozens of good restaurants along this extraordinary stretch of beach. The following is a very small and varied sampling to get you started in Biloxi (traveling from west to east):

Keppner's Gasthaus German Restaurant, 1798 Beach Boulevard, has the best authentic German food. It offers a children's menu and is open Tuesday through Saturday. Call for hours at (228) 436-4878.

Believe it or not, there is a small "landlubbers' get away" too! Just north of all the gambling and beachside glitter is a small but beautiful park containing the **James Hill Bayou Walk and Fishing Pier.** Located at Switzer Road near Jeff Davis Junior College and covering several acres, this park contains a tennis court, playground equipment, and picnic tables along the bayou. There are also a pavilion and good parking. The fishing pier is open from 6:00 A.M. until 10:30 P.M.

The French Connection, 1891 Pass Road, serves a grilled, open-hearth cookery of seafood and beef in an intimate setting. Be sure to try the "house potato." It is open from 5:30 P.M. until 10:00 P.M., Monday through Saturday. Reservations are recommended. The telephone number is (228) 388-6367.

A tradition in this area for more than 25 years, the superb food and service at **Mary Mahoney's Old French House and Cafe,** 110 Rue Magnolia, have never wavered. Dishes are traditional but excellent. Tucked away from the hullabaloo of the gambling casinos just across the street, this circa-1737 house of handmade bricks is a cozy, charming piece of history.

In the shady courtyard with lush plantings underneath is a magnificent live oak tree. In the restaurant is a snug, brick-walled bar, private dining rooms with ancient plaster walls, and a beautiful glassed-in porch overlooking the walled courtyard.

Specialties include Stuffed Red Snapper, Eggplant Eileen (shrimp and crab), and Sisters of the Sea au Gratin. For lunch, try the superb Lump Crabmeat Salad. Don't dare pass up the bread pudding. This café is open from 11:00 A.M. to 9:30 P.M. on weekdays, but never on Sundays. The telephone number is (228) 374-0163.

A bookstore that deals in rare books is very rare indeed . . . **Spanish Trail Books** is one such rare bookstore. In the oldest commercial building in Biloxi (circa 1894), Pat and Mike Hunter, owners, handle 100,000 new, used, and rare editions with unrivaled expertise in book business.

Seldom will you find an independent, full-scale bookstore offering research, appraisals, collection development, and restoration of volumes you hold dear or would like to own. The Hunters have been in business since 1970, and after complete restoration of their building you may venture a guess they will be there for many more years. The address is 781 Vieux Marche. Check weekend hours, but weekdays they are open from 11 A.M. until 5 P.M. The telephone number is (228) 435-1144.

Gumbo Research Project

In the never-ending search to bring you the best in dining along the coast, the authors contacted two independent tasters to find the best gumbo. Excellent gumbo abounds along this stretch and the decision was not an easy one. For seafood gumbo: Boss Oyster in Apalachicola, Florida; Characters on Perdido Key, Florida; Good Time Diner in Mobile, Alabama; Miss Kitty's in Lillian, Alabama; and Trapani's in Bay St. Louis, Mississippi. Armands in Waveland, Mississippi, is noteworthy for their Duck and Andouille Sausage Gumbo.

Mississippi Gulf Coast Gambling

Not since Hurricane Camille in 1969 has anything hit the Mississippi Gulf Coast with such force as casino gambling.

Casinos are now playing to packed houses with matching hotels and more in the works. Overnight the casinos have sprung up, stretching from Biloxi to Bay St. Louis, with the beautiful, old historic homes looking quietly upon the spectacle before them. The contrast only adds more flavor to this Gulf Coast smorgasbord.

The Isle of Capri was the first casino to open and has a tropical atmosphere. Pink dolphins dancing in a fountain mark the entrance to the Capri's Crown Resort Hotel. If you come by boat, dockage is available at the Point Cadet Marina.

Next door to The Isle of Capri is **Casino Magic–Biloxi,** which is the "sister act" to the Casino Magic–Bay St. Louis. Twin towers with huge Palladian windows are the hallmark of Magic Biloxi and contemporary Aladdins come to see if the "magic" is going to be here.

First of the two Grand Casinos come next. The **Grand Casino–Biloxi** has as much flash as its counterpart in Gulfport, plus a theater with 2,500 seating capacity. Big names are booked the whole year and live bands play every night.

Lady Luck is next door to the Grand Casino–Biloxi. You would think it would be diminished by its giant neighbor, but many people prefer the smaller casinos over all the hoopla of the larger ones. Lady Luck has an Oriental theme with a fire-breathing dragon that moves in and out of its cave at the entrance of the casino. The inside is dark and sensual with a feeling of privacy.

Coming down the strip of U.S. 90, the next casino will be the **Mirage,** opening sometime in 1998. The Mirage will seal the fate of gambling on the Gulf Coast and assure even more growth.

Another jumbo-sized casino along the strip is **Treasure Bay.** The mast from the pirate ship can be seen for miles and at night the ship is bathed in a purple glow. Inside, the casino has glittering treasure chests and one-eyed pirates everywhere. Over the bar is another gigantic pirate ship suspended in mid-air with moving clouds above.

Next on the strip is the **President,** which is a local favorite, perhaps because it is located at the popular old Broadwater Beach Resort and Marina. The facade of the President has changed from a paddleboat motif to a presidential mansion with crystal chandeliers.

Copa Casino is an old ocean liner docked at 877 Copa Boulevard on the Gulf side. The road to the casino is about half a block from the big neon sign on U.S. 90. The ship is all white with employees dressed in white with shiny buttons. The low, twinkling ceilings and thick carpets make the Copa acoustically pleasant and you feel as if you are on a cruise.

Just past the Copa is the **Grand Casino–Gulfport,** a 13,000-ton floating casino. It is a high-tech structure with neon buzzing everywhere like lightning. Some say this casino is the swankiest along the strip and is a favorite of the Louisiana crowd.

After Gulfport, the next casino is **Casino Magic–Bay St. Louis.** The drive takes about 15 minutes along the highway with the beach on one side and beautiful homes on the other. This is the original Casino Magic. On this rambling 340 acres, the casino offers a 200-room hotel, nationally broadcast boxing matches and concerts, an 18-hole Arnold Palmer golf course and clinic, a 100-space RV park, and a camp for kids ages three months to 12 years.

Three casinos are not directly on the strip but are located on Biloxi's Back Bay and can be reached by turning off U.S. 90.

Palace Casino is just across from Isle of Capri. The outside of the Palace looks like it is made of mirrors with a big, pink dome on the roof.

Boomtown is on Back Bay and can be reached by turning off U.S. 90 to Bayview Avenue from Interstate 10. At Boomtown, everything is Western style, catering to the family more than most other casinos.

Imperial is a new, giant casino that opened in early 1998. You can easily spot this huge casino after coming off the Biloxi exit from Interstate 10.

The Mississippi Gaming Commission makes sure regulations concerning casinos are strictly monitored and background investigations on all employees are automatic. As one officer at the Commission said, "It is probably as well regulated an industry as there is."

All the casinos have the same scenario, wall-to-wall slots with gambling tables of blackjack, craps, roulette, baccarat, and poker, and all have very good restaurants. The difference lies in the presentation—viva là difference! Casino-hop until you find your favorite one.

Try not to be too philosophical about this giant industry and just remember three things when you visit: 1) it is pumping money into the economy; 2) all the glitz is designed to relive you of your money; and 3) never play "sucker bets" (whatever that means).

Gulfport

A planned city, Gulfport has broad streets laid in a pattern paralleling the seawall. This sparsely settled section of Mississippi was transformed when the railroad came to Gulfport in 1902. In the 1920s, Gulfport turned to the resort business and after World War II the luxury motels took over.

Gulfport is the county seat of Harrison County and a major world banana terminal. The Mississippi Gulf Coast, with Gulfport at its center, is best described as the year-round playground of the South. In spite of its recent growth, Gulfport still remains a fisherman's paradise.

Turn off U.S. 90 for only two blocks to the small Old Courtyard Corner and you will find the most wonderful gift gallery. **Sernac Galleries,** which is not your run-of-the-mill antique/gift shop, is owned by John (he's a photographer too) and Lisa Majure.

Now don't be put off by the sedate exterior. Inside, besides some of the loveliest-ever English antiques, are simply fabulous, affordable, and different accessories for your home or for a not-to-be-forgotten gift. Here are beautiful ceramic pieces, wonderfully priced cloisonné, stone fish objets d'art, hammered wind chimes, and on and on.

Lisa is adamant about keeping a wide variety of prices. "I have really worked hard to find distinctive gifts that are not expensive," she says. "I have some great-looking buys for under 10 dollars." She also has good-looking traditional pieces—leather boxes, lap desks, some fabulous magnifying glasses with antique silver and bone han-

dles, lamps, and mirrors. Don't miss this shop. It is located at 402-B Courthouse Road and is open Tuesday through Friday from 10:00 A.M. until 4:30 P.M. and on Saturday from 10:00 A.M. until 12:00 noon. The telephone number is (228) 896-2838.

The phrase "That's for the birds" takes on a whole new meaning when you step into **Lydia's Audubon Shoppe.** Located at 344-A Courthouse Road, this small shop has virtually everything you could possibly need or want for the care and feeding of wild birds.

Lydia Schultz has been in business since 1982, selling bird products—feeders, houses, bird baths, and bird food (she even has her own custom blend). Prior to 1982, she was just an interested bird watcher whose husband made copper bird feeders for her (they, too, are available in the shop).

Lydia also has an extensive selection of field guides and other bird books, wind chimes, binoculars, weather vanes, sparrow-proof bluebird boxes, and kits for making birdhouses. There is a small but excellent selection of Audubon prints and a children's corner with T-shirts to color and ant farms. Butterfly and hummingbird plants are available during the spring. Don't miss this!

Lydia's Audubon Shoppe is open from 10:00 A.M. until 5:30 P.M., Monday through Thursday, and from 10:00 A.M. until 5:00 P.M. on Friday and Saturday. The telephone number is (228) 497-BIRD.

For lunch, try **Lil' Ray's Po-Boys** (500-A Courthouse Road) for a family-style menu and delicious seafood, including boiled crabs, shrimp, and crawfish (when in season). Be sure to try the trout po' boys. Lil' Ray's Po-Boys is open Monday through Saturday, from 10:00 A.M. until 9:00 P.M. and has a children's menu. The telephone number is (228) 896-9601.

The Blow Fly Inn was started as a happenstance operation (originally named Hickory's Bar-B-Que) more than 40 years ago by Albert and Mary Malone.

As the story goes, Al's good friend, Mac (who had a restaurant in the vicinity), was constantly being asked, "Where is Al's place?" One day, after far too many inquiries, Mac gave in to his frustrations and replied, "Yeah, I'll tell you. Just follow the blow flies to the end of Washington Avenue and you will find it."

(continued)

> Before long, Hickory's Bar-B-Que was better known as the "Blow Fly Inn." For years, Al tried unsuccessfully to list his "Blow Fly" with the telephone company, but was told that the name was "inappropriate." Mr. Al has since passed on and Mrs. "Bert" has retired to her fishing camp. (Permission to print the history of the Blow Fly Inn was given by Joan Ferrara.)

Joan Ferrara purchased the **Blow Fly Inn** and added a new menu consisting of Southern cooking with lots of good fresh fish dishes. The house specials are worth a try, especially the Eggplant and Crab Beauvoir, veal, crabmeat, and asparagus with Creole hollandaise.

Besides the menu, nothing else has changed at Blow Fly Inn—even the friendly staff is the same and, of course, the big plastic flies appear on every plate.

The Blow Fly Inn is located at the end of Washington Avenue on Bayou Bernard and is shaded by 150-year-old oaks. Prices are moderate and hours are from 11:00 A.M. to 10:00 P.M. every day of the week. If you must, you may call (228) 896-9812, but accommodations are usually available without reservations. Nobody seems to know why the Blow Fly Inn is so named; it has never been an inn.

It looks like the Port of Gulfport just might become top banana! As you casino-hop into the Grand Casino in Gulfport, nearby you will see lots of fruit trucks parked along the waterfront. This is the **Banana Terminal,** which was built in 1962.

Dole, West Lake Village, and Chiquita brands have all imported significant amounts of bananas through Gulfport for more than 20 years. Now it seems that Mississippi's state port might settle for the title of Number-One Banana Port in the nation. With the 1997 addition of banana importer Turbana Corporation, Gulfport's banana volume could jump to more than 800,000 tons a year. That order will fill a lot of lunch boxes! (Information courtesy of Mississippi State Port Authority.)

Vrazel's, located at 3206 West Beach Boulevard, is fine dining on the beach. Vrazel's offers the finest French, Italian, and Cajun cuisine . . . the Eggplant LaRosa is superb. For dessert, try Cherries Jubilee or the bread pudding. Children's portions are available and reservations are accepted. It is open for lunch, Monday through

Friday, from 11:00 A.M. until 2:00 P.M. and for dinner, Monday through Saturday, from 5:00 P.M. until 10:00 P.M. The telephone number is (228) 863-2229.

Coast Books is yet another independent bookstore you will find dotting towns along the Gulf Coast road. Family-owned bookstores are getting as hard to find as hen's teeth and it is always a pleasure to find one. Of course finding Coast is especially nice because the **Espresso Cafe** is connected and you can always browse and eat your lunch to your heart's content.

No dark corners can be found at Coast Books, just big lighted spaces where everything is easy to find. A fun children's section with clever projects usually hang on the wall, and the "Trashy Beach Book" section is there for people who just want to grab a quick read. Coast Books has full services with emphasis on special orders. It is located at 2700 13th Street. The hours are Monday through Friday from 10 A.M. to 6 P.M. and Saturday from 9 A.M. to 5 P.M. The telephone number is (228) 822-0040.

If you are traveling along the beach road in the spring and summer, you will see several locations where portions of the beach have been roped "off limits" to human visitors. The Mississippi Coast Audubon Society has erected these ropes in order to welcome another kind of visitor—the least tern.

Thousands of these pale, little birds love to nest on the Mississippi beaches and the Audubon Society makes it possible. The Society has even erected signs that proclaim "Nest in Peace." Do stop and look, for it is very interesting. If you spot some larger, darker birds swooping among the "visitors," they are full-time resident black skimmers welcoming the tiny terns to the Gulf Coast.

Golf Courses

Good golf courses flourish on the Gulf Coast and the following is a list of some of them, courtesy of The Fairways Golf Company, Don Faggard, President.

The Mississippi Gulf Coast Area Golf Courses

The Bridges at Casino Magic. Designed by Arnold Palmer, this course offers a challenging round amid natural wetlands. Located next to the Casino Magic. Bay St. Louis—(228) 463-4047.

Edgewater Bay. Overlooking scenic Biloxi Back Bay. Gently rolling course, moderately wooded. Smallish greens make short games very important. Biloxi—(228) 388-9670.

Mississippi National. Formerly named Hickory Hill. Recently rated one of the 10 best courses in Mississippi. Rolling fairways lined with pines, oaks, and dogwoods. Gautier—(228) 497-2372.

Pine Island. Well-kept, beautiful setting, built on three islands. Plentiful wildlife. Designed by renowned architect Pete Dye. Ocean Springs—(228) 875-1674.

Treasure Bay Royal Gulf Hills. Dense trees line the bay side. Seventeenth hole ranked as one of the most challenging in the country. Ocean Springs—(228) 875-4211.

Windance. Designed by PGA player Mark McCumber. Host to Hogan and Nike events since 1990. Lightning-quick greens. Gulfport—(228) 832-4871.

Shoo-Fly

The dictionary defines *shoo-fly* as: 1) a child's rocker, 2) the name of a popular song, and 3) a pie. But in Coastal Mississippi, "shoo-fly" means something entirely different. Popular around the turn of the century, shoo-flies were built under and around the huge live oak trees along the coast. Constructed of wood and lattice, they were gathering places in the late afternoons when leisure time was an art. These structures were built up about four or five feet from the ground, so that one could escape the mosquitos near the ground, while catching the evening breezes.

Although there once were many shoo-flies in private yards, time, tides, and hurricanes have been responsible for their demise. There are only a few along the Gulf Coast today—one is on private property, another is on a small piece of public property in downtown Biloxi, and one is on the grounds of the old City Hall in Bay St. Louis.

Sadly, none of these shoo-flies are old, but happily, two have been reconstructed to help us envision how, in times past, the ladies (wearing their shoo-fly dresses) would meet their friends underneath a shady tree at dusk for polite conversation. (Information courtesy Charles Gray, Hancock County Historical Society.)

Long Beach

The history of Long Beach is a colorful part of the stories and history of the entire Louisiana territory. Historical legend traces the origin of Long Beach back 250 years to the time when it was an Indian village, a trading post, and happy hunting grounds for several Indian tribes that roamed the forests and fished in the Gulf.

Long Beach was also the reputed hideout of a vicious pirate named "Pitcher," and the treasure he hid from his men has yet to be found. Long Beach, the city, was created by farmers. The town was known nationally as a trucking center for radishes, carrots, beans, and other produce shipped daily to markets around the country.

Don't miss seeing the coast's most famous tree, **Friendship Oak,** which is located on the grounds of the Gulf Park Campus of the University of Southern Mississippi. This magnificent live oak is 500-plus years old—just think, it was alive when Christopher Columbus sailed into the Caribbean! The tree has a 50-foot height, the circumference of its trunk is 17 feet, and it forms almost 16,000 square feet of shelter.

A perfect choice for casual dining is **Beachside Pizza,** 300 East Beach Boulevard. Beachside Pizza has some terrific pizza with unusual topping choices. It also offers lasagna, spaghetti, and Italian sandwiches. It is open at 11:00 A.M., Monday through Saturday, and at 11:30 A.M. on Sunday. The telephone number is (228) 868-9997.

While in Long Beach, you should visit two especially attractive restaurants: **Chappy's** and **Chimney's.** Chappy's, located at 624 Beach Boulevard, serves a variety of dishes, including seafood and fresh game. Noteworthy are its made-from-scratch desserts and its comfy, homey cocktail lounge with leather sofas. Chappy's is open seven days a week for lunch and dinner, including champagne brunch on Saturday and Sunday. Reservations are accepted for parties of six or more and there is also a children's menu. The telephone number is (228) 865-9755.

High up on stilts at the Long Beach Harbor is Chimney's—where you can dine on fresh seafood and steak on the deck overlooking the water or in the cozy dining room with a marvelous beach view. There is a nice but small bar and the whole restaurant has a good feel. Try the Trout Bon Vivant or the Oysters Chimney's. Chimney's is open seven days a week for lunch and dinner and accepts reservations. The telephone number is (228) 868-7020.

Pass Christian

Pass Christian has been charming visitors to the Gulf Coast since the 1800s. Early Indian groups lived in the area, but the city's dominant influence has been from the French. Pass Christian (pronounced "Christienne," with the accent on the last syllable) was named for Nicholas Christian, a carpenter from New Orleans, who settled on Cat Island in 1745. One of two deep-water channels, or passes, through oyster reefs to shore became known as the "Pass of Christianne."

Today, the "Pass," as it is known to Coastians, is a town rich in culture and that boasts many gracious homes along its waterfront. The city's colorful harbor and stately oaks add to the charm of the Pass. (Information obtained from an article in *Destination: Mississippi Beach 1993*, page 19. Original author is Mildred Klyce, editor of the Southern Poetry Association.)

As one beach town blends into another, you can become absorbed in the splendor of the beautiful mansions overlooking the tranquil, sandy beaches. But don't overlook the lovely, quiet city of Pass Christian. There is an interesting historic section right along the beach road on West Beach Boulevard.

Take time to look at the **Pass Christian Harbor** while you are here. It is one of the oldest and most picturesque marinas on the entire coast. There is a boat ramp and under development is a recreation area and playground; public fishing is also permitted. If it looks like a lot of boats are docked here, you are right. The harbor consists of seven piers, four for pleasure boats and three for commercial boats. There are 468 slips and a skiff pier is planned. Walk down and take a look around. You'll be glad you did.

Across the street from the Pass Christian Harbor, at 126 West Scenic Drive, you will find **The Harbor Oaks Inn,** which has been in existence since the 1840s. According to owner Tony Brugger, many European visitors have signed the guest register. For more information about this antebellum inn, call (228) 452-9399.

Housed in another giant mansion a few steps away from The Harbor Oaks Inn, you will find **Letty's Food and Spirits at the Blue Rose** in a 10,000-plus-square-foot mansion that also houses **Blue Rose Antiques.** After you browse through the shop, Letty's is conveniently waiting to whet your appetite with the likes of seafood, specialty pasta dishes, and sandwiches or you might prefer "English Tea," which is served Tuesday through Saturday (tea reservation 24 hours in advance, please). The restaurant is open from 11:00 A.M. until 3:00 P.M., Tuesday through Saturday, and from 5:30 P.M. until 10:00 P.M., Friday, Saturday, and Sunday. A Champagne brunch is served on Sunday, from 11:00 A.M. until 3:00 P.M. The telephone number is (228) 452-0335.

Oyster Reefs

This area's productive oyster beds have historically been documented on maps since D'Iberville and Bienville chartered these waters in 1699.

The early French explorers to the area called the water passage in the Sound "Passe aux Huitres." Translation for the offshore pass was suitably named the "Oyster Pass." For hundreds of years the numerous oyster reefs have afforded a source of supply to the coastal region.

Today there are nine principal reefs comprising an area of about twenty square miles. This group of reefs are the most important in the state, both in production and acreage. During the oyster seasons, as many as 150 fishing boats and tonging skiffs can be seen just off shore. (Dan Ellis, *Pass Christian—Tricentennial* [Pass Christian: Ellis Enterprises, 1997], 7-8. Permission to reprint granted.)

Oyster harvesting takes place almost year-round. Oysters in shallow waters are picked up with tongs that open and close somewhat like scissors. Oysters in deeper waters are brought up by dredges. Most oysters are sold unshelled and highly skilled oyster shuckers are in great demand. (Dan Ellis, *Pass Christian—Tricentennial* [Pass Christian: Ellis Enterprises, 1997], 7-8. Permission to reprint granted.)

If you're in the mood for some more shopping, walk over to **Valentino's Fine Gifts** across from the yacht harbor. "The Colonial Revival brick structure is adorned by a gable roof and a beautiful inset gallery. This picturesque dwelling, which duplicates the preserved and famous Tullis Toledano house in Biloxi, complements the manors and cottages of Scenic Drive." (Dan Ellis, *Pass Christian—Tricentennial* [Pass Christian: Ellis Enterprises, 1997], 61-62)

Proprietor Edward Valentine Jurkowski has filled his shop with unique and affordable gifts for all occasions. He also has a large selection of decorating accessories for the home. Valentino's is located at 116 West Scenic Drive. It is open Monday through Saturday from 10:00 A.M. to 5:30 P.M. and Sunday from 12:00 noon to 5:00 P.M.

On the corner of Scenic and Market is **Morning Market,** a sunny place filled with organically grown fruits and vegetables. Janet Gordon, owner, grows some of the produce herself and some is shipped from organic farms in California. In the back are vats of rice, beans, and lentils, which you can buy in bulk. She also carries all kinds of juices and homemade jellies, jams, and breads.

Morning Market stocks natural beef and quail, as well as fresh fish of the area. If you like everything in your life to be natural, you may want to purchase the toilet paper. The Market is open from 10:00 A.M. to 6:00 P.M., Monday through Saturday. The telephone number is (228) 452-7593.

The **Inn at the Pass** overlooks one of the oldest yachting harbors in the South. The inn, built in 1879, is on the National Register of Historic Places and is furnished with period antiques. There are three rooms in the main house (two on the first floor) and a cottage on the grounds. Each morning you'll be treated to a gourmet, family-style breakfast.

Vivacious owner Brenda Harrison will direct you to beaches, shops, and restaurants—all within walking distance. Within a short drive are casinos, the Stennis Space Center, and an oceanarium.

The inn is also available for small weddings, receptions, and other events. It is located at 125 East Scenic Drive and the telephone number is (800) 217-2588 or (228) 452-0333.

On your way up Scenic Drive, do stop and look over the wonderful white iron fence at the Union Quarters house. Not open to the public, but well worth gazing at, this beautiful old antebellum home was used as quarters for the Union officers during the occupation of the city in 1862.

Continue up Scenic Drive (about a block) to a "must-see" shop called **The Hillyer House,** which represents 175 American artists who create jewelry, pottery, and handblown glass (demonstrations on Saturdays).

Est. 1970

In business for more than 20 years, Katherine Reed and her daughter Paige have a stunning collection in their circa-1930 building. Unbelievably, every 30 to 60 days the artists send new collections. You can browse through jewelry (look for a "gumbo necklace"), pottery (casseroles and wind chimes), and some really exciting watercolors. Look also for the Walter Anderson designs in stained glass (*see* Walter Anderson Museum).

Paige and Katherine will offer you lemonade or coffee and then leave you alone to wander. Please note their displays about the artists— a short biography and picture of each one, which is a nice touch.

The Hillyer House is open Monday through Saturday from 10:00 A.M. until 5:00 P.M. and on Sunday from 12:00 noon until 5:00 P.M. It is located at 207 East Scenic. The telephone number is (228) 452-4810.

The Legend of Spanish Moss

Legend has it that Spanish moss came from the times when, according to custom, an Indian princess cut her long hair on her wedding day and draped it from a gigantic oak tree. Unhappily, the bride and her new husband were killed on their wedding day and buried beneath the oak tree. Her hair, hanging from the branches, turned gray and began to grow and spread, and spread, and spread.

Fact has it that Spanish moss is actually an air plant and, contrary to popular belief, does not kill the trees. Believe it or not, Spanish moss is kin to the pineapple family (probably a distant cousin).

Going east on Scenic Drive, you will come to Davis Street; take a right onto Davis and you will find a string of smart shops called **Regatta Row.** All of the owners are originally from New Orleans.

Great's is a clothing shop for women with a good line of attractive casuals and accessories. Almost all of the clothes are made of cotton and linen, under the labels of Eileen Fisher, Joan Voss, Kathleen Sommers, and PA of Boston. The shoes cover a wide price range, from Cole Haan to Saga clogs. Great's also has a good stock of sterling silver jewelry. It is open from 10:00 A.M. to 5:00 P.M., Monday through Saturday. The telephone number is (228) 452-0680.

Jackie's has a combination of children's fancy clothes and gifts. The children's clothes include casual as well as handmade and smocked dresses for important occasions. Jackie's gift selection includes linens, silver and pewter trays. and crystal—all of which can be monogrammed. It is open from 10:00 A.M. to 5:00 P.M., Monday through Saturday. The telephone number is (228) 452-4304.

Parker's, Inc., is "fine and fun jewelry," says owner Mimi Parker. She showcases the work of artists from all over the country, including David Yurman's cable jewelry. Mimi has been interested in jewelry since she was four years old. Her grandmother gave her a jewelry kit for Christmas, she progressed to stringing Mardi Gras beads, and the rest is history.

In addition, Mimi has some of the best faux jewelry along the Gulf Coast as well as handmade glass Christmas ornaments from Poland and Czechoslovakia, mirrors, and silver baby things. Her collection of Limoges boxes is extensive and her imported accessories are just right for a spot in your home. Parker's, Inc., is open from 10:00 A.M. to 5:00 P.M., except Sunday and Monday. The telephone number is (228) 452-7979.

Next door to Parker's is **The Stitch Niche,** a full-service needlepoint store. Vivacious owner Jeanne Hines is very knowledgeable and can help you with any project. She has a huge selection of hand-painted canvasses and a full array of colors in Paternayan, Appleton, and Medici yarns. She also carries a large variety of novelty fibers, books, and great gift items. Check out her fabulous Nutcracker series.

If you're a novice, she'll teach you! The Stitch Niche is open from 10:00 A.M. to 5:00 P.M., Wednesday through Saturday. The telephone number is (228) 452-3100.

After perusing the streets of Pass Christian, **Cafe Du Soleil** is a most agreeable spot to have lunch and try one of the eight gourmet coffees. Excellent cappuccino is served as well as several ice creams.

The favorite sandwich of the regulars is Curry Tuna on one of the grain breads or a bowl of Black Bean Soup. Whatever your taste, Cafe Du Soleil is a peaceful place that you will come back to whenever you are in the area. It is open from 9:00 A.M. to 5:00 P.M., Monday through Saturday. The telephone number is (228) 452-5002.

On the corner of Market and 2nd Street is a great "combination" shop—**Lynda's Cookery** and **Blue Skies Gallery.** Lynda Cook, owner of the Cookery, says, "This is food and art, a total connection." Blue Skies is in front with wonderfully displayed art and photos.

The Cookery has it all—kitchenware, butcher blocks, aprons, cookbooks, and gadgets, as well as necessities. Beyond the light and sparkling display room is the large test kitchen where classes are held. Behind the stove, artist Addie Connell has painted four bright "cookbook murals." Chef Bill Hahne is the resident chef, who offers regu-

larly scheduled classes. Guest chefs from the area's fine dining establishments often join him.

Chef Bill also teaches a wide variety of specialized classes—"Kooking for Kids," bread making, and gourmet pizza to name a few. You might want to take the New Orleans Cajun-Creole class, where you'll learn to make gumbo, jambalaya, bread pudding, and pralines. *Laissez les bon temps roulez!* The shop is open from 10:00 A.M. to 5:30 P.M., Monday through Saturday. For class information, call (228) 452-7382.

Shrimp La Linda

⅓ cup olive oil
1 tsp. each:
    rosemary
    oregano
    thyme
    fresh ground black pepper
    garlic salt
1 bay leaf, broken up
4 lb. medium to large shrimp, peeled
½ tbsp. flour
½ cup water
½ cup white wine or dry vermouth

In a heavy-bottomed pot, sauté the seasonings in the oil over low heat for 3 minutes. Add shrimp and simmer for 15 minutes, stirring often. In a cup mix flour and water and add to shrimp. Blend well, add wine, and simmer 5 minutes. Can be served as is for an appetizer, in patty shells, or over rice for an entrée. Serves 6-8.

Remember: Do not cook with any wine that you would not drink.

Bay St. Louis

The actual Bay of St. Louis was discovered in 1699 by the French on the Feast Day of St. Louis. Later, in the 1700s, the Spanish arrived and in 1811 the area became part of the United States. Although the town was incorporated as Shieldsboro in 1858, the name Bay St. Louis appeared later and remained.

Numerous large hotels and summer homes for New Orleanians were built along the beachfront. The hotels have long since been destroyed, either by fire or hurricanes, but many elegant Victorian residences remain. You will need to get off the beaten path of U.S. 90 in order to find "Old Town" Bay St. Louis. On the west end of the bridge, turn left onto North Beach Boulevard. The gracious homes along here provide a glimpse of times past.

One of these homes is the **Bay Town Inn,** a bed and breakfast overlooking the bay. Listed on the National Register of Historic Places, the inn has seven guest rooms with queen-size beds and private baths. Owner Ann Tidwell says she also offers "military rates and Southern breakfasts." The telephone number is (228) 466-5870 or (800) 533-0407

Just about a block away are a couple of nice restaurants. Lunch is a must while you are at "The Bay." If you are ready to savor a giant hamburger or some fried seafood, you might try **The Dock of the Bay** (119 North Beach Boulevard), where you can eat on a deck over-

Bay Town Inn
Bed and Breakfast

looking the bay. Owner Melba Fisher's husband, Jerry, provides the entertainment. Jerry, by the way, was once the lead singer for the band Blood, Sweat & Tears. The Dock of the Bay serves from 11:00 A.M. until 9:30 P.M., Tuesday through Saturday, and from 12:00 noon until 9:30 P.M. on Sunday. A band plays on Saturday night beginning at 10:00 P.M. The telephone number is (228) 467-9940.

Legend of the Po' Boy

In New Orleans, years ago, the neighborhood bars would give each customer a sandwich with their purchase of nickel beer. The working men would go in for lunch for five cents. Bar owners would refer to them as "poor boy's lunch" . . . thus, the name "po' boys" came into being.

In a wonderful, old (circa 1906) building just as you enter town is **Trapani's Eatery.** Walk into this casual, friendly restaurant, seat yourself, and an attentive waiter will come right over. You'll need a little while to look over the full menu, so just begin right away with a cup of great gumbo or some fried green tomatoes while you decide.

You can't go wrong with the po' boys—great (New Orleans) French bread piled high with shrimp, oysters, or fish and the Muffaletta is huge and good. Nothing is overgarnished or oversauced—it is all good, solid Southern food.

Trapani's is open Monday and Tuesday from 10:00 A.M. to 4:00 P.M. for lunch; Wednesday through Sunday from 10:00 A.M. to 9:00 P.M. for lunch and dinner. Entrées include steak, seafood, veal, crawfish cakes—you get the picture. For alcohol, beer only is served; or you can BYOB wine. The telephone number is (228) 467-8570.

Fishing buddies Tony Trapani and Steve Pucheu are co-owners. Says Tony, "Come enjoy our restaurant and if you don't think it's the best meal you ever had, then the coffee is half price!"

Across from the courthouse you might want to stop by the **Hancock County Historical Society** in the Kate Lobrano House (108 Cue Street). Charles Gray, president of the society, will gladly fill you in on any information you might need. "We're usually open," Charles says, "although we do take a long lunch hour on Wednesdays and Fridays." It is open from 8:00 A.M. to 4:00 P.M., Monday through Friday. The telephone number is (228) 467-4090.

Behind the courthouse, do find **Ruth's Cakery** on Court Street. Right outside this "cakes only" bakery is a beautiful and rare weeping bald cypress tree that you will want to see.

Also nearby is **Evergreen.** This antique shop is in an old building that has been restored to its original state. The building itself is noteworthy, but the collection of antiques and jewelry is particularly outstanding. The owner of Evergreen, Sandy Smith, travels extensively throughout the South to acquire special pieces for her shop. Evergreen is open from 11:00 A.M. until 5:00 P.M., Thursday through Saturday, and from 12:00 noon until 5:00 P.M. on Sunday, or by appointment. The telephone number is (228) 467-2834.

Speaking of long lunch hours, we hope you won't be in a big
hurry when you visit the charming little town of Bay St. Louis,
because "they" aren't in a hurry. "They" (the residents and shop
owners of Bay St. Louis) are a relaxed bunch of folks who live
along this exquisite stretch of the Gulf Coast. Only a few stores
are open on Mondays and there doesn't seem to be any real
hurry to open on Tuesday mornings. You will find that the
townsfolk are so pleasant, personable, and helpful that you will
forget the slightest delay and find the atmosphere refreshing.

From Evergreen look to the west a couple of doors. You'll see the
Blue Dish restaurant and you won't want to miss it. It is located in one
of the many quaint "shotgun" houses that are scattered throughout
the town. Head on up the steps past pots of herbs and across the
shaded porch. When you enter, go on to the back counter and place
your order before sitting down (there will be fresh flowers in a Coca-
Cola bottle on your table).

This pleasant, unpretentious restaurant serves up maybe the best
"sandwich" you'll ever have. These sandwiches are pieces of hollowed-
out, melt-in-your-mouth, crispy French bread. In the "hollows" are
the most delicious concoctions—a yummy broccoli something and a
superb crawfish combination to name two. Get the light house salad
with raspberry vinaigrette as a side. Blue Dish also serves quiches,
soup, a large variety of coffees, and a delicious ginseng tea. A dessert
case is overflowing.

Blue Dish, 112 North 2nd Street, is open from 7:30 A.M. to 6:00
P.M., Monday through Saturday. The motto here is "Sip, Tip and Be
Hip!" The telephone number is (228) 467-1989.

Around the corner at 116 Ullman Avenue is another nice bed and

Coffee House Café

breakfast. The **Heritage House** offers three spacious bedrooms on the second floor. Housed in the old Drake Home, built around 1900, Heritage House has several common rooms and a beautiful, shaded veranda and it is only steps away from the beach. The telephone number is (228) 467-1649 or (888) 702-2686.

At 126 Main Street is **Serenity,** a fine arts gallery owned by Jerry Dixon. Jerry opened this gallery after being located in the New Orleans French Quarter for 25 years. Here you will find a large variety of unusual art forms. Along with some unique but excellent paintings, Jerry has assembled some great sculptures and wood carvings.

Be sure to walk down the "Yellow Brick Road" corridor painted by Pat George and through her "Malachite Door," where a large brass Buddha presides over even more art. The corridor is lined with a variety of paintings and along the way you'll pass by artist Robert Waldrop's great concrete crocodile bench. The gallery is open from 10:00 A.M. to 5:00 P.M., Monday through Saturday, and from 12:00 noon through 5:00 P.M. on Sunday.

As you exit this shop, be sure to notice artist John McDonald's fabulous mural on the back of the bank building. It depicts early settlers and present-day inhabitants who seem to be socializing. Yes, the "bricks" have been painted on!

Next door to Serenity is **Old Books and Curiosities,** owned by Nancy Marie and Zoe Bowers. This nook is packed with old books, postcards, and magazines and a good supply of fabric for quilting. Everything is carefully labeled and organized so browsing can be more fun. Nancy has stacks of sheet music with old favorite tunes reminiscent of earlier times. Old Books and Curiosities is open from 11:00 A.M. to 5:00 P.M., Wednesday through Monday. The telephone number is (228) 467-9791.

Vicki Niolet explains her shop as "fun antiques, not fine antiques." She really hits the nail on the head. If you are of a certain vintage, the items in **Paper Moon** will be as familiar to you as bobby pins and hankies.

More than 40 percent of the collectibles in Vicki's shop are everyday things that she has accumulated over the years. You will be glad to see them again and can easily afford to buy something sentimental from the past. Give yourself some time to browse through Paper Moon—it is worth it. The shop is located at 220 Main Street and has regular business hours during the week. If you wish to find a treasure from the past, call (228) 467-8318.

Quarter Moon is a gallery of contemporary crafts by established, regional artists. Ellis Anderson, owner and artist in her own right, has a gathering of several artists from New Orleans whose talents are being recognized all over the United States.

Here you will find Kathy Schorr's exquisite silk scarves (which can be worn or hung like a fine piece of art), Gabriel Q's Venetian masks (he has perfected gold leafing from studying the methods used centuries ago in Venice), Barbara Stone's handwoven vests and light jackets, Tracy Thomson's "little" hats, and Ellis Anderson and four other jewelry designers (each with his own original gold and silver pieces).

Quarter Moon is a shop for the collector who loves to invest in wearable art by quality craftsmen in their field. The shop keeps steady hours and is open every day (except Tuesday) from 11:00 A.M. to 5:00 P.M. and from 12:00 noon to 5:00 P.M. on Sunday. The telephone number is (228) 467-7279.

On the service road adjacent to U.S. 90, tucked behind a white picket fence, is a treasure—**Bookends** (111 U.S. 90). Bookends resides in a turn-of-the-century row house. "Probably a 'company house' for the cannery or the railroad," says owner Susan Diagre. You enter Bookends from a cozy screen porch complete with ceiling fans, books, and rocking chairs.

Inside the four-room house, books are displayed in old cabinets that came from a dry goods store in the New Orleans French Quarter. On the shelves are all of the best sellers and there is a great children's room and a fascinating room of history books—new and used. There is also a selection of first editions, many of which are signed by the authors.

Don't miss the kitchen. On the baker's racks are cookbooks, new, used, and out of print. Beside the door is located a good selection of old Victorian romance novels. Bookends is open Monday through Saturday, from 10:00 A.M. until 5:30 P.M.

Next door, **The Kid Company** is a good establishment that has been in Bay St. Louis for more than 12 twelve years. Owner Anne Truett Mann has children of her own and is always up-to-date with clothes from preschool to elementary. She has comfortable, knockabout clothes in cotton and knit that are never trendy—and children love to wear them. Anne also carries interesting pick-up toys and games that you do not see everywhere. The Kid Company is open from 10:00 A.M. to 5:30 P.M., Monday through Saturday. The telephone number is (228) 467-6786.

Waveland

You are sure to notice the serene, rose-colored building at 141 U.S. 90—**Armand's.** Don't miss it—for brunch, lunch, or dinner. Step inside to an elegant, softly carpeted room with dark green walls, ceiling fans, and soft music in the background. Tucked into a large corner is a comfy bar with some table seating and old photos on the walls of Bay St. Louis houses in the early 1900s.

Maître d' Philip Folse will seat you—charming you all the while with his soft Louisiana accent. Once seated, you'll discover that the service is great and surpassed only by the food. For lunch or dinner, have the Turtle Soup, which comes with its own miniature carafe of sherry. Then you might want to order the Gulf Stream Pasta or the Crab Nova Salad.

Chef Armand Jonte, who came from the Gautreaux's Restaurant in uptown New Orleans, changes the menu daily and usually features veal, filet mignon, and seafood. If it is on the menu, don't miss Eggplant Eloise or the sweetbreads for an appetizer. If you're lucky, you will have timed your visit well enough to have the Mississippi Pinecone—a redfish sensation. Prices are moderate to expensive. Lunch is served Tuesday through Friday from 11:30 A.M. until 2:30 P.M., Sunday brunch is served from 11:30 A.M. until 2:30 P.M., Dinner is served Tuesday through Saturday from 6:00 P.M. until 9:30 P.M. Although you may call for reservations, they are not required. The telephone number is (228) 467-8255.

Next door to Armand's Restaurant is **Countryside Antiques** (151 U.S. 90), the oldest shop in the county, although the building is circa 1978. Keeping the same hours as Armand's, this wonderful antique shop features a wide assortment of American antiques (1790-1890), art glass (especially notable is the Tiffany), some fabulous old wicker pieces, and an extensive selection of sterling silver.

Owners Mike Mayo and Tom Cottom will welcome you into their distinctive building, which also showcases a few European pieces and some estate jewelry. The telephone number is (228) 467-2338.

The **Stennis Space Center** is NASA's primary center for testing and flight, certifying large rocket propulsion systems for the space shuttle and future generations of space vehicles. The center was designated as a national rocket test site in 1961 and, in 1966, the first *Saturn V* rocket booster was tested for the Apollo lunar landing program. Today you can tour this huge, isolated facility. The center, named for John Stennis, senator from Mississippi, occupies nearly 14,000 acres and is surrounded by a unique 126,000-acre acoustical buffer zone for safe testing of large rockets and rocket engines.

There is a visitors center with interesting exhibits (don't miss the moon rock), including the *Apollo IV* command module. Visit the Hall of Achievements and trace the history of NASA and space flight. Be sure to go up to the six-story observation deck and just absorb the vastness of this place, although minuscule in relationship to the vastness of space. But you need to get on the tour bus to see it all; a 45-minute trip will take you out to the three massive concrete-and-steel vertical rocket propulsion test stands.

The Stennis Space Center was a historic steppingstone in America's path to the moon. The first and only human beings to ever set foot on the moon rode above a rocket that had been tested and proven capable right here in the swamps and marshes of southern Mississippi. There was a saying going around during the 1960s: "To get to the moon, you've got to go through Hancock County, Mississippi."

The center is located 14 miles west of Bay St. Louis. To get there, take the Alabama 607 exit off Interstate 10 and follow the signs. It is open from 9:00 A.M. to 4:00 P.M., Monday through Saturday, and from 12:00 noon to 4:00 P.M. on Sunday. It is closed Easter, Thanksgiving, and Christmas. Reservations are encouraged for groups of 15 or more. To schedule a tour, call (800) 237-1821.

> The energy released by the three shuttle engines at full power, in units of watts, is equivalent to the output of 23 Hoover Dams.

If you are planning a visit to the Mississippi Gulf Coast and need information on accommodations or otherwise, contact Mississippi Gulf Coast Convention and Visitors Bureau at (800) 237-9493; web site: http://www.gulfcoast.org; e-mail: tourism@gulfcoast.org.

The Northern Gulf Coast area has an annual rainfall of 64 ½ inches. Now this may sound unfortunate, but a local meteorologist said, "We actually have more sunny days on average than many areas such as the Northwest Coast, where there are prolonged periods of drizzle."

The Gulf Coast does not usually have such wimpy rainfall. In fact, the rain here is quite macho—rain drops do not fall on your head, they plummet! The summer thunderstorms are impressive also, but happily for everyone concerned, unless there is a stalled front overhead, the sun can be shining minutes after the last drop.

Of course, the azaleas and oak trees thrive on these "gullywashers" and the semitropical air. The growing season is unusually long, with the first frost usually not occurring until the end of November and the last about the end of February.

The coldest month is January, with an average temperature between 60 degrees Fahrenheit and 42 degrees Fahrenheit. July is the hottest month, with an average temperature between 90 degrees Fahrenheit and 74 degrees Fahrenheit. Usually, the driest month is October, with an average rainfall of 3 ¼ inches; and July is the wettest month, with an average rainfall of 7 ½ inches.

There are two things about the Gulf Coast climate that one does not mention—the two Hs—humidity and hurricanes.

There is nothing that can be done about either one of them. However, when the humidity is high, you can take comfort in the fact that everything is air-conditioned and it is probably the most efficient air conditioning in the country.

With hurricanes, you can only pray and get out of the way!

Index